Yorùbá Music in the Twentieth Century

Eastman/Rochester Studies in Ethnomusicolgy

Ellen Koskoff, Series Editor

Eastman School of Music

(ISSN: 2161-0290)

Burma's Pop Music Industry:
Creators, Distributors, Censors
Heather MacLachlan

Yorùbá Music in the Twentieth Century:
Identity, Agency and Performance Practice
Bode Omojola

Yorùbá Music in the Twentieth Century

Identity, Agency, and Performance Practice

BODE OMOJOLA

UNIVERSITY OF ROCHESTER PRESS

First published 2012
Reprinted in paperback and transferred to digital printing 2014
Reprinted in 2019

University of Rochester Press
668 Mt. Hope Avenue, Rochester, NY 14620, USA
www.urpress.com
and Boydell & Brewer Limited
PO Box 9, Woodbridge, Suffolk IP12 3DF, UK
www.boydellandbrewer.com

ISSN: 2161-0290
hardcover ISBN: 978-1-58046-409-3
paperback ISBN: 978-1-58046-493-2

Library of Congress Cataloging-in-Publication Data
Omojola, Bode, author.
Yorùbá music in the twentieth century : identity, agency, and performance practice / Bode Omojola.
     pages cm. — (Eastman/Rochester studies in ethnomusicolgy, ISSN 2161-
     0290 ; v. 2)
     Includes bibliographical references, discography, videography, and index.
     ISBN 978-1-58046-409-3 (hardcover : alkaline paper) 1. Yoruba (African
people)—Music—20th century—History and criticism. 2. Music—Africa, West—
20ᵗʰ century—History and criticism. I. Title. II. Series: Eastman/Rochester studies
in ethnomusicology ; v. 2.
     ML355.W47O46 2012
     781.62'96333—dc23

                                                             2012032747

A catalogue record for this title is available from the British Library.

To the memory of my late father, Mathew Omojola,
for setting me on the path of honor,
and to "Unilorin 49" for defying tyranny with courage.

Contents

Acknowledgments

I have benefited from the support, advice, and assistance of many individuals and institutions in the course of writing and conducting research for this book. I would like to acknowledge the assistance and support of all the musicians and resource persons with whom I worked in Nigeria and the United States (see appendix A); Mount Holyoke College, for sponsoring my research visits to Nigeria, and for providing financial assistance toward the completion of this book; the Alexander von Humboldt Foundation in Bonn, Germany, for a research fellowship; Professor Kofi Agawu of Princeton University, for reading parts of the book and for his numerous suggestions; Professor Akin Euba, for his guidance and support; Professor Kay Kaufman Shelemay of Harvard University, for her constant support and encouragement; Professor Anna Drews, for hosting me in Berlin; and Chrissa Godbout of Mount Holyoke College for helping with the production of the CD. Thanks are also due to Dr. Tunde Adegbola, for reading parts of the book and for his very valuable suggestions; Olori Funke Osin of Emùré-Èkìtì, for her support; "Baba" Wole Adetiran of the Ibadan Polytechnic; Dr. Femi Faseun of the Lagos State University; Dr. Oyin Medubi of the University of Ilorin, who read parts of the book and made valuable suggestions; Dr. Femi Abiodun of Kwara State University; Bisi Adeleke, for sharing his knowledge of dùndún drumming with me; Dr. Sunbo Loko, Dr. Doyin Aguoru, and Mrs. Kehinde Faniyi, for their support.

I must also express my gratitude to Dr. Michael Olatunji, for permission to use the photo of Ekundayo Phillips; to Sir Victor Olaiya, for permission to use his music and photo; to Bisade Ologunde (a.k.a. Lagbaja), for permission to use his music; and to Tunde Afolayan for creating the images of Fela Anikulapo-Kuti and Lagbaja. I am also grateful to Professor Rowland Abiodun of Amherst College for his support and his insightful discussions on various aspects of Yorùbá culture. I have enjoyed the tremendous support of colleagues in the music department at Mount Holyoke College. I am particularly thankful to Professor Linda Laderach for her support and encouragement. I am very grateful to Ryan Peterson, Tracey Engel, and Suzanne Guiod of the University of Rochester Press for doing such a great job and for their numerous suggestions.

Finally, I must thank my wife, Abimbola, and our three lovely children, Oluwafunto, Oluwatosin, and Oluwaseun, for their love and support.

Note: An audio CD no longer accompanies this book. Audio files can now be accessed at http://hdl.handle.net/1802/34724. All references to the CD in this book now refer to the online audio files.

Introduction

The issue of identity, a central theme in this book, is a familiar topic in eth-nomusicological literature, one that continues to generate considerable interest among scholars who seek to understand how music defines individual traits and group affiliation; how music articulates the relationship between self-identity and social identity; and, on a cognitive level, how musical concept, behavior, and sound translate into, enhance, or reveal a capacity for self-reflection.[1] With specific reference to Yorùbá culture, one immediate concern is how to deal with the notion of an assumed homogeneous identity, a hegemonic "framework for cultural identity" that laminates the plethora of local and individual identities that lie beneath.[2]

What do we mean, for example, when we speak of a Yorùbá identity? Are we referring to a unified, homogeneous identity, or are we musing about the many types and levels of group affiliations, framed by such cultural identifiers as gen-der, religion, ethnicity, place, and professional guilds, to mention but just a few? In engaging the ramifications of these questions, Christopher Waterman, who has done extensive work on this topic, reminds us about the constant engage-ment between the "internal face of identity" and the "socially constructed iden-tity."[3] The dynamic between the notion of the "self" and that of the "person" draws attention to the ways in which identity is constructed on different levels and shaped by social contingencies and competing interests. Given the nature of Yorùbá history and society and the ways in which various Yorùbá musical tra-ditions are organized, my discussion throughout this book analyzes the ways in which the process of identity construction is guided by the principle of "nested cultural formations"[4]—it is framed simultaneously by a desire to unify and differentiate. It is informed by a strategic process that ultimately entails what Thomas Turino describes as "the partial and the variable selection of habits and attributes that we use to represent ourselves to ourselves and to others as well as those aspects that are perceived by ourselves and by others as salient."[5] This two-tiered approach to identity construction is ethnographically mirrored in the ways in which the average Yorùbá person describes himself or herself. In situ-ations involving non-Yorùbá persons from within or outside Nigeria, the label Yorùbá is often used by the people to categorize themselves. But in situations involving fellow Yorùbá people within or outside their native hometown, labels like Ìjèṣà, Èkìtì, Ìjèbú, or Àkókó, which refer to specific Yorùbá ethnic groups, may be preferred for self-identification. The basis for this dual approach is historical, political, and cultural, as I explain later.

As exemplified in the Yorùbá example, the delineation between "us" and "them" occurs on different levels, and helps to shape the nature of social relations between individuals, social organizations, and ethnic groups. Identity narratives in the form of musical performances as well as the concepts and behaviors that are associated with them are thus inherently exclusive rather than inclusive, and strategic rather than altruistic. They are often oppositional and competitive even within relatively homogeneous and small communities. In exploring the issue of musical identity among the Yorùbá, I am interested in how musical practices reflect different interests even when they draw on certain widely shared elements. My discussion is informed largely by the notion of competing musical identities—that is, the ways that individuals and groups reconfigure received and imposed musical practices and styles to articulate specific individual interests and those of nested groups. I seek to investigate how Yorùbá musical practices reflect a process of critical engagement between individuated choices and cultural norms, as well as how creative and performance strategies are constitutive of socially motivated actions in a rapidly changing cultural, social, and political environment. To provide a context for a discussion of the role of music in how Yorùbá people "see themselves, how they are seen by others, and how they imagine themselves to be seen by others,"[6] we must begin with a brief discussion of Yorùbá history and culture.

The Yorùbá People

The Yorùbá people are comprised of many semiautonomous ethnic groups that occupy southwestern Nigeria and parts of the Benin Republic and Togo. In Nigeria, Yorùbá ethnicities include the Èkìtì, Ìjèṣà, Ègbádò, Òyó, and Ìjèbú, to mention just a few. Descendants of Yorùbá people also live in parts of the Americas and the Caribbean, notably in Brazil and Cuba, following the slave trade that took place between the sixteenth and the nineteenth centuries. Members of all the various Yorùbá groups speak a variant or a dialect of the Yorùbá language, believe in a common ancestry, and share a common traditional religion.[7] Although human occupation of Yorùbá territories in Nigeria dates to the fourth century BC, the roots of Yorùbá identity are grounded in the ninth century, in the kingdom of Ilé-Ifè, the place now generally regarded as the ancestral home of all Yorùbá. The first king to rule Ilé-Ifè was Oduduwa. Oranyan, one of his descendants, is believed to have founded the kingdom of Òyó in the mid-fourteenth century.[8] The Òyó kingdom emerged as the most powerful of all Yorùbá kingdoms in the seventeenth and eighteenth centuries.[9] As Louis Munoz has explained, the political ascendancy of Òyó was probably due to its geographical location in "the savanna [which] extends to the coast, [and] which allows not only easier communication but also the use of cavalry in raids and punitive expedition."[10] Ọ̀yọ́'s political status declined considerably, however, in the early nineteenth century. Ìlọrin, a major part of the kingdom, was taken over by Islamic jihadists from Northern Nigeria, led by Othman dan Fodio, thus forcing the relocation of the political headquarters of the kingdom from Ọ̀yọ́-Ilé (Old Ọ̀yọ́) to the present location of Ọ̀yọ́ city in 1836.

There is no evidence to suggest that the various towns and kingdoms comprising the Yorùbá ever existed as a united political entity, even during the golden era of the Ọ̀yọ́ kingdom. Indeed, the word "Yorùbá" is foreign in origin, and its use relatively recent; it was coined by the Hausa people of northern Nigeria in the nineteenth century to refer to the people of the Ọ̀yọ́ kingdom. The gradual emergence of the notion of a pan-Yorùbá society (as suggested in the adoption of a collective name for the people) at the beginning of the twentieth century was tied strongly to the onset of the British colonization of Nigeria.[11] It was during the colonial era that the word "Yorùbá" became popular, following its adoption by the British colonial and missionary institutions as a collective name for the people of various kingdoms, towns, and communities.[12] Also aiding the formation of a pan-Yorùbá consciousness was the adoption and promotion of the dialect of Ọ̀yọ́ as the standard Yorùbá language for radio broadcast, as a medium of instruction in schools, and for journalism and literature.[13] The formation of the Ẹgbẹ́ Ọmọ Odùduwà (Society for the Descendants of Oduduwa) in 1945 by Chief Obafemi Awolowo, the man who has been described as the first leader of a pan-Yorùbá ethnicity, provided a major boost for this new consciousness.[14] By the time of Nigeria's independence in 1960, the "centripetal tendency"[15] toward a pan-Yorùbá identity within a competitive Nigerian federal structure comprising at least two hundred ethnic groups was clearly in effect.

Although the notion of a pan-Yorùbá identity has become accepted nationally and internationally, the constituent Yorùbá ethnic groups continue to maintain their unique cultural and linguistic traditions, a factor which must be taken into consideration in any discussion of Yorùbá identity. Recent political and administrative changes in Nigeria seem to have helped bolster this sense of relative group autonomy. The creation of smaller states to replace old regional divisions is particularly significant in this regard. Today, the Yorùbá people occupy the states of Ọ̀ṣun, Èkìtì, Oǹdó, Ògùn, Ọ̀yọ́, Lagos, and parts of Kwara, Edo, and Delta. These smaller states have been created since 1970 to replace the old Western Region, one of the four regions formed during the colonial era and sustained for a while after independence. The creation of these smaller states tends to undermine the notion of a pan-Yorùbá identity that was promoted by the former administrative structure (the old Western Region) and by the endorsement of Ọ̀yọ́ as the standard language; most of the newly created states are dominated by a single Yorùbá ethnic group or by a few closely related ones, an arrangement which

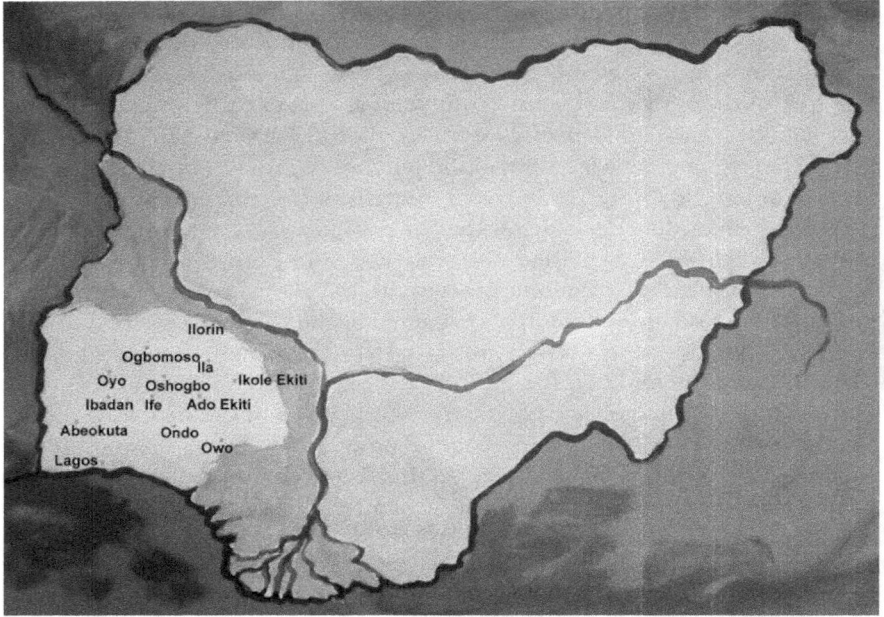

Figure I.1. Map of Nigeria, showing Yoruba. Reproduced with permission from Tunde Afolayan.

has helped to promote a sense of relative autonomy among the ethnic groups. The new arrangement also provides a favorable social and political environment for the promotion of ethnic-specific cultural traditions, including language and music. For example, although the Ọ̀yọ́ dialect remains the official vernacular language and the dominant language of broadcast all over Yorùbáland, other ethnic dialects, including Èkìtì, Ìjẹ̀ṣà, and Ìjẹ̀bú, are now featured more regularly on the radio and television in their respective states. In addition, non-Ọ̀yọ́ ethnic musical traditions from these smaller states are also featured very prominently at national events like the annual national arts festival and the annual Abuja Carnival, and now enjoy a visibility that was not possible in the old Western Region.[16]

Thus, behind the veneer of a homogeneous Yorùbá identity is a complex and multifarious structure of relationships among various ethnic groups. Needless to say, ethnic diversity parallels diversity in gender and class relationships, issues on which I elaborate in this book. Before examining how music is used to nego-tiate social identities, it is important to assess how Yorùbá music has fared in ethnomusicological scholarship. In the next section, I focus mainly on major trends, rather than attempting an exhaustive review.

Yorùbá Music in the Ethnomusicological Literature

Yorùbá Drumming

Of the various aspects of Yorùbá music, it is drumming that has been discussed most extensively in the academic literature. Ethnomusicological interest in Yorùbá drum music was part of a general wave of inquisitiveness on the part of early visitors to the continent (including missionaries, colonial officers, and anthropologists); drumming was considered intriguing and even mysterious. In 1923, Captain Sutherland Rattray stated that "there is hardly any other West African art or custom that has aroused more widespread wonder and curiosity, nor any concerning which such almost universal misconception still prevails, as that connected with the wonderful West African Drum Language."[17] Rattray's own work on Ashanti music helped to pioneer and entrench what would become a sustained academic interest in West African drumming, as shown in the works of W. E. Ward[18] and Arthur Morris Jones.[19] For example, Rattray's comment foreshadowed that of Jones, who, thirty-one years later, observed, in a now-famous quote, that "rhythm is to the African what harmony is to the Europeans."[20] Kofi Agawu has amply documented the curiosity of such early scholars about African rhythm, as well as the persistent interest in the subject.[21] That interest continues today, highlighted in the works of John Chernoff, Willie Anku, David Locke, Kofi Agawu, and Patricia Tang, to mention just a few.[22]

Early studies on Yorùbá drumming ranged from introductions to the concept of musical instruments as speech surrogates and the role of the lead drummer[23] to discussions of the acoustic and physical properties of musical instruments and the social contexts in which they are used.[24] The musical principles of Yorùbá drumming were not studied until the early 1960s; Anthony King, who did his field research in Ìfàkì-Èkìtì, a small hinterland town, was the first scholar to provide a substantial transcription and analysis of Yorùbá drum patterns. King analyzed the significance and functions of repetitive patterns played on support drums as well as the structure of speech-based narratives and improvisations played on the lead drum in a *dùndún* ensemble of hourglass-shaped drums, consisting of the *ìyáàlù* (lead drum), *aguda*, and *kànàngó* (support drums).[25] He observed that while the rhythmic patterns played on ìyáàlù (and sometimes aguda) reflect a process of continuous variation, the kànàngó (the highest-pitched in the ensemble) reiterates an asymmetric pattern that he referred to as the "standard pattern" (known as *konkolo* in Yorùbá). King suggested two particular reasons for the structural significance of the standard pattern: first, its "length, being 12 quavers, allows combination with phrases two, three, four or six in length"; and second, "when played in combination with other rhythmic phrases as suggested above, its irregular division (seven and five units) ensures that there will always be a fair amount of cross rhythms."[26]

King's study provided an important analytical premise for subsequent works, notably those of Yemi Olaniyan and Akin Euba.[27] Olaniyan's study also derives from an extensive transcription of performances from the Ọ̀yọ́ region, and discusses different varieties of the "standard pattern" and the compositional-performance techniques of the master drummer. His study also covers the role of the ṣẹ̀kẹ̀rẹ̀ (Yorùbá gourd rattle) as used in the expanded dùndún-ṣẹ̀kẹ̀rẹ̀ ensemble. Of all the studies devoted to Yorùbá drumming, Euba's work remains the most extensive. Based on repertories from the Ọ̀yọ́ region, Euba's work provides detailed analytical transcriptions and a wide-ranging discussion that covers the acoustic properties of drums, the training of musicians, ensemble practices, the interaction of text-based and nonlexical musical phrases, standard patterns, as well as the social and religious dimensions of musical performance. Amanda Villepastour's recent study on bàtá drumming (an ensemble of conically-shaped drums) is most significant in its documentation of the "remarkable speech surrogacy technology" of bàtá and its exploration of the relationship between bàtá drumming and ẹnàán bàtá, a form of coded speech used exclusively by bàtá drummers.[28] Villepastour's study also charts a tripartite and dialectical relationship between the Yorùbá language and ẹnàán bàtá, the ways in which ẹnàán bàtá translates into drum strokes, and how drum strokes prescribed by ẹnàán bàtá are decoded into the general Yorùbá language.

The studies of Yorùbá drumming discussed above emphasize the combination of duple and triple rhythmic figurations in the "standard pattern," a feature described by Rose Brandel as "the African hemiola."[29] Hemiola formations are also reflected in the structure of other repetitive patterns in drum performance, and the narrative sequences of the lead drummer. The focus on the konkolo rhythm foreshadowed recent theoretical interests in the "standard pattern", as illustrated in Agawu's study, which analyzes the structural and cultural dimensions of the "standard pattern" by discussing its "morphology and . . . [the] habits of (its) perception."[30]

Most of these earlier ethnomusicological studies analyzed musical structures and the organization of Yorùbá ensembles. A recent study by Debra Klein, however, departs from this trend by focusing on the lives and musical activities of a group of Yorùbá bàtá drummers from Ẹ̀rìn-Ọ̀ṣun (the town of Ẹ̀rìn in the state of Ọ̀ṣun). Klein's study traverses local and global boundaries in an ethnographic journey that mirrors the collapsible cultural boundaries within which Ẹ̀rìn-Ọ̀ṣun drummers now perform. Thus, in addition to exploring transnational collaborative interactions that involve Ẹ̀rìn-Ọ̀ṣun artists and Western scholars, artists, students, and anthropologists, she discusses the local variants of such collaborations between the artists and indigenous Yorùbá entrepreneurs and government institutions within Nigeria. In identifying the global dimensions of collaboration, Klein distinguishes between a homogenizing "globalization" and a liberating "global connection," as defined by "a culturally specific set of communities and a set of practices." Her discussion of the global networks involving Èrìn-Òṣun artists thus focuses on the documentation and analysis of the roles of committed individual participants in the process of forging a Yorùbá culture movement that challenges "coercion and stereotype."[31]

Vocal Music

Studies on Yorùbá vocal music have tended to emphasize the poetry and performance practice of *oríkì* (praise recitatives) and the linguistic and musical properties of *orin* (metered melodies). Prominent scholars of vocal music include Adeboye Babalola, Oludare Olajubu, and, most comprehensively, Karin Barber.[32] Barber's study, while building on the works of previous scholars, discusses a variety of oríkì performances in Òkukù, a Yorùbá town in Òṣun. Although her study, like those of Babalola and Olajubu before her, does not engage in technical musical analysis, it discusses important compositional and performance techniques, the central role of women in the sustenance of the genre, and the changing social and religious contexts in which vocal music is performed. Barber explains and demonstrates key performance features of *oríkì*, especially those of "fluidity, boundarilessness and centrelessness."[33]

Technical attention to the musical properties of Yorùbá vocal music exists, however, in the works of Ekundayo Phillips, which I discuss extensively in chapter 5. These and studies by Fela Sowande, Ulli Beier, Mary Adebonojo, Tunji Vidal, Ademola Adegbite, Akin Euba, and David Welch devote considerable attention to the tonal properties of song and the relationship between linguistic and melodic contours.[34] Several of these authors note that although the inflectional principles of Yorùbá speech often dictate the melodic contours of songs (Yorùbá being a tonal language), linguistic factors do not entirely account for melodic properties. Sowande observed that "the tonal interval of a Yorùbá word is not a precise musical interval; it is approximate. Hence each word has what we may call an 'interval period' within which it retains the same meaning. Musical intervals are eventually determined by musical context."[35] Welch, in a study of Yorùbá praise music, also emphasized this point, stating that although the "performer is inherently aware that a disregard for speech tone will alter the meaning of the words, within the limits of tone, there are still adequate chances for creativity. For example, the tonal structures may be transposed up or down as long as the tonal patterns of the word remain constant."[36] These early observations on Yorùbá music are similar to those of scholars who have investigated the relationship between text and tone in other West African examples, including Erich von Hornbostel, Marius Schneider, Nissio Fiagbedzi, Lazarus Ekwueme, and Kofi Agawu.[37]

Neotraditional Music

Research interest in modern Yorùbá musical genres rooted in indigenous forms has continued to grow since the last few decades of the twentieth century. Akin Euba must be given the credit for pioneering a series of studies that discuss the incorporation of indigenous elements in Yorùbá Christian church music; the interface of traditional and modern elements in the works of modern Yorùbá composers of art music; the impact of Islam on Yorùbá popular music; and the emergence of modern forms of folk opera.[38] An overarching theme of these works is the analysis of modern Yorùbá music as neotraditional forms in which indigenous Yorùbá performance and compositional practices are incorporated. Other scholars of modern Yorùbá music include Afolabi Alaja-Brown, who produced the first major study on *jùjú* (a genre of Yorùbá popular music); Christopher Waterman, whose book on jùjú music has become a standard piece in ethnomusicological literature; Michael Veal, who produced the first major study on Fela Anikulapo-Kuti's Afro-beat; and Tejumola Olaniyan, whose study on Fela Anikulapo-Kuti's work is richly informed by a personal experience of the music in Nigeria.[39] Alaja-Brown's work on jùjú explains the historical and cultural roots of the genre and its transformation into a pan-Yorùbá tradition, notably through the music of Isaac Kehinde Dairo (a.k.a. I. K. Dairo), while Veal's work on Fela Anikulapo-Kuti interweaves biographical information with a discussion of the political themes of the music. The study by Waterman is particularly significant in its use of the methods of historiography and ethnography to generate insight into the aesthetics and performance practices of jùjú music as shaped by the sociopolitical climate of the later half of the twentieth century. Euba and Mosunmola Omibiyi-Obidike focus on the impact of Islam on Yorùbá music, and discuss the historical development of newly evolved Islam-affiliated idioms like *àpàlà*, *sákárà*, *fújì*, and *wákà*.[40] Focusing on oríkì and fújì, Barber and Waterman discuss the relationship between neotraditional forms and indigenous traditions, and analyze how Yorùbá musicians have synthesized modern musical elements and indigenous performance practices, a technique which underlines their role as "culture producers."[41] Drawing on Ulf Hannerz's theory of creolization,[42] Barber and Waterman explain that modern Yorùbá musicians are engaged in a constant process of selective adaptation involving local and transnational forms. They express historically and socially contingent experiences through their music, thus "traversing" boundaries and "domesticating difference."[43]

I will later explain the specific ways in which my study of Yorùbá music in this book revisits, expands on, and departs from the issues and approaches highlighted above. Suffice it to state here that a central narrative pervades my discussion of disparate musical genres: the exploration of the connection between performance practice (a term I explain in the next section of this chapter) and identity, and the privileging of the agency of performers with a view to reorienting the discussion of Yorùbá music toward its understanding as individual and group creativity within a larger social network. In addition to studying a variety of musical forms and genres in a single study, a radical departure from most studies on Yorùbá music, I adopt a historically situated approach that interrogates the continuous engagement between music and social dynamics as exemplified in the music and activities of specific individuals and groups. My study is guided by a set of critical perspectives, which I discuss below.

Performance Practice, Agency, and Social Action in Music

Performance practice, as I define it in this book, is a multifocal term, which covers the context and ambience of performance, the ways in which an ensemble is organized, the role of the participants, the form and structure of the music, and how the music is communicated and mediated. Integral to this multifocal approach is how music constitutes social action, an issue in which ultimately lies the humanistic and social significance of musical performance. Closely linked to the issues of performance practice and identity is the agency of the musicians who create and perform the music. Stressing the situational significance of African music and the social value of musical participation, John Chernoff explains that the music is not merely a reflection of a fundamental African sensibility. Rather, as a "social force, music helps shape [the African] sensibility."[44] In the same vein, Martin Stokes stresses the processual nature of music and explains that it does not merely represent preexisting social categories, a view which departs from a structuralist-oriented interpretation of the relationship between music and society. Following Pierre Bourdieu and Michel de Certeau,[45] Stokes explains that music, as a form of "social performance," is a "practice in which meanings are generated, manipulated, even ironised, within certain limitations," providing the space within which social "hierarchies are negotiated and transformed."[46] These observations serve to privilege the significance of musicians as actors whose work represents neither "the mere execution of the model" that guides it, nor "a marker in a prestructured space."[47] The efficacy of music as a form of social action thus derives from its performativity, and from the situational sensitivity of the individuals who create and perform it. As a form of self or group representation, musical performance often constitutes a social strategy designed and deployed for particular purposes in a given situation at a specific point in time. Stressing the role of individual musicians as agents in the sustenance and transformation of musical traditions, Kay Kaufmann Shelemay has observed that "as ethnomusicologists we do not study a disembodied concept called 'culture' or 'place' but rather a stream of individuals."[48] Thomas Turino has likewise observed that the shaping of society suggests an ongoing dialectical interaction between individuals and their social and physical surroundings.[49] In the same vein, Christopher Waterman, writing about Yorùbá jùjú music, has analyzed how individual perception of the Yorùbá social order has guided jùjú musicians in negotiating their "collection of rights and duties."[50]

As noted by Bruno Nettl, individual roles have not always been stressed in ethnomusicological literature.[51] In 2004, Gregory Barz made a similar observation, stating that "in textbooks and ethnographies about African music, individual musicians are often masked behind labels that characterize anonymous individual behavior as collective behavior," while "musicians and dancers are represented as generalized groups."[52] Although the situation has improved significantly, and although not every scholar of African music is guilty of this charge, accounting for the role of individuals in Yorùbá music is a research approach yet to be significantly explored.[53] I should quickly add that my discussion of individual ensembles and musicians is also informed by the knowledge that agency gains social significance only when individuals work together as part of a network. As Ingrid Monson has explained, "There is also a collective component to agency, since people must be able to coordinate their efforts with others to create collective projects."[54] Against this background, I explore how individual and group musical activities transform into or relate to wider cultural networks, shaped by specific interests. Rather than embarking on a comprehensive study of Yorùbá music, I have thus focused mainly on selected ensembles and musicians whose music and performances I consider representative of the major genres, trends, and developments in Yorùbá music since the beginning of the twentieth century.

Musical History and Change

My discussion of Yorùbá music is guided by an implicit analysis of musical change. Musical practice, by its very nature, is dynamic in both microscopic and macroscopic terms: individual performances outline a dynamic temporal process in the course of their enactment; and individual musicians constantly revise their musical styles, while musical traditions change over a period of time. In all of these situations, the musician deals constantly with the dynamics of temporal change, whether in the processual flow of a specific performance or in the longer and broader process of change within a given community. In its rootedness in ethnographic methods, however, ethnomusicological research has a curious, perhaps even nebulous, attitude to history and to the dynamics of change. Sarah Weiss goes so far as to suggest the possibility of an "inherently ahistorical" dimension to ethnomusicological research, due to its usual emphasis on the "ethnographic present," which represents only a "node in the historical development of musical culture."[55] Making a work "stand still" tends to de-emphasize or even totally ignore what musicians do "between those historical nodes" upon which our understanding of musical history depends.[56] Furthermore, the oral nature of the musical traditions that ethnomusicologists mostly study and the fact that such performances often exist "only in the articulation of its makers" pose additional challenge for an historical inquiry.[57] Weiss suggests that ethnomusicologists "need to think [more] about process as much as result, to think about getting to historical nodes as much as about the nodes themselves, and in particular, to interpret the attitudes and goals of the hybridizers themselves."[58]

My discussion in this book entails a comprehension of the habits, concerns and challenges that anticipate and accompany the nodes of musical change. As John Blacking has observed, musical change "epitomize[s] the changing conditions and concerns of social groups, perhaps even before they are crystallized and articulated in words and corporate action."[59] To account for musical change is to analyze the musical evidence of change and provide the basis for such a change. It entails analyzing musical traditions or genres in terms of their "nature as aesthetic constructs" and locating them in their specific "social universe, which is the ground of their existence."[60]

Although my discussion in this book relies considerably on a study of a series of "ethnographic presents," there is also an inherent diachronic inquiry that helps to account for the "synchronic reality of social and musical processes."[61] Indeed, implicit in my arrangement of the various chapters of the book is a consideration for musical change. Thus, while the opening four chapters focus on musical traditions whose origins are rooted in precolonial forms, the remaining four chapters focus on musical genres bearing Western and Islamic influences. The accretive nature of the Yorùbá musical landscape provides a good foundation for evaluating the degree of change. For although new musical practices continue to emerge and indigenous idioms are themselves not static, traditional musical practices provide a model against which I continuously assess the degree and significance of change in new and old musical genres and styles.

The Insider Dilemma and the Ethnographic Experience

I consider it important to explain the ways in which my experience as a Yorùbá has influenced my work in this book. The insider-outsider relationship, or the emic-etic distinction, a residual of Romantic hermeneutics linked to René Descartes' philosophical distinction between the "ego and the other,"[62] resonates differently with native scholars engaged in the study of their own culture. For such scholars, the "field" experience is shaped by a combination of epistemological and ontological factors linked to the desire to gain a refreshing insight and a much deeper knowledge of one's own culture. Such a desire is motivated by the need to probe beyond the unquestioned assumptions one has acquired growing up in a particular society.

I was born and bred in Yorùbáland, and have had a long and sustained engagement with Yorùbá music in its various ramifications. Growing up in the Èkìtì region of Yorùbáland, I participated in traditional musical storytelling sessions, followed masquerades, danced and sang actively at annual yam-eating festivals, attended traditional naming, marriage, and funeral ceremonies, and took an active part in school cultural groups. In the 1960s and 1970s, these were the main contexts and avenues within which indigenous musical performances took place. Like most of my peers, however, my experience of Yorùbá music was not restricted to indigenous types. I was also a chorister in an Anglican church, singing Yorùbá adaptations of British hymns as well as indigenous songs composed by local musicians for use in the Christian liturgy. As an undergraduate university student majoring in music, I studied Western classical music, took part in indigenous musical ensembles, and performed with modern highlife bands.

"Native" ethnomusicologists like me are relatively few and are rarely accounted for in theoretical reflections about field research. Take, for example, the observation by Timothy Rice, who, in reflecting on the dynamics of ethnographic work, once observed that "bounded cultures contain insiders in relation to which the researcher, whether anthropologist or ethnomusicologist, is an outsider."[63] I must note, however, that native scholars are often neither insider nor outsider. For in spite of a native scholar's relative familiarity with the cultural terrain of her or his field, she or he may not necessarily be "inside" enough to understand the more restricted aspects of the musical traditions being studied. In addition, a native scholar's knowledge gained by growing up "at home" often does not amount to a professional understanding of the music. Such a position of being neither fully outside nor inside may translate into a dilemma, the management of which can be daunting. Humility, patience, and a good sense of balance are vital if one is to overcome this challenge. It entails not taking things for granted; watching and participating in as many performances of the same tradition as possible; and asking as many questions as possible, even when such questions generate unnerving curiosity on the part of local research assistants. A native scholar must therefore learn to develop an outsider mentality that builds on the advantages of his or her insider experience of the culture. Thus, although this research has benefited immensely from my considerable knowledge of the various musical traditions studied here, I have privileged the views of the musicians and the communities who constitute the social agents that sustain and nurture Yorùbá music in its various forms. My role has been primarily to discuss and analyze the music based on the expert knowledge of these real insiders and performers within their respective communities.

Focus and Departures

This book derives mainly from extended field research in various parts of Western Nigeria conducted over two decades, the details of which are provided in appendix A. Apart from chapter 5, which focuses mainly on historical resources and musical scores, each of the remaining chapters derives from or captures specific ethnographic material. Analytical resources include interviews, performances, musical transcriptions, recordings, and published literature. It is important to note that twentieth-century Yoruba music, in scope and practice, extends beyond the calendar boundaries of the twentieth century. Many of the social practices and cultural processes associated with that century are still relevant today; likewise, the performance practices that define the music continue even now. Thus, although many of the musical performances studied in this book were recorded after 2000, my emphasis is on explaining the ways in which social, cultural, and political developments of the twentieth century have helped shape contemporary Yoruba musical practice. A companion CD, details of which are provided in appendix B, contains recorded music to be used along with the book. My discussion of each of the various musical genres explores the relationship between identity, agency, and performance practice. My focus on these three elements guarantees that my discussion throughout this book encompasses not only the social and cultural perspectives of music making, but also "the music itself." Drawing organic relationships between these components provides the framework for understanding how Yorùbá music reflects social and cultural identities and constitutes a form of social action. In chapter 1, I discuss how bàtá drummers define themselves in opposition to dùndún drummers as part of a survival strategy that traditional drummers have devised in their bid to sustain and improve the relevance of their music in a fast-changing social and political environment. I explore this issue further in chapter 2 by analyzing specific examples of bàtá and dùndún drumming in relation to the new wave of identity negotiation discussed in chapter 1. My discussion of Yorùbá drumming in the first two chapters draws on specific events encountered during my fieldwork to explore the links between performance practice, group identity, and socioeconomic factors. I examine the recent schism within the rank and file of Yorùbá drummers—articulated during a meeting of the Association of Bàtá Drummers in Ibadan—as it relates to the increasingly competitive socioeconomic climate of postcolonial Yorùbá society. I investigate the new ensemble configurations of bàtá drummers as a socially motivated musical response to the increasing domination of modern performance spaces by their dùndún counterparts. I discuss the ability of drummers to generate a coherent and an engaging musical performance rooted in the phenomenon of àlùjó—a musical aesthetic that integrates the functions of dance-drumming and speech-surrogacy. Through comparative analyses of examples of bàtá and dùndún music, I develop the concept that the social advantage that dùndún drummers enjoy over their bàtá colleagues derives ultimately from their capability to fully explore the contemplative potential of àlùjó.

The drum ensembles that I discuss in chapters 1 and 2 are exclusively male. In chapters 3 and 4, I focus on the roles of women and gender in Yorùbá musical culture. My discussion of Yorùbá vocal music explores the question: In what ways do Yorùbá vocal traditions delineate ethnic, group and individual identities?

To address this question, I focus on the issue of gender as manifested in two vocal genres from the town of Emùré-Èkìtì. I analyze the ethnographic situations within which specific examples of Yorùbá song are created and performed, the structure of selected examples, and the ways in which the organization of vocal ensembles helps to delineate group identities. I discuss how the process and dynamics of communal creativity, song-structure, and song-texts express gendered and hierarchical identities in two specific cohorts, namely, female chiefs (*olóyè obìrin*) and the numerous wives (*olorì*) of the king within the Emùré-Èkìtì community. I discuss the collaborative nature of the process through which new songs are created, the topicality of song texts and the ways in which song performance provides the context for the mediation and articulation of social boundaries.

Chapters 5 and 6 focus on the impact of Christianity on Yorùbá musical practice. In chapter 5, I discuss the early attempts by some elite Yorùbá musicians to create a Yorùbá Christian musical liturgy using standard musical notation and indigenous Yorùbá musical elements. I examine the results in terms of the elitist orientation of the church leaders of the time and of the prevailing cultural hegemony of Ọ̀yọ́-Yorùbá. Chapter 6 focuses on the construction of a new form of identity in the Yorùbá Africanist church, forged in opposition to the elitist orientation of the early Yorùbá church musicians discussed in chapter 5. Based on an ethnographic study of a specific group, I look at musical performances in latter-day Yorùbá "white-garment" churches known as *Aladŭra* (prayer band). Such performances constitute a space of sanctuary, a zone of empowerment, and an encased cultural form whose "creolized" musical language speaks to the forging of a new form of aesthetics—a counteraesthetic that gives valence to the expression of individual voice, agency, and identity within a desperate social and economic environment of postcolonial Nigeria.

Chapter 7 focuses on specific examples of Yorùbá popular music, with an emphasis on the songs of Victor Olaiya, Fela Anikulapo-Kuti and Bisade Ologunde (a.k.a. Lagbaja), three individuals who represent key nodes in the historical development of neotraditional Yorùbá popular music. I begin by highlighting the significance of Yorùbá popular music as a symptom and resister of colonial oppression. The themes of nationalism and politics constitute critical prisms for understanding the role of these three musicians as social actors within the Yorùbá public sphere of the twentieth century and the present. While the works of musicians like Lagbaja, Sunday Adeniyi (King Sunny Ade), and Ebenezer Fabiyi (Ebenezer Obey) may be seen to signify a newly emerging pan-Yorùbá identity that is shaped distinctly from imposed colonial musical forms, those of Fela Anikulapo-Kuti and the numerous performers of Yorùbá Islamic popular music articulate social and cultural divisions within the Yorùbá society, and indeed Nigeria as a whole. But these categories are not mutually exclusive of each other: the music of Fela Anikulapo-Kuti, for example, though focused mainly on internal divisions, often strongly projects anticolonial themes.

All the genres of popular music discussed in chapters 7 and 8 constitute musical hybridities or syncretic expressions. As Stokes has observed, the social significance of musical hybridity derives from its inclination toward "simultaneity, heterophony (and thus, pastiche, irony, multivocality, contradictions), its collective nature (and thus imbrications with everyday lives)," as well as "its capacity to signify beyond the linguistic domain."[64] Popular music genres are particularly imbued with these postmodernist attributes because they often integrate diverse cultural elements that match the increasingly interdependent relationship between communities. But the real significance of musical syncretism lies in how its constituent elements are combined and shaped, and how they reflect on the social experience that provides the context for its formation. Are such elements randomly put together, or are they synthesized to develop "a social base" which becomes the context "for borrowing and reinterpretation?"[65] And for what purpose—economic, cultural or political—is syncretism or hybidrity deployed in a piece of music?

In engaging these questions, I provide an extensive discussion of selected works by Victor Olaiya, Fela Anikulapo-Kuti, and Bisade Ologunde. My discussion thus departs from most of the studies on Yorùbá popular music earlier reviewed by generating extensive analyses of specific examples as a means of demonstrating how musical form indexes social and ideological identities. I also complicate the notions of pan-Yorùbá identity and compositional altruism by explaining how works that aspire to such ideals often reflect hegemonic and partisan interests.

The final chapter discusses the impact of Islam on Yorùbá music through analyses of recorded examples as well as through an ethnographic study of a specific musical ensemble in the Yorùbá town of Ikirun. I explore how Yorùbá musicians have engaged the dynamics of Islam, and explored the interstice between àṣà (social reality and cultural practice) and ẹ̀sìn (spiritual devotion and religious belief) to project new modes of musical expressions marked by a religious piety that is liberating rather than limiting. Yorùbá Islamic popular music forms tend to undermine or reinterpret many of the features of Western-influenced genres like highlife, jùjú, and Afro-beat by focusing on performance practices that appeal to the tastes of their listeners.

Chapter One

Yorùbá Drumming

Performance Practice and the Politics of Identity

In the Beginning Was Drumming: *Òrìṣà* in Yorùbá Music

It is generally believed that the first Yorùbá drummer was a man named Àyànàgalú. His status as the progenitor of all Yorùbá drummers—indeed, the Yorùbá deity of drumming—is acknowledged and commemorated in the adoption of his name by traditional Yorùbá drummers whose names begin with the prefix "àyàn."[1] Yorùbá drummers routinely perform appeasement rituals in his honor, seeking to invoke his authority to secure good luck and fortune (*orí ire*) in their daily work as drummers and custodians of his musical legacy. As Akin Euba has observed, Àyànàgalú's status symbolizes a tripartite identity: deity, spirit of the drum, and ancestral father of all Yorùbá drummers.[2] The strong attachment of music to Yorùbá deities (*Òrìṣà*), as depicted in the spiritual and ancestral legacy of Àyànàgalú, represents a natural starting point for my discussion of Yorùbá music, because it provides the background for understanding the religious significance of indigenous Yorùbá music, and for my exploration of the ways in which Yorùbá drummers have sought to negotiate for themselves new and competing identities in recent times.

The diverse character of Yorùbá deities speaks to the dynamic nature of Yorùbá religion itself and how it has evolved over many hundreds of years. Many Òrìṣà have emerged over a long period of time often as a result of pragmatic human responses to important events. Powerful kings, great warriors and famous women have transmuted into Òrìṣà, joining an array of over one thousand hierarchically structured pantheons, some of whom have existed, it is believed, from the very time of creation.[3]

The unbroken chain between Òrìṣà and humans is symbolized in the institution of *egúngún* (ancestor-venerating masquerades) whose significance is rooted in the belief that departed beings, though physically dead, continue to intervene in the affairs of humans; protecting, rebuking and reforming as occasion demands. Ancestral spirits work in concert with Òrìṣà, functioning as intermediaries between the domain of social experience and the supernatural world of spirit beings, both domains of which are under the sole authority of Ọlọ́run or Olódùmarè, the owner of heaven and the master of the universe.[4]

Òrìṣà fall into three main categories. In the first one are primordial beings that have been in existence with Olódùmarè since the creation of the universe.[5] They include Ọbàtálá, arch-divinity and deputy to Olódùmarè, who is empowered with the task of creation, and of molding of humans. Others include Ọ̀rúnmìlà, the Òrìṣà of divination and knowledge, and Èṣù the unpredictable Òrìṣà of fate and human conduct. Èṣù acts as a link to other deities, and provides the pathway for the navigation of a complex and multidimensional protocol of interaction amongst deities, and between humans, deities and Olódùmarè. Alana has observed that Èṣù often "receives a portion of the sacrifices offered to other divinities so that he might not stand in the way of the sacrifices" made to such other gods.[6] The second category of deities consists of those regarded as spiritual reincarnation of departed heroes. Examples in this category include Ṣàngó, the Òrìṣà of thunder, lightning and retribution, and Ògún, the Òrìṣà of war and iron implements. In the third category are those believed to be manifestations of the power of the natural phenomena. These include Oya, Òrìṣà of the Niger River and Ṣàngó's wife; and Òkèbàdàn, the mountain deity of the people of the city of Ìbàdàn.[7]

Every major Òrìṣà in Yorùbá religion is associated with one or more specific instrumental ensembles or a set of musical practices.[8] For example, religious rituals in honor of Ọbàtálá are accompanied by and conveyed through the music played on the *ìgbìn* (three-legged drum ensemble); while those of Ọ̀rúnmìlà are accompanied by the *ìpèsè* (cylindrical drum ensemble). *Ògìdán* drums (also cylindrical in shape) and *ìjálá* (hunters' chants) are performed to honor and appease Ògún, while the bàtá ensemble (of conically-shaped drums) performs in connection with Ṣàngó.[9] The attachment of specific ensembles to each of these deities is indicative of the significance of music in Yorùbá religion, and of how the spiritual identity of individual deities is musically delineated. In the same vein, musical form and performance procedures are often defined and shaped within the context of religious protocols, a fact which hints at the liminal position of drummers as a link between humans and deities. It is also important to note that many Yorùbá sacred drums are, traditionally, rarely performed outside the shrines and the sacred rituals with which they are associated. Adegbite has observed, for example, that *àgbá-ọbalùfọ̀n* and ìpèsè (both cylindrical in shape) are, in traditional contexts, not to be performed outside the religious ceremonies and shrines of Ọbalùfọ̀n and Ọ̀rúnmìlà to which they are respectively dedicated.[10] The structure of a musical performance and the format of religious rituals are thus often mutually deterministic of one another as we will see in chapter 2. More significantly, the identity of drummers as a group of musicians is often strongly tied to their sacred roles as drummers for the Òrìṣà. Yorùbá master drummers exploring the tonal capabilities of their instruments often intone religious chants and praise on their drums, drawing from their extensive knowledge of sacred texts.

But as I explain further below, the significance of traditional religion has waned considerably since the colonial era, as a result of which Yorùbá drummers have been seeking a renegotiation of their roles and status in the society. The activities of bàtá and dùndún drummers, perhaps the two most important categories of Yorùbá drummers today, are illustrative of the competitive nature of this process of repositioning. Bàtá drummers, originally almost exclusively associated with sacred performances, now also perform in a variety of new social contexts, while their dùndún counterparts, who had hitherto performed mainly at social events, now also appear very prominently in sacred contexts.

The recent polarization of identity amongst bàtá and dùndún drummers is evidence of how they have been redefining their roles in response to the demand and dynamics of a rapidly changing social and economic environment of postcolonial Nigeria. Relying on the self-reflexive narratives of drummers and the views of nondrummers, I discuss how bàtá musicians in particular have responded to what they perceive as an emerging and worrisome domination of Yorùbá drumming by their dùndún counterparts. I discuss the development of new performance practices by bàtá drummers as an evidence of this development, and as an acknowledgment of the power of speech surrogacy in Yorùbá drumming. My analysis draws on specific ethnographic contexts as presented in live performances, a meeting of the Bàtá Drummers Association in Ìbàdàn, and traditional Yorùbá festivals that I witnessed and recorded in Òṣogbo, Ìbàdàn, Ìkìrun, and Ìbà, all located within the core bàtá and dùndún drumming areas. As a background to my discussion of the emerging competitive relationship between the two categories Yorùbá drummers, it is instructive to provide a brief reflection on Yorùbá traditional music.

Roots of Pan-Yorùbá Musical Practice

As I explained in the introduction, the Yorùbá people do not constitute a wholly homogeneous society. Rather, they exist as a number of subethnic groups whose members often refer to themselves by names like Èkìtì, Ọ̀wọ̀, Ìjèbú and Ìjèṣà. Self-identification as Yorùbá by the people began to gain currency only at the beginning of the twentieth century, and mainly in interethnic, national, and international contexts in which they have to identify themselves as a distinct group, different from non-Yorùbá groups. What is often referred to today as Yorùbá music by scholars is indeed a constellation of a few widely shared traditions, mainly those that were dispersed from the Ọ̀yọ́-speaking area. The Yorùbá intertribal wars of the nineteenth century, which significantly facilitated the movement of people from Ọ̀yọ́ to non-Ọ̀yọ́ areas, provided a major fillip for the transmission of such Ọ̀yọ́-derived musical practices. We know, for example, that captured territories were often placed under the leadership of chiefs that were posted from the city of Ọ̀yọ́, as in the case of Ede, which was placed under Timi, one of Ṣàngó's war generals.[11] The Ọ̀yọ́ cultural hegemony, which was initiated during the political ascendancy of the kingdom of Ọ̀yọ́ in the seventeenth and eighteenth centuries and sustained by the British during the colonial era, helped to create a situation in which the cultural practices of Ọ̀yọ́ were often projected as standing for the entire Yorùbá culture. While it is true that some Ọ̀yọ́-derived musical traditions have been popularized across different parts of Yorùbáland, it is important to note that each of the subethnic groups that constitute the larger Yorùbá ethnicity has its own distinct musical traditions. Unfortunately, these other traditions are rarely discussed in research work on Yorùbá music. Christopher Waterman, who has done extensive work in this aspect of Yorùbá music, corroborates some of these points by explaining that what "most scholars and government cultural officers refer to as Yorùbá music is an amorphous category comprised of numerous, often quite distinctive local practices. When ethnomusicologists write about 'traditional Yorùbá music' they are generally referring either to a set of genres disseminated over a wide area (by the indigenous empires of the eighteenth and nineteenth centuries (for example, dùndún or bàtá drumming and certain specialized styles of praise singing) or to localized styles performed by and for people who would identify themselves as Yorùbá only in inter-ethnic contexts and certainly not while participating in community-based ceremonial events."[12]

The process of popularizing Ọ̀yọ́-based musical practices in non-Ọ̀yọ́ areas of Yorùbáland has also been accounted for by Joel Adedeji with specific reference to an ancient masquerade (egúngún) sacred performance, which was developed during the reign of Alaafin Ogbolu, the king of Ọ̀yọ́ in the first half of the seventeenth century. Although initially restricted to the palace, this musico-dramatic genre was, with the king's permission, later performed to audiences outside the palace.[13] This new form later became known as *alárìnjó* (roving entertainers), a name which reflects the itinerant lifestyle of the performers who helped to popularize it in different parts of Yorùbáland. Alárìnjó performances feature bàtá drumming and acrobatic dances by masked performers known as *eégún ọ̀jẹ̀* or *eégún apidán* (masquerades with magical displays).[14]

Recent oral accounts narrated to me during my field research have corroborated the main point of this historical account. A respected bàtá drummer, Pa Dafidi Ayandola, whom I interviewed in Òṣogbo, explained that he started his career as a bàtá drummer in 1935, and later became the leader of a bàtá ensemble that accompanied a group of eégún ọ̀jẹ̀.[15] As itinerant performers, he and his group traveled from Ìrèsì, where he resided at that time, to towns such as Òṣogbo, Ẹdẹ, Èfòn-Alàyè, Òró, Ìjáráàsin, Ìlá-Ọ̀ràngún, and Èsìẹ́.[16] They traveled initially on foot and, much later, when vehicular transportation became more accessible, by bus. Alárìnjó performance was later adopted by performers of a modern Yorùbá traveling musical theatre to evolve a new musico-dramatic genre, which reworked traditional mythology, chants, songs and storytelling for modern stage presentations. This modern operatic genre, now often referred to as Yorùbá folk opera, was first popularized by Hubert Ogunde in the late 1940s, and reached its apotheosis in the operas of Duro Ladipo and Kola Ogunmola in the 1960s and 1970s.[17] These three key personalities hail from different Yorùbá ethnic groups, namely Ìjèbú (Ogunde), Òyó (Ladipo), and Èkìtì (Ogunmola), a fact which highlights the spread of this tradition across different parts of Yorùbáland. The process of musical dispersal made possible by alárìnjó performers was complementary to the one facilitated by the Yorùbá intertribal wars of the nineteenth century.

Similar oral information regarding kìrìbótó, an ensemble of gourd-resonated membrane drums, was provided during my field work in Òyó town. Kìrìbótó drummers explained to me that the ensemble was initially performed exclusively for the Alaafin within the palace.[18] In the early nineteenth century, however, the king gave permission for it to be performed for the public outside the palace.[19] The popularization of the kìrìbótó ensemble paved the way for its transmission to other parts of Yorùbáland like Ègbá and Ìjèsà, communities where the instrument is still performed.[20] A most visible evidence of the dispersal of ancient Òyó performance traditions to other parts of Yorùbáland is the Òjétúndé bàtá group, based in the town of Èrìn-Òsun. In her study of this group, Debra Klein asserts that the "Òjétúndé group's 'tradition' is the alárìnjó tradition" and attributes the dispersal of alárìnjó to the migration of Òyó people, who, having been forced by the Fulani invasion of the late eighteenth century, had to seek new settlements in "previously unsettled southern regions, including Èrìn Òsun."[21]

The diffusion of the Òyó musical tradition as shown in these accounts is framed by what could be described as vertical and lateral patterns of musical transmission. Musical traditions that had hitherto been performed exclusively for the king (Alaafin) of Òyó and the Òyó elite were later made accessible to ordinary members of the society, thus paving the way for their adoption by a wider, cross-ethnic range of musicians and participants. The bàtá and dùndún drumming traditions are perhaps the two most visible symbols of an emergent pan-Yorùbá musical culture historically linked to Òyó-Yorùbá. In chapters 7 and 8, I will elaborate on the concept that neotraditional Yorùbá music as manifested in new forms of popular music must be seen against the background of the spread of Òyó-based musical practices to other parts of Yorùbá land. Here, I focus on the activities of some specific bàtá and dùndún musicians as a basis for illustrating how Yorùbá drummers have been redefining their identities and roles as part of a strategy to be socially relevant and economically fulfilled in a modernizing social environment.

Bàtá: Ferocious Deities and a "Difficult" Instrument

Hornbostel has observed that musical traditions that have a strong religious association are generally more antiquated in their origins than those used for social purposes.[22] Corroborating Hornbostel's observation, Adegbite categorizes Yorùbá drums as (1) those invented for a specific deity from time immemorial; (2) those played in connection with a variety of deities throughout the history of the Yorùbá people; and (3) those recently introduced to the Yorùbá culture.[23] It is important to note, however, that these categories are not mutually exclusive, as highlighted in the case of the bàtá. Oral history explains that it was invented by and originally performed for Èṣù, who later gave permission for it to be used by adherents of Ṣàngó.[24] On the other hand, dùndún, now often performed in religious ceremonies, was initially used mainly for social, nonsacred purposes. It is quite striking that dùndún, unlike all the other main Yorùbá drums, is the only one not culturally attached to any specific deity, a fact which tends to support the theory about its non-Yorùbá origin.[25]

Bàtá drummers are often eager to assert that their instrument is the oldest of all Yorùbá drums, and that it has been associated with ancient Yorùbá religious practices for as long as human memory can recall. They also often stress that bàtá is a difficult instrument to master. The drummers reiterated this point to me many times, drawing my attention to the relatively large size of their instrument, the need to suspend the drum around the neck and shoulder and play its two drum heads simultaneously, and the challenge of making the instrument "talk." It is generally believed that playing the drum demands considerable stamina; bàtá performances are sometimes led by two master drummers who take turns playing the ìyáàlù bàtá.[26]

Bàtá drummers also draw connections between the challenging conditions of playing their instrument, the piercing sound of the music, and the use of bàtá drumming to communicate with deities. The spiritual "power" of the instrument is often illustrated by narrations of how it was used by ancient Yorùbá warriors. Bàtá drumming, it was believed, had the power to energize warriors in battle. Commenting on the power of the bàtá, Oyewo, an expert on Yorùbá traditional culture, has observed that "the ferocious sound of the beats and the intimidating shape of the drums together with the rigorous beating are attuned to the ferocious disposition attributed to Ṣàngó himself."[27]

While the use of the bàtá for war purposes now seems to be a thing of the past, the instrument continues to perform important sacred functions. In Òṣogbo, for example, bàtá drums still accompany the town-wide procession of gbógorù (a sacred masquerade), believed to be spiritually powerful. Because of the cultural perception of the bàtá as an instrument of extraordinary power, bàtá musicians affirm strongly that their drum is not a musical instrument for the weakling. Only men who combine physical strength with an ability to connect with spiritual powers are considered fit to play the instrument.

Figure 1.1. Ayanlere's bàtá ensemble. *Center*, Ayanlere, ìyáàlù bàtá; *left*, Ayanwole, omele abo; *right*, Ayanyemi, omele-aḳọ. Ìbàdàn, 2010, photo by author.

The status of the bàtá as a source of spiritual energy is often contrasted with the entertaining role of its sister drum, the dùndún, which is viewed by many bàtá drummers as the instrument of ìgbádùn (enjoyment), a reference to the prominence of the dùndún in social ceremonies. This view also carries an implicit notion that dùndún drumming is less difficult to master than bàtá drumming. As I explain below, perceived differences in the acoustic properties and the speech-representing capabilities of these two instruments are critical to the ways in which bàtá and dùndún drummers have redefined and reformulated their musical roles and performance practices in recent times.

Talking and Stammering Modes of Drumming

The bàtá and dùndún are both double-membrane, or bimembranophonic, drums. But the bàtá is "ambi-percussive," because both of its two drumheads are played, while the dùndún is "uni-percussive," as only one of its heads is normally played.[28] Both drums consist of a hollowed-out wooden frame that is covered on both ends with a goatskin stretched to permanent tension. The membrane heads of both drums are held in place by strips of leather cordage that help pin them to the wood. The similarities between the two instruments end there, however. Dùndún's unique acoustic properties derive basically from its capability to produce a wide range of tones through the manipulation of the leather strips that connect its two drumheads. Bàtá drums lack this tone-producing mechanism and are therefore unable to properly imitate the inflectional patterns of the Yorùbá language. Yorùbá people often distinguish between these two performance qualities by referring to the bàtá as a stammering instrument (akólòlò). The comparison between bàtá and dùndún drums in terms of their speech capabilities has featured fairly well in academic literature. Ulli Beier, a German anthropologist writing in 1954, explained that "it is much more difficult to talk (on the bàtá) and far more difficult to understand."[29] In the same vein, Euba, who is considered the greatest academic authority on Yorùbá drumming, has observed that "the tonal capacity of the bàtá drum is limited to two fixed pitches and additional pitches can only be obtained by muting."[30]

Commenting on the same issue, Adegbite explains that "the reason for the [recent] adoption of dùndún by some religious sects is that it is easier to understand its language. According to him, while "Iya'lu [mother drum] of Dùndún can speak certain phrases intelligibly, the Iya'lu of the Bàtá set needs the help of Emele ako to be . . . intelligible when playing these phrases. It is for this reason that Iya'lu of Bàtá is often referred to as akò lòlò."[31] Kolawole and Ladipo have also described the bàtá as a "stammer drum."[32] Although the word kòlòlò (derived from the noun akòlòlò) translates as "stammer," it is important to note that the use of the word in this context is figurative rather than literal. It is intended to capture the limited speech capability of the drum, not to imply that the drum's speech resembles a stutter.

In my field research I observed that many average Yorùbá listeners, both young and old, agree with this conclusion—they say that it is more difficult for them to understand the speech of bàtá drumming than that of the dùndún.[33] Many bàtá drummers, however, reject the claim that their instrument cannot "talk" coherently. Some go so far as to say that the bàtá can "talk" far more eloquently than the dùndún. Such testimonies may not, however, be unconnected with the politics of identity involving bàtá and dùndún drummers, an issue on which I elaborate later in the chapter. Musibau Ayanlere, an Ìbàdàn-based bàtá drummer with whom I have worked closely, agrees with the suggestion that it is far easier for the average Yorùbá listener to understand "what the dùndún is saying than what the bàtá is saying." This view is supported by Amanda Villepastour who, although she challenges the "notion that the bàtá has difficulty talking," has observed that it is "indisputable that the bàtá is more difficult to understand for most Yorùbá speakers than the dùndún." This, according to her, is "due to the dùndún's large pitch range and gliding capacity, which make it more aurally accessible to Yorùbá speakers. The bàtá, with its narrower pitch range, has a different technique for representing tone glides and is less accessible to listeners unfamiliar with its mode of speech."[34] In order to understand the sonic structure of bàtá music, the basis for its label as a "stammer drum," and why it is quite challenging for the average Yorùbá listener to comprehend its mode of talking, it helps to have an understanding of how the drum ensemble is organized.

The Yorùbá Bàtá

A bàtá ensemble typically consists of four or five instruments (depending on how they are counted), with each instrument named according to its function. The ìyáàlù bàtá (the bàtá mother-drum) leads and propels bàtá performances through text-based and nonlexical musical narratives. Other drums in the ensemble, which support or accompany the ìyáàlù, are known collectively as the *omele*.[35] These secondary instruments, in their order of hierarchy, are: the omele abo (female support drum), which is usually next in size to the ìyáàlù, and two small drums, the omele ako (male support drum) and the omele kúdí (child support drum). The omele ako and kúdí (often collectively referred to as *omele méjì*, that is, two omele) are usually tied together and played by one drummer as a single instrument, often providing a steady ostinato. Another instrument of the ensemble is known as the *èjìn*, which is generally about the same size as the ìyáàlù; its main function being to provide a deep and regular "grounding" beat. The players of the ìyáàlù and èjìn often alternate their roles, especially in extended performances demanding extraordinary stamina on the part of the ìyáàlù player. By taking turns, each of the two players can take a rest and regain their energy at regular intervals.

The larger of the two drumheads of the ìyáàlù bàtá (and that of the omele abo bàtá) is known as the *ojú òjò*. It is played with the palm of the right hand. The smaller drumhead of the ìyáàlù bàtá (like that of the omele abo bàtá) is known as the *ṣáṣá*, and is played with a leather or plastic beater (*bílálà*), held usually in the left hand.[36] Its relatively high and sonorous sounds complement the low pitch areas of the bigger drumhead. The placing of *ìda*, a black tuning paste, on the ojú òjò, and the simultaneous use of the two drumheads are devices that help the lead drummer generate a limited number of pitch areas, often barely distinguishable from one another. Different hand techniques are used to generate such pitch areas on the ojú òjò. They include the use of the lower part of the palm to generate an "open" pitch at the fringe area of the drum surface. A marginally higher sound is produced by muting the fringe area of the drum head, and a still higher tone is made by striking the inner area of the drumhead with the upper part of the palm. These playing techniques have been described as "open," "mute," and "slap" respectively.[37] The categorization of the bàtá as a "stammering" drum occurs in connection with the difficult challenge of "talking" with the instrument, a problem clearly related to the paucity of clear pitch levels and the corresponding lack of tonal clarity. The use of multiple omele drums, tied together to form the *omele méta* (three omele drums) and the *omele méfà* (six omele drums) is, as I was informed by my research assistants, a relatively new development. I discuss this issue further later in the chapter.

The Ìyáàlù and Omele Abo in the Bàtá Ensemble

In order to fully understand the inner workings of the bàtá ensemble, it is important to understand the nature of the relationship between the ìyáàlù bàtá and the omele abo bàtá.[38] As an additional "voice" within the bàtá ensemble, the omele abo is, as earlier mentioned, often described by bàtá drummers as the *ògbùfò* (speech assistant), whose duty is to help make clearer the "speech" utterances of the ìyáàlù bàtá. The use of the omele abo bàtá is, however, often much more variable than as suggested in the concept of *ògbùfò*. Describing the role of the omele abo to me, Musibau Ayanlere, an Ìbàdàn-based bàtá drummer with whom I have worked extensively, explained that it alternates between providing "ridim" (rhythm) and joining the ìyáàlù bàtá to "talk." According to him, the omele abo may join the ìyáàlù bàtá at the beginning, the middle, or toward the end of a phrase. Thus, although the drum often duplicates the phrases of the ìyáàlù bàtá, it also often provides repetitive and beat-articulating patterns.

Unlike the omele akọ bàtá, whose part is mostly repetitive, the omele abo bàtá often plays a dynamic part. This arrangement contrasts with what obtains in the dùndún ensemble, in which the functional demarcation between the ìyáàlù dùndún and the omele drums is generally much more distinct. Although an omele drum may, in a dùndún ensemble, play limited variations, it does not normally engage in substantial dialogue with the ìyáàlù in the manner that the omele abo does in a bàtá ensemble. The challenge of interpreting the utterances of bàtá is complicated by the dialogical and often overlapping relationship between the part of the ìyáàlù bàtá and that of the omele abo bàtá, providing the basis for the relatively complex structure of bàtá drumming.

The challenge of decoding bàtá's "speech" inevitably draws attention to its traditional sacred functions. The restricted nature of its utterances is not incompatible with its role as an instrument traditionally associated with secret sacred rites and performed by a restricted group of musicians. Indeed, bàtá drummers continue to define themselves as an exclusive circle of musicians through the use of a body of linguistic codes known as *enàan bàtá*, a form of spoken language that is exclusive to bàtá drummers. Enàan bàtá, which Villepastour suggests may have originally served "to transmit musical information,"[39] is often employed as a form of communication among bàtá drummers in nonmusical situations. The restricted and sacred nature of bàtá drumming parallels the use of an exclusive linguistic code among its players.[40]

The obscurity and exclusivity of bàtá music stand in contrast to the relative clarity and accessibility of dùndún drumming. I subject this last point to some scrutiny later in the chapter.

Narratives of Identity and Fury

The domination of modern Yorùbá social and performance spaces by dùndún drummers has been a source of concern to many bàtá drummers. At a meeting of the Ọ̀yọ́ State Bàtá Drummers Association held in Ìbàdàn, Yorùbá's second largest city after Lagos, in 2007,[41] the topic of discussion was how to reverse this trend and what the drummers saw as the declining patronage of bàtá music. I use the word "patronage" here to refer to different forms of support, including opportunities and invitations to perform at social or religious occasions and educational institutions; as well as encouragement and financial support from individuals, government departments as well as cultural and philanthropic bodies. This meeting, one of the largest congregations of bàtá drummers in Nigeria in recent times, attracted drummers from the core areas of bàtá drumming, including Ọ̀yọ́, Ṣakí, Ìkìrun, Ìlá, Ògbómọ̀ṣọ́, and Ìbàdàn. Present were leading bàtá drummers like Pa Ayantayo Amusa, the Baálẹ Alubàtá (chief of bàtá drummers) of Ìbàdàn—the chief host for the meeting; Pa Ayanleye Shittu, the Ààrẹ Alubàtá (chief of bàtá drummers) of Ìṣẹ́yìn, and the President of the Ọ̀yọ́ State Bàtá Drummers Association; Pa Ayanwola Azeez, the Ààrẹ Oníbàtá of Ìgànná; Pa Ayansola Tafa from Ìṣẹ́yìn; and Pa Ayanriola Yekini Adigun from Ìbàdàn. Musibau Ayanlere was also present at the meeting. The drummers identified two groups of "enemies" behind their misfortune: dùndún drummers, whom they constantly referred to as "our counterparts" (àwọn ẹnìkejì i wa); and government agencies (àwọn ìjọba). Bàtá drummers explained that their "counterparts" were depriving them of the prestige and respect that they deserved as members of an ancient and prestigious Yorùbá drumming tradition. They complained that dùndún drummers often relegated them to the background by making them play accompaniment patterns (omele) in joint ensembles involving dùndún and bàtá. In such ensembles, a dùndún, rather than bàtá player, was often allocated the leading role—the part that does the "talking."

The government was accused of not according the same level of recognition to bàtá drummers as to their counterparts. At the end of the meeting, bàtá drummers advised their members to resist all forms of marginalization, and urged agencies of government to be more inclusive in their patronage of traditional musicians.[42] It is important to note that the group of bàtá drummers that converged for this meeting was parallel to a much larger one comprising both bàtá and dùndún drummers. The tone of the Ìbàdàn meeting suggested a high degree of frustration with the umbrella group, and a felt need to consolidate an association that would be exclusive to bàtá drummers and within which issues

Figure 1.2a. Bàtá Drummers Association. *From left:* Ayanwọla Azeez (Ààrẹ Oníbàtá of Ìgànnáland), Ayangbekun Adigun (Ààrẹ Alubàtá of Ògbómọ̀ṣó), Ayantayọ Amusa (Baálẹ̀ Alubàtá of Ìbàdàn), Ayanṣọla Tafa (standing, Alubàtá from Ìséyìn, now deceased), Ayanlẹyẹ Shittu (President, Oníbàtá of Ọ̀yọ́ State), and Ààrẹ Alubàtá of Ìséyìnland. Ìbàdàn, 2007, photo by author.

specific to their own interests could be tackled. It was very clear to everyone at the meeting, which I was privileged to attend as an observer, that this smaller group affiliation was needed to protect the interests and project the identity of bàtá drummers and resist what they saw as the dominant status of their dùndún counterparts.

In order to gain insights into how bàtá drummers conceive their role and position in contemporary Yorùbá society, it is instructive to analyze some of the statements of the musicians as articulated during the Ìbàdàn meeting of the Ọ̀yọ́ State Bàtá Drummers Association. The self-reflexive nature of these statements strikingly shows how these bàtá musicians have been reacting to the changing dynamics of their social and cultural environment. Their narratives begin with a reaffirmation of their belief in the primacy of bàtá drumming in Yorùbá culture. The claim to the custodianship of Yorùbá drumming constitutes part of a strategy to strengthen their quest for a greater stake in

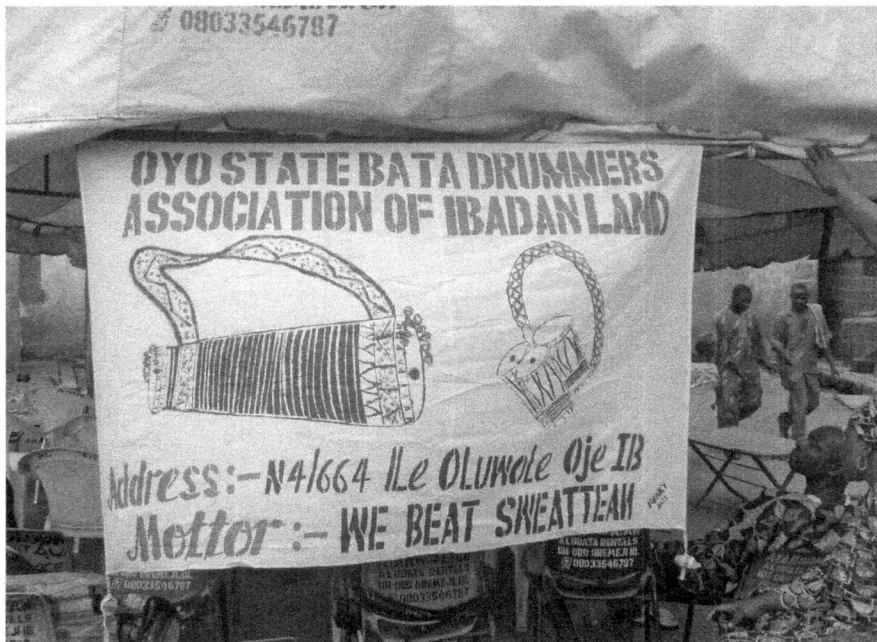

Figure 1.2b. Banner at the Bàtá Drummers Association. Ìbàdàn, 2007, photo by author.

contemporary Yorùbá drumming. These issues resonate strongly in the series of statements made by the drummers during the meeting, samples of which I analyze below.

The following exemplifies bàtá drummers' classic touting of their instrument's primordial roots: "Dùndún came to the world at noon; we (bàtá players) were on earth since morning. Bàtá is the king of all drums." In addition, many bàtá drummers informed me that bàtá is "àgbà ìlù" (elder drum), in contrast to dùndún, which was described as "ọmọdé ìlù" (child drum). In Yorùbá culture, seniority in age begets honor and respect, a fact which is often articulated in Yorùbá proverbs. The popular Yorùbá proverb "Ẹni a bá bá lábà ni baba," which roughly translates as "The earliest person is the leader," is a case in point. Elderly men and women are considered for positions of responsibility over younger ones, and lines to royal and chiefly positions are decided on the basis of seniority in age. Wisdom, it is believed, comes with age. In explaining this, another Yorùbá proverb asserts that "the wisdom of an old man is the cumulative of knowledge gained from other people over a long period of time."[43] This emphasis on seniority in age and experience provides the backdrop for understanding the cultural roots of the assertion by bàtá drummers that bàtá's seniority should naturally guarantee them an undeniable leadership claim to the custodianship of Yorùbá drumming.

"There are many drums: koso, dùndún, ṣẹ̀kẹ̀rẹ̀, but bàtá is king." In this statement, bàtá musicians reiterate their conviction that their music is superior to other types of Yorùbá instrumental music, represented here by dùndún, ṣẹ̀kẹ̀rẹ̀ (Yorùbá gourd rattle), and koso, a single-headed tension membrane.[44] The statement hints at the dominance of bàtá drumming in the precolonial Yorùbá culture and its strong attachment to religious, political, and social institutions of the time. But political and social institutions of societies, being neither static nor sacrosanct, remain susceptible to internally and externally generated change, as evident in the declining fortunes of Yorùbá bàtá drummers, most noticeably since the last two to three decades of the twentieth century. In spite of their constant reminisces about a glorious past, bàtá drummers do admit the reality of their dwindling relevance, as clearly revealed in the next statement.

"Bàtá was the first to arrive on earth; we used to be the ones that invited our counterparts [dùndún players] to come and eat." Although this statement consolidates the historical claim of previous expressions, it goes on to admit the alteration of the social equation that, in the past, privileged bàtá over dùndún drummers. Dùndún musicians, this statement suggests, were the ones who in the past struggled for social relevance and economic survival. Their survival depended on the magnanimity of bàtá drummers who were kind enough to allow dùndún drummers to benefit from the material gains that accrued to them as the exclusive beneficiaries of institutional patronage in precolonial Yorùbá society. To "invite to come and eat" is a statement that emerged as part of a new Yorùbá discourse during the economic downturn of the 1980s and 1990s. It means to help someone secure employment, get a political appointment, or win a profitable government contract. In making this statement, bàtá drummers evoke the buoyant economic conditions of the past to reflect on their declining status. This statement is thus loaded with meanings that attest to the changing social conditions and the evolving identity of Yorùbá musicians. Dùndún musicians, as suggested in this statement, are the beneficiaries of an emergent social and economic order in postcolonial Nigeria.

As the statements progress, the tone of bàtá drummers becomes sharper and more biting: "Dùndún people have turned us into trash; we said we would henceforth have nothing to do with them. If a drummer calls a dancer a fool, the dancer should not dance in a manner that corroborates such a label [Bí onílù bá tilẹ̀ ń lu a mà rọ́bọ, ẹni tí óń jo kìí ṣọbọ]." In accounting for the decline in their social and economic status, bàtá drummers accuse dùndún drummers of insulting and debasing them. The second line of the statement conveys this feeling through another Yorùbá proverb. Bàtá drummers must now stand up to their antagonists.

We should not allow them to dip our heads inside a hole. They hate us, would keep us at the backside and make us play redundant rhythms. They made themselves treasurer, representative, secretary; but nothing for bàtá. They used us as rainwater. Now we have lit the lamp and can see the posterior of the chicken. No man here could say that a dùndún man has done him any good. They kept us at the back line of the ensemble and made us play redundantly (tó tó tó tó). We are not bastards and we should not behave like bastards. Let us work together.

The remaining statements develop these themes with increasingly powerful symbolisms. With reference to how administrative positions are allocated within the umbrella association of dùndún and bàtá drummers, they complain that important positions, such as those of treasurer and secretary, are often allocated to dùndún drummers, while "there is nothing for us." Moving away from a narrative of self-pity, the drummers seem to suddenly rediscover their ability to "liberate" themselves. Thus, they express a new resolve to "work together" and do something about their plight. They affirm: "Now we have lit the lamp and can see the posterior of the chicken."

As these narratives clearly show, bàtá drummers believe that there has been a gradual but sustained erosion of their social relevance and domain of influence. The status of traditional Yorùbá religion, to which bàtá is historically attached, has been declining due to the rising profile of Christianity and Islam. This is destabilizing for bàtá music, which for hundreds of years was systematized as sacred music, and whose musical repertoire was for a long time conceived as an integral aspect of the protocols and liturgy of indigenous Yorùbá religion. Thus, apart from the issue of bàtá's limited capability for speech surrogacy, it should also be noted that the performance constituency of bàtá as traditionally defined has diminished in popularity, especially because modern-day listeners lack sufficient knowledge about the ancient rituals and Yorùbá texts to understand the music based on these texts. The dislocation between the social dispensation of modern listeners and the cultural significance of an ancient ensemble is a familiar story in many African postcolonial societies where instrumental ensembles that were initially tied to ancient religious cults and ritual ceremonies have declined in their social relevance. In many such cases though, indigenous drummers have been able to redirect and even alter the content and context of their musical performance to conform to the changing needs of their environment. For example, Patricia Tang, in her study of Senegalese music, has explained that *sabar* drumming, which was originally associated exclusively with indigenous social and religious institutions, has found a new outlet in *mbalax* music, a new urban-based social dance music.[45]

The ability to understand and evaluate speech-based drumming is often related to how conversant a listener is with the context and cultural foundations of the performance. With specific reference to the Yorùbá drum language, it is important to note that speech-based "melo-rhythmic" patterns are generally interpretable and accessible only through sustained familiarity with their immediate and remote musical and cultural contexts.[46] Furthermore, a single melo-rhythmic pattern could convey a variety of meanings, depending on the specific nature of the context of performance. The clarity and communicability of a performance thus derive as much from the extent to which melo-rhythms are able to capture tonal and rhythmic patterns of speech as from the application of the knowledge of the cultural milieu of performance to the task of interpretation. The marginalization of the religious contexts of bàtá performances in modern Yorùbá society, and the limited tonal capability of the instrument have posed a considerable challenge to the practice of bàtá drumming in the past century. In order to capture the contrasting social and cultural spaces within which bàtá and dùndún drumming traditions tend to thrive, I now provide two ethnographic cases that are typical, though not exhaustive, of the performance contexts of each of the ensembles.

Performance Contexts: Two Contrasting Ethnographic Examples

A Bàtá Performance in Ìbà

This account focuses on an eégún òjè performance that I watched in a small village called Ìbà, a rural agricultural community close to Ìkìrun in Òṣun state, on July 25, 2007. The performance featured masked male dancers accompanied by bàtá drumming. As in many parts of Africa, Yorùbá masquerades are regarded as symbolic representations of ancestral spirits.[47] On the day of the performance, I traveled from Òṣogbo, the capital of Òṣun, arriving at Ìbà at about 6:30 p.m. I was struck by the sight of villagers sitting in front of their houses in a relaxed mood, enjoying the cool breeze of the evening, a remarkable contrast to the hustle and bustle of the city of Òṣogbo, just a few kilometers away. I exchanged greetings with some of them and proceeded to a little mud house roofed with rusty corrugated iron sheets. All the four male masked dancers lived in this house; the drummers came from a nearby town, Ìkìrun. The performance started when the four masqueraders danced from inside the house into the open courtyard in front. As soon as they were sighted, the drummers began to play. I looked around at this point and realized that, apart from the performers, I was the only person in the vicinity.

The masqueraders were three men and a young boy, all of whom were covered from head to toe in colorful (mainly red) attire that was richly decorated with black and white stripes. Their hands were concealed by gloves, and their faces by velvet cloths with small perforations through which they could see. The leader of the masquerade started the performance with a rather showy acrobatic dance, and the others soon followed, taking turns doing a variety of acrobatic movements with legs, arms and the torso. These movements were often sharp and swift, matched to the piercing staccato sounds of the bàtá. Those who were not

Figure 1.3. Eégun Ọ̀jẹ̀, with bàtá drummers. Ìbà, 2007, photo by author.

dancing at any given time sang in a call-and-response format. Vocal performance functioned rather peripherally, however; it was rendered sporadically to motivate the other dancers into action.

Each solo dancer interacted intimately with the leader of the drum ensemble, generating an intertextual dialogue in which dance steps functioned as visual representations of drum strokes. The more agitated the rhythms were, the more intensely the masqueraders danced. About twenty minutes into the performance, the dancers progressed into more spectacular acrobatic displays—running, jumping, and somersaulting.

Suddenly, I realized that a very sizable audience had formed a ring around the performers. The audience was a mixed one, consisting mostly of young boys and girls and a few elderly men and women. *Eégún ọ̀jè* (a masquerade designed to entertain), unlike its more potent counterpart, *eégún alágbo* (a masquerade involving the power of witchcraft), may be watched in performance by any member of the community, because its main purpose is to entertain. Many members of the (participating) audience expressed their appreciation by clapping, shouting, or coming into the dance arena to do a few steps or to drop money for the performers. The performance ended at about 7:30 p.m. The audience, which had now grown into a large crowd, burst into a loud ovation as the masquerades danced back into the house, while the sounds of the drums stopped rather reluctantly.

As this account illustrates, bàtá drumming remains strongly attached to ancient traditional performances like eégún òjè. Its patronage is thus still strongly defined within traditionally derived performance contexts in which it is performed as part of indigenous religious (or quasi-religious) event. Although eégún òjè performances are conceived largely as social events, Yorùbá masquerades, whether entertaining or spiritually potent, are regarded as representations of ancestral spirits. Thus, while bàtá drumming remains popular in traditional Yorùbá musical life, its typical performance contexts are removed from the more lucrative world of urban modern music, in which dùndún has fared much better. It is also important to note that dùndún drummers, partly because of their ability to generate easily understood praise poetry on their drums, are generally more comfortable—and indeed more daring—in exploring new contexts for well-paid performances. These differences are brought into sharp relief in the ethnographic account of a dùndún performance.

A Dùndún Performance in Ìbàdàn

The dùndún performance that I have chosen to describe took place, ironically, during the Bàtá Drummers Association meeting that I earlier discussed. This performance illustrates how dùndún drummers create performance opportunities even in the most difficult and unwelcoming circumstances. Midway into the meeting, two dùndún drummers suddenly showed up—uninvited, of course. That they were not invited was not the problem; dùndún musicians often show up uninvited at social ceremonies with the sole intention of making money by praising people, including strangers. No one could have imagined, however, that dùndún drummers would show up at a meeting of bàtá drummers that was being held specifically to map out strategies to resist them. Although the two "interloping" dùndún players were not privy to the agenda of that meeting, their decision to interrupt the meeting of a large group of bàtá drummers speaks to their legendary ability to force their way into an otherwise restricted social space for the purpose of enacting an economically profitable performance. Without hesitation, the two dùndún drummers began to play their drums to praise the bàtá drummers and some others, including myself. Their mode of operation was typical: move around, identify a potential "patron," and cast a probing eye on him or her to identify physical attributes that might provide topics for praise-drumming. They soon zeroed in on me, moved closer, and began to praise me with their drumming. They drummed that my slight obesity is a sign of wealth, and that my "fair skin" reminds them of the "adorable redness of palm oil." They stopped praising me with their drums after I had given them "a little change,"

Figure 1.4. Raimi Ayanniyi Adepoju (*hidden*), and Lamidi Alayande, two uninvited dùndún drummers performing for leaders of the Bàtá Drummers Association. Ìbàdàn, 2007, photo by author.

and moved on to another person to repeat the same process. They moved around the fringes of the arena for another fifteen minutes or so, and then, to everyone's surprise, headed straight to the high table, where the executive members and zonal leaders of the Bàtá Drummers Association were seated.

Cognizant of the fact that an important meeting was going on, they engaged each of the executive members sitting at the high table, playing praise narratives that addressed the leaders' physical features, and moving on to the next person only after they had been rewarded monetarily. To my great surprise, each of the executive members responded without apparent hostility. They gave money and nodded in appreciation of each sequence of praise-drumming. The hostility articulated in the narratives above was suspended during the series of short and focused renditions of the two dùndún drummers.

This dùndún "outing" (*ìjáde*) contrasts sharply with the bàtá performance earlier described in a number of ways. First, eégún òjè performance represents a ready format for bàtá drumming. The performance conventions of eégún òjè are relatively fixed. In the dùndún example, however, what we see is a group of drummers proactively identifying, defining, and controlling an arena of performance. Bàtá drummers are also known to show up uninvited at social events, but dùndún drummers are far more likely to be seen in such contexts.

Dùndún drumming enjoys highly visibility in urban neotraditional forms such as jùjú and fújì, and it also features far more prominently than bàtá at social ceremonies such as namings, marriages, and house-warmings. Again, bàtá drummers also participate in new neotraditional popular music, notably fújì, but to a lesser extent. Itinerant dùndún drummers, moving as soloists or in groups, often go uninvited to entertain guests at such ceremonies, making money by praising individuals and groups and providing peripheral performances that compete favorably with those of the invited bands at such ceremonies. Furthermore, educational institutions, eager to expose their students to traditional Yorùbá drumming, often engage dùndún drummers, not bàtá drummers, as instructors; and Christian churches across Yorùbáland now commonly feature dùndún drummers, both during worship services and at Christian social gatherings outside the church. Bàtá drums have yet to attract significant patronage at these modern performance spaces.[48] To explore further the social and cultural disparities between dùndún and bàtá drummers, I present below biographical sketches for two drummers with whom I worked closely in the course of conducting field research for this book in Nigeria.

Sule Ayantunde: A Dùndún Drummer's Story

Born in 1943, Sule Ayantunde, who hails from Láàrọ̀ Street in Ìsàlẹ̀ Ọ̀ṣun in Òṣogbo, is the current Àrẹ̀ẹlu (chief of drummers) for Òṣogbo. Ayantunde is a member of the Oluawo Ayanka Oyetade, one of the families of prestigious drummers from which the Àrẹ̀ẹlu may be selected. Ayantunde started learning the art of drumming at the age of six, when he followed his elder brothers and cousins to performance engagements and occasionally played the konkolo pattern on secondary instruments (omele).

Ayantunde left for Ilé-Ìfẹ̀ in 1956, when his father moved there. Although he was enrolled at different elementary schools, including the Salvation Army School at Òkè Àmàlà, Modákẹ́kẹ́, and later, the St Paul's Primary School, Ayégbajú-Ìfẹ̀, he never abandoned drumming. He combined schooling with drum apprenticeship under master drummers Lasisi Ayandokun, Kehinde Olowolagba, and Buremoh Adedokun, all of whom were based in Ilé-Ìfẹ̀ at the time. Apart from playing traditional-style dùndún, he also spent time playing gángan (small-size hourglass drum) in neotraditional jùjú music ensembles that combined Yorùbá and Western instruments. Ayantunde recalls with nostalgia his stint with a man called Iyiade, who led a jùjú band in Ilé-Ìfẹ̀ in the early 1960s. He explained that playing with Iyiade equipped him with the skills needed to jam with jùjú and fújì musicians.

Figure 1.5. Ayantunde Sule, the Àrẹẹlu of Òṣogbo, performing at the Òṣun Òṣogbo festival. Òṣogbo, 2008, photo by author.

Ayantunde finished his primary school education in 1960 and, one year later, proceeded to the Seventh Day Secondary Modern School for his secondary education, which he was unable to complete for lack of money. He returned to Òṣogbo in 1963 with a serious illness. Following his miraculous healing by a traditional herbalist, Ayantunde decided to train as an herbalist himself, a mission which lasted from 1963 to 1969, and which further deepened his knowledge of Yorùbá drum repertories, especially those associated with Òsanyìn, the deity of healing and medicine. He went back to Ilé-Ìfẹ to continue his professional life as a drummer, and also engaged in other jobs. Indeed, until recently, Ayantunde has combined his work as a drummer with other vocations; he worked as a cook and waiter at the Mayfair Hotel in Ilé-Ìfẹ, as a bicycle repairer in Òṣogbo; and in 1976, as a water-pump operator with a construction company at Iwo, near Òṣogbo. Like many traditional Yorùbá drummers who also work as carpenters, tailors, and barbers, among other trades, Ayantunde realized that he needed to supplement his work as a drummer in order to make ends meet. Ayantunde returned to Òṣogbo in 1979 to finally settle down, a decision that brought him back to his family roots and stood him in good stead to champion the traditional

Figure 1.6. Ayantunde's dùndún ensemble. *From left:* Yunisa Ayanbiyi, aguda (or kẹríkẹrì); Ayansola Oladosu, kánran ìṣáájú; Sule Ayantunde, ìyáàlù dùndún; Laisi Ayanwale, gúdúgúdú. Osun grove, Òṣogbo, 2006, photo by author.

role of his family as the principal guardian of dùndún drumming in the town. As at 2009, members of Ayantunde's dùndún ensemble included Ayansola Oladosu, who played kánran ìsáájú; Yunisa Ayanbiyi, who played aguda (also known as kẹríkẹrì) and Laisi Ayanwale, who played *gúdúgúdú* (a pot-shaped drum).[49] The dùndún music examples that I study in chapter 2 derive from the performances of this group. The most important traditional function that Ayantunde performs as Àrẹẹlu is that of leading and coordinating the principal dùndún ensemble for the annual Òṣun festival, a duty which Ayantunde has performed since 1987. Prior to his selection as the Àrẹẹlu earlier this year, Ayantunde performed that role in an acting capacity, standing in for his uncle, Olaniyi Ayansiju, who was too ill to discharge his duties as the Àrẹẹlu. (Ayantunde's confirmation as the chief of drummers followed the death of Olaniyi Ayansiju.) A number of important points have emerged from this brief biography. Ayantunde, although a professional drummer, is constantly aware of the need to engage in other vocational activities in order to make ends meet. As a child, he went to a Western-style school with his age-mates in Western Nigeria, the only part of the country to have a successful free education program at that time, thanks to the visionary leadership of Chief Obafemi Awolowo, the first premier of the Western region. While at school, he continued to train under different master drummers after school hours and on weekends, when most of the social ceremonies at which dùndún drummers perform normally take place. This form of bicultural education typifies the career of many Yorùbá drummers.

The career of Ayantunde clearly shows that professional drumming activities in Òṣogbo are male-dominated, and that education in drumming is a privilege associated with one's family. For Ayantunde, becoming a drummer was a predetermined fact. He was born into it, and virtually every male within his extended family was involved in the art of drumming. His father, uncles, cousins, and brothers were all involved in sustaining a well-guarded family tradition. Also worthy of note is the role that the factor of age plays in the process of selecting who becomes the chief of drummers. Older drummers are generally preferred even if there are more competent younger ones. Ayantunde does not receive a salary or any form of regular compensation for his role as the lead drummer for community events in Òṣogbo. Although Yorùbá drummers may receive some nominal rewards from town chiefs and audience members when they perform within traditional contexts, they often engage in other (nonmusical) vocations. In addition, they often seek nontraditional performance spaces where they can make more money for their musical work. Ayantunde often performs with modern jùjú and fújì bands because such new contexts pay better than traditional religious activities do. To meet the expectations of participants in these nonsacred contexts, he has explored the power of the oríkì, the Yorùbá praise poetry, which represents perhaps the most important tool of social engagement in Yorùbá performance: drummers are handsomely rewarded for their ability to praise people. Ayantunde explained to me many times that the dùndún drum has the greatest capability of all Yorùbá drums to reproduce the Yorùbá oríkì, and that he finds that to be a major advantage for him as a drummer. His ability to play in praise-singing jùjú bands is, according to him, closely linked to this advantage.

Ayantunde's use of his drum to generate oríkì is not limited to popular events. I remember one instance in which he turned a sacred performance in honor of Ṣàngó in Òṣogbo into an opportunity to make some money; as soon as the sacred part of the festival was over, he and his ensemble began to move round the venue of the festival, praising individual participants, including myself, for instant monetary reward.

Musibau Taiwo Ayanlere: A Bàtá Drummer's Story

Musibau Taiwo Ayanlere was one of the bàtá drummers present at the meeting of the Bàtá Drummers Association described above. He has worked consistently to cope with the challenge of a declining patronage of bàtá music by embracing and popularizing two relatively new configurations of bàtá ensemble, namely, *omele mẹ́ta* and *omele mẹ́fà*. These configurations both consist of a row of multiple omele drums (three in the case of omele *mẹ́ta* and six in the case of omele *mẹ́fà*); they have evolved as part of the attempt to boost the capability of the bàtá ensemble to imitate Yorùbá speech and generate a more effective drum language. Ayanlere has also been playing with modern popular bands and seeking opportunities to perform internationally. Compared with those of Ayantunde, Ayanlere's career activities reflect a stronger sense of urgency and a more concerted effort to keep his music relevant in the modern world.

Born in 1965 into an Àyàn family, Musibau Taiwo Ayanlere is today a notable professional bàtá player in Ìbàdàn. He went to stay with his grandfather, Ayantegbe Lasisi, following the death of his father in 1968, and by age four, had started learning how to play the bàtá. As is customary, Ayanlere started with the omele category of drums, playing repetitive standard patterns within an ensemble headed by his grandfather. He also devoted attention to the construction and repair of bàtá drums. Ayanlere explained to me that he started learning bàtá drumming first by playing a single omele drum, and graduated to playing two omele drums. At that stage he was capable of accompanying key bàtá drum styles, including *lábóó, elékóto, ẹlẹ́ṣẹ̀,* and *kògbà.*

Ayanlere's training as a bàtá drummer was not restricted to working with members of his family. Like Ayantunde, he worked with other prominent drummers in Ìbàdàn, including Pa Otolorin of the Oke Bioku compound of Beere; Pa Yesufu Ayantola and Pa Lalude, both of the Alájé compound of Ọ̀rányàn area. Ayanlere was particularly fortunate in the sense that he was exposed to and trained in the three allied traditions of the bàtá: his mother was a highly proficient bàtá music dancer, while his grandfather combined virtuosic bàtá drumming with a remarkable ability to perform a form of chanting known as *ẹ̀ṣà*, which goes with bàtá drumming. In mastering these aspects, Ayanlere benefited largely from the tutelage of his mother and grandfather. Ayanlere's brilliant mastery of bàtá drumming was also helped by the fact that his grandfather relied exclusively on family members for all bàtá outings rather than hiring bàtá drummers from outside their family to complement family strengths, as was customary then. This put enormous pressure on Ayanlere and his brothers; they had no choice but to master an exhaustive repertoire and develop a wide range of techniques within a relatively short time. By the age of thirteen, when he commenced formal Western education, he had attained a significant proficiency level, performing at private and public events along with his grandfather and mother. At eighteen, he was already performing on the master drum, the ìyáàlù bàtá. Like Ayantunde, Ayanlere combined instruction in traditional music with Western-style schooling. He attended the CAC School II in Ìtabaálẹ̀ Olúgbọdẹ, Ìbàdàn, from 1978 to 1984, and later, Aperin Oniyere Commercial Grammar School from 1984 to 1989, obtaining the West African School Ordinary-Level Certificate that same year. Ayanlere has continued to perform at traditional festivals like Egúngún,

Ṣàngó, and Òkèbàdàn in Ìbàdàn. In addition, he has played with neotraditional bands. For example, he played with the Young Adeayo Band, a jùjú band based in Ìbàdàn; and later with a fújì band, the Fújì Merenge band, touring Ghana, Ivory Coast, and the Republic of Benin, all of which have significant Yorùbá migrant populations.

In 1991, Ayanlere joined the Ọ̀yọ́ State Arts Council, a government-owned institution based in Ìbàdàn and charged with the responsibility of preserving and promoting traditional culture. Working with the center has given him a level of visibility not enjoyed by the average bàtá drummer. It has also afforded him a variety of performance opportunities that many of his counterparts do not have. He has thus been one of the most prominent Yorùbá bàtá drummers active in the process of popularizing the use of newly configured bàtá drum rows. He explained to me that the use of a drum row consisting of multiple drums (usually three or six), each of which produces at least one clear pitch, enables him to make bàtá "talk" eloquently, and generate pulsating dance rhythms. Bàtá drum rows have also found greater appeal than traditional bàtá ensembles in popular jùjú and fújì bands, in both of which Ayanlere has performed extensively.

Ayanlere also performs regularly at the yearly National Festival of Arts and Culture, the annual Abuja Carnival, and at numerous engagements of the Ọ̀yọ́ State Arts Council. His role as one of the most nationally visible performers of "omele mẹ́ta" (three-drum rows) and "omele mẹ́fà" (six-drum rows) bàtá ensembles was acknowledged with the award of a gold medal for his brilliant performance at the National Festival for Arts and Culture (NAFEST) in 1997. Ayanlere's performances are not limited to national and state-level engagements. He has also traveled to countries like Cuba and Brazil where Yorùbá bàtá drumming has become part of a totally new culture and is practiced differently than it is in Nigeria. In those countries, Ayanlere often performs in omele mẹ́ta and omele mẹ́fà configurations, thus demonstrating to foreign audiences how bàtá drumming has been evolving within Nigeria. As part of the Ọ̀yọ́ State Arts Council troupe, Ayanlere has also visited many other countries, including India (1994), Libya (1996), London (2003), Venezuela (2006), France (2006), and Cuba (2010), participating in concerts, workshops and numerous cultural exchange programs between Nigeria and these countries.

In addition, Ayanlere privately leads a bàtá ensemble of three players in Ìbàdàn. The other two members of the group are Amusa Ayanwole, who plays the omele abo; and Kasim Babatunde Ayanyemi, who plays the omele akọ. Ayanwole, who was born in 1965, hails from Iganna, a town in the northern part of Ọ̀yọ́ State. He has played the bàtá since he was a child, and now combines bàtá drumming with his work as a dry-cleaner. Ayanyemi, born in 1985, is a native of Ọ̀póo Lábíran in Ìbàdàn. A primary school (middle school) certificate holder, Ayanyemi started playing the bàtá when he was three years old. The bàtá music examples that I discuss in chapter 2 were performed by Ayanlere's group.

Figure 1.7. Oyo State Cultural Center, Ìbàdàn, one of the modern institutions promoting indigenous Yoruba musical traditions in Nigeria. Ìbàdàn, 2007, photo by author.

Ayanlere's career choices align with the goals of the Bàtá Drummers Association. His musical decisions and activities are reflective of the force of individual agency, and grounded in the collective struggle that binds members of the bàtá drummers association together. His career activities also demonstrate how the musical decision of an individual (the preference for new bàtá configurations) emanates from, and is reflective of the goals of a collective social action (deployed toward economic survival and social relevance). Compared with Ayantunde, who enjoys a relatively higher level of patronage because of the popularity of dùndún drumming, Ayanlere has been more explorative in his desire to "survive." His international engagements and his creative approach to ensemble organization can be linked to the declining fortunes of bàtá drumming at home and his determined effort to survive socially and economically. His decision to explore new opportunities within Yorùbá neotraditional idioms of the fújì and jùjú, performance spaces that remain dominated by the dùndún, also speaks to a desire to compete more favorably with his dùndún counterparts.

The Wood of Commerce and the Father of Drums

The preceding discussion highlights a number of important issues relating to the practice, transmission, and patronage of bàtá and dùndún drumming. These include the constantly evolving nature of performance contexts, the ways in which the activities and experiences of individual drummers reflect the interests of, and the challenges faced by, the group to which they belong, the relationship between social action and musical choices, and the economics of musical performance as defined in postcolonial Nigeria. It should be noted that the Ibàdàn meeting of bàtá drummers and the decision taken at that meeting to be more aggressive in promoting bàtá drumming constitute a form of social action geared toward redressing the declining fortunes of a major tradition of Yorùbá drumming. In drawing attention to this, bàtá drummers often cite a proverb that states that the "dùndún is the wood of commerce, while the bàtá is the father of all drums." The word "*bàbá*" (father) describes the bàtá in terms of seniority, hinting at its historical advantage over the dùndún. This proverb provides insight into the attitude of bàtá drummers toward their own music and toward dùndún drumming, and even more significantly, about how the bàtá is conceptualized in the traditional Yorùbá society. The proverb, like many of the statements of bàtá drummers earlier discussed, derives from what could be described as "mythical and historical modes of consciousness,"[50] from which emanates the belief that their music represents the more authentic version of Yorùbá drumming. The notion of the dùndún ensemble as an instrument of commerce, though inherently condescending, is nevertheless an acknowledgment of the increasing popularity and economic viability of the dùndún.

The domination of Yorùbá neotraditional performance spaces by dùndún ensembles highlights the transformation of dùndún from a subsidiary musical genre into the status of the most patronized Yorùbá drum ensemble today, a fact acknowledged by bàtá drummers themselves. It must be noted that bàtá drummers' complaint of marginalization is conditioned largely by economic factors. In spite of the encroachment of dùndún drummers into the sphere of sacred performance, bàtá drummers still play a major role in sacred performances and festivals. Spiritually powerful masquerades such as Lábúàtá and Gbógorù in Òṣogbo, to mention a couple, remain attached to bàtá ensembles exclusively. Furthermore, theatrical performances involving eégún ọ̀jẹ̀ masquerades are still completely dominated by bàtá drummers. But these performance contexts exist at a considerable social distance away from the affluent world of urban social ceremonies where dùndún ensembles hold sway. Bàtá drummers would like to play a role that goes beyond being bearers of ancient customs and rituals.

I am not suggesting that the financial needs of dùndún drummers are totally or even significantly met through their work as musicians. Indeed, for many of them, this is far from being the case. As shown in Sule Ayantunde's biography, many dùndún drummers, like their bàtá counterparts, still have to combine their work as musicians with other vocations such as tailoring, carpentry, farming, and auto repair. But by constantly adjusting their musicianship to engage the changing contexts of performance in Nigeria, a feat which depends largely on the expressive power of their instrument to praise, dùndún musicians have been able to achieve greater social visibility in modern-day Yorùbáland, and integrate themselves more successfully into the economic system of modern Nigeria.

In spite of the rhetoric about the historical primacy of their music, many bàtá drummers are quite pragmatic in their bid to remain relevant and survive economically as musicians. They seem to have realized that their status as custodians of traditional religion should not prevent them from proactively responding to the dynamics of a fast-changing society. The Ìbàdàn meeting was not the initiatory platform for this new mode of thinking. It was one of many efforts to reaffirm a group commitment to a cause that had begun to take shape decades before. That meeting constituted thus only a dramatic moment within a process of reflection and adjustment that had long been in the making. Although bàtá drummers continue to function in their capacity as master drummers for religious rituals, they are also poised to working their way along the economic and social contours of modern musical practice in Nigeria. And as shown in the works of Klein and Villepastour, there is a growing international interest in bàtá drumming.[51]

The resolve of bàtá drummers to chart a more competitive approach to the practice of their music is noticeable in the changes that have taken place in the organization of the bàtá ensemble. Such changes seem to acknowledge the need to boost the capacity of their drums to function as speech surrogates and generate a more engaging mode of performance. Evidence of this new approach exists in the increasingly popular miniature bàtá ensembles that are configured around three or six small omele instruments in a manner that somehow reverses the erstwhile leading role of the ìyáàlù bàtá. In these new configurations, the ìyáàlù bàtá, when present, may be used as an èjìn (deepener), providing bass ostinato patterns that help to energize the performance. Musibau Ayanlere explained to me that, in its new drum row configuration, the bàtá is a lot more eloquent at imitating Yorùbá speech because of the clarity of the tones of each of the instruments in the drum row. In addition, the newly configured drum row, because of the small size of the drums, is much lighter to carry and less energy-sapping than the more traditional form of the ensemble. It is also more economical to manage, since a single player manipulates each drum row.[52]

I watched a performance by one such ensemble during the Ọ̀ṣun Òṣogbo festival in 2007. It consisted of only two drummers playing four bàtá drums. The lead drummer was a young man who played the triadic drum row. An elderly man, the second member of the ensemble, played the ìyáàlù as the èjìn, providing an accompaniment rather than attempting to "talk." This relatively new configuration is already becoming popular in modern popular bands. Although trailing the dùndún in such contexts, its emergence has signaled a new approach to the use of the bàtá. It is important to note that the drum row configuration exists side by side with the more traditional form of bàtá drumming. The use of three or six omele drums to "talk," and the use of the ìyáàlù bàtá to provide accompaniment within the new configuration demonstrate a reversal of roles, and constitute a concrete musical practice that parallels the desire of bàtá drummers to redefine their identity and fashion a new mode of performance.

In addition to such innovations, bàtá drummers have also been exploring new social contexts of performance beyond the shores of Nigeria as a means of boosting their social status and redefining their identity within the country. Klein, in her study of a group of bàtá drummers from Èrìn-Òṣun, Western Nigeria, discusses how the musicians have "strategically" explored a global network to "manage and enhance their positions within the local market" against the background of declining material gain. She explains that although the social and musical world of Èrìn Òṣun artists is "defined by local specificity," their art has started to be shaped by a perspective in which "the global becomes a space of imagined opportunity and material gain" as they "work the gap between local and overseas markets."[53] This strategy speaks to bàtá drummers' awareness about how local performance and daily life issues are shaped by the global networks in which the artists are involved. Although Èrìn Òṣun drummers continue to perform ancient repertoires, especially for their occasional overseas patrons (individuals and academic institutions in Europe and the United States who often prefer "authentic" indigenous repertoires), they have also been infusing their performances with "stories about their ventures overseas"[54] to satisfy the expectations of their more progressive local audiences.

The narratives and activities of bàtá drummers as discussed above speak to the dynamics of "[social] structure and agency in the creation of social life";[55] illustrate the status of music as a form of social behavior "grounded in a flow of activity continually shaped by actors' interpretations of, and reactions to constraints and incentives encountered in the world";[56] and constitute a form of "active power negotiation and contestation."[57] The statements and decisions of bàtá drummers, the acts of reconfiguring the bàtá ensemble, and the exploration of new performance spaces are all indicative of a socially responsive strategy, spurred by the need to root for a renegotiated identity, one that benefits from their status as bearers of ancient customs while attuning to the socioeconomic realities of modern society. As a major plank for articulating such a strategy, the Bàtá Drummers Association provides a unique forum within which the drummers share their experiences, sharpen their capability to analyze the social dimensions of their musical practice, and map out a plan of action for collective survival. As I mentioned in the introduction, Ingrid Monson has stressed the critical significance of this form of dialectic between individual action and group solidarity by drawing attention to the "collective component to agency."[58] Although the Ìbàdàn meeting represents but one auspicious moment, a loud and dramatic reflection on the twentieth-century social dynamics of Yorùbá drumming, it signals the desire of bàtá drummers to work as individuals and as an integral part of a project of collective survival. The Ìbàdàn meeting thus represents a dramatic illustration of how nodes of musical change are preceded by, and organically related to, collective agency and social action.

Chapter Two

Talking and Stammering

Toward an Analysis of Yorùbá Drumming

The incursion of dùndún ensembles into sacred performance spaces originally exclusive to bàtá and other sacred drums, and the domination of modern, neotraditional performances by dùndún drummers both represent a significant development in twentieth-century Yorùbá music. This development is linked to dùndún's capability to imitate Yorùbá speech more accurately than its sister drum, bàtá, the so-called stammer drum, and, ultimately, to the significance of drum language in the conception, practice, and mediation of Yorùbá music. In analyzing selected examples of bàtá and dùndún drumming in this chapter, I explore the musical ramifications of speech surrogacy by drums, and demonstrate the link between performance practice and identity politics in Yorùbá drumming traditions. Although it is generally known that speech surrogacy is a vital aspect of West African drumming, its realization is far from being uniform across West Africa. David Locke, who has done extensive work on Ewe drumming in Ghana, has observed, for example, that among the Ewe, "usually, only drummers know the texts" that generate rhythmic patterns. He further explains that "even Ewe speakers cannot understand drum language just by hearing the music—they must be told."[1] In addition to the power of secrecy, "which makes restricted information valuable and powerful,"[2] the relative lack of accessibility to the linguistic basis of Ewe drumming could also be due to the fact that Ewe drums, which are upright and without the tone-producing tendons of hourglass drums like the dùndún, lack the capability to clearly imitate the tonal inflections of speech found in hourglass drum traditions.[3] John Miller Chernoff, discussing Dagomba drumming, also in Ghana, has noted that "for some dances like *Zhem*, the drum language is a secret, and drummers may be able to beat the drum without knowing the meaning." He explains that Dagbamba drummers often "did not know the meaning" of their sounds, and had to travel "to Yendi to consult the chief drummer of the Paramount Chief of the Dagbon" to find out.[4] The Yorùbá

drumming tradition, however, contrasts sharply with these two Ghanaian examples in the sense that an effective mediation of the music is linked strongly to the
disposition of performers and audiences to comprehend and interpret drum
language in musical and linguistic terms. My main argument in this chapter is
that a Yorùbá drummer must activate this power of contemplation or active listening through an effective integration of nonlexical and speech-based patterns.
The socio-aesthetic discourse from which this contemplative element of Yorùbá
drumming derives must be analyzed and understood in order to properly situate
the emerging politics of identity within the fold of Yorùbá drummers.

The process of understanding how speech-based drum phrases relate to, differ
from, or complement nonlexical drum phrases has generated considerable interest among scholars, including Anthony King, Kwabena Nketia, John Carrington,
Akin Euba, David Locke, Kofi Agawu, Tunde Adegbola, and Patricia Tang.[5] In
his study of Akan drumming, Nketia identifies three different modes of communication, namely, those of speech, signal, and dance. The speech mode refers to
the use of drum patterns to convey lexical meanings by imitating speech rhythms
and tones. The signaling mode, which may also be speech-based, refers to the
use of the drum to convey messages such as those that cue dancers in the course
of a performance; while the dance mode refers to purely musical drum patterns,
lacking lexical meanings and often interpreted through the expressive mode of
dance.[6] Expanding on Nketia's tripartite model, Agawu discusses how speech-
based rhythmic phrases and nonlexical phrases interact, and explains that the
different modes are not mutually exclusive in the manner in which they operate.
For example, speech-based phrases and drum signals are often musically significant. Focusing on the music of the Northern Ewe, Agawu also observes that
speech-based drumming operates differently from ordinary speech.[7] Although
they are rhythmically and tonally similar to speech patterns, drummed speech
patterns cannot adequately represent speech syllables, because drums obviously
cannot talk like humans. Akin Euba makes the same observation with regard to
Yorùbá dùndún drumming, noting that "only a few of those features of ordinary
speech that aid comprehension are present in ìyáàlù speech" since the drum
lacks the biological functions of the human voice.[8] Thus, unlike the ordinary
speech, the speech mode of drumming often functions in a symbolic manner,
since "its meaning [may be] known only to a given number of people within
the same community, thus moving towards Nketia's signal mode."[9] The status
of drummed speech as a form of coded language is particularly well illustrated
in the Yorùbá bàtá drumming tradition, in which drum strokes may be used to
represent ẹnàan bàtá, a form of coded language used for communication among
bàtá drummers within and outside the context of musical performance. In cases
such as this, when the Yorùbá texts from which drum strokes are generated are
inaccessible to the ordinary listener, the speech mode of drumming assumes a
doubly coded form of expression whose full comprehension is restricted to a
close circle of initiates. It is also important to note that speech-based drumming

is often interspersed with nonlexical musical phrases in Yorùbá drumming. The interruptions that derive from such juxtapositions add to the coded character of the drummed texts, since the listener must be able to isolate and separate purely musical phrases from speech-based patterns in order to comprehend the intertextual structure of drum phrases and its impact on the performance as a whole.

In exploring how these issues resonate within the context of musical structure and performance, I expand on Agawu's observation on the interdependence of the three modes of drumming by exploring the significance of the Yorùbá concept of àlùjó (literally, dance-drumming or drumming for dance). Although my research derives mainly from a series of field trips to Nigeria during which I worked closely with a group of drummers, my analysis and conclusions in this chapter have benefited immensely from Akin Euba's monumental and pioneering study of Yorùbá dùndún drumming.[10] Euba, who is generally regarded as the foremost authority on the subject, has indeed explored many of the issues touched in the present study and the ways in which modern musical traditions, notably art and popular music, draw on indigenous Yorùbá drumming.

I argue that àlùjó denotes a form of musical aesthetics, somewhat akin to Agawu's "autonomous mode."[11] Although àlùjó melo-rhythmic patterns often do not convey independent speech-based meanings, they do comment on, and accentuate the lexical meaning of, the speech-based phrases that appear before or after them within a musical performance. Furthermore, the complementary relationship between nonlexical àlùjó patterns and speech-based phrases speaks to the multidimensional role of the Yorùbá master drummer. While speech-based drum patterns are often directed to members of the audience when performed in social contexts, in sacred performances, the same phrases are deployed to appease or praise deities. Although sacred texts tend to be sacrosanct and undiluted in strictly traditional performances, modern-day Yorùbá drummers often incorporate them within social entertainment or, reversing the protocol, introduce àlùjó elements within performances that feature sacred texts. The increasing tendency to combine the sacred and the secular constitutes an important performance strategy that serves to popularize and propagate religious ideas within modern social performance spaces. It is important to note that as a result of this performance practice, Yorùbá drummers have been able to stimulate the interest of modern-day audiences in ancient Yorùbá religious beliefs, in spite of the overall declining profile of traditional Yorùbá religion in modern Yorùbá community life. Dùndún drummers, exploiting the considerable capability of their instruments to "talk," are most adept at this mediating and modernizing role. My analyses of selected examples of dùndún and bàtá drumming below shed more light on these issues. All the examples discussed in this chapter derive from specially arranged performance sessions with Sule Ayantunde and Musibahu Taiwo Ayanlere and their groups. Those by Ayantunde were performed at his house in Ìsàlè Òṣun and at the Odò Òṣun (the

Ọ̀ṣun grove), both in Ọ̀ṣogbo. Although my analysis focuses specially on these arranged performances, my discussion also derives from many years of working with Ayantunde, whom I have interviewed many times and watched perform at various events, including the Ọ̀ṣun and Ṣàngó festivals in Ọ̀ṣogbo, since 2006. Likewise, Ayanlere and his group performed all the bàtá pieces studied here at specially arranged sessions at Ìjokòdó in Ìbàdàn. My discussion also benefits from my work with Ayanlere's group dating from 2007. I have also watched this group perform at various traditional events, notably the annual Eégún and Òkèbàdàn festivals in Ìbàdàn.

My Musical Transcriptions

I should at this point provide some explanations regarding the musical transcriptions discussed in this chapter. In order to transcribe very fast polyrhythmic dùndún and bàtá performances, I asked Ayantunde and Ayanlere to play the pieces phrase by phrase to generate the versions presented in this chapter. The negligible differences between those phrase-by-phrase versions and the versions performed without a break can be observed by comparing my transcriptions and the corresponding audio examples provided on the accompanying CD. Such minor differences show the ways that well-known pieces change from performance to performance without losing their individual identities. Furthermore, in all of my transcriptions, pitch representations are relative, conveying the contour patterns of melo-rhythms rather than representing exact intervallic relationships. In spite of these minor discrepancies, all musical transcriptions are representative of the corresponding bàtá and dùndún audio examples. The letter *r* shown in the musical transcriptions denotes a drum roll. And although my discussion focuses specifically on the performances of Ayantunde and Ayanlere (whose biographies I discussed in chapter 1), my understanding and conclusions are enriched considerably by the many years of my interaction with a wide range of Yorùbá drummers, including Bisi Adeleke, a Yorùbá master drummer now based in Atlanta. Further details about each musical transcription are provided below.

Ọ̀ṣun Drumming

Ọ̀ṣun, the deity of healing, fertility, and protection, is celebrated annually in many different parts of Yorùbáland. Annual festivals in honor of the deity provide a grandiose and dramatic closure to daily, weekly, and monthly religious events spread around the entire year. The parts for the ìyáàlù (lead drum) and the omele (secondary drums) in the music of Ọ̀ṣun are shown in example 2.1. The parts played by the *kánran ìṣáájú* and *kánran àtẹ̀lé*, two of the secondary drums, are basically the same, except that they are played at different pitches (about a third apart), and start at different interlocking points. As the musical transcription shows, the gúdúgúdú's part combines these two patterns. The *aguda*, the biggest drum of the ensemble, plays low-sounding regular sounds, every fourth of which is played with the left hand (marked H in ex. 2.1), rather than with the stick. Like the aguda, the gúdúgúdú consistently plays a sixteenth-note.[12]

Many of the more well-known features of West African drumming can be observed in the omele parts of example 2.1. The gúdúgúdú and aguda articulate the smallest unit of durational movement, a feature that has been characterized variously as the African "metronome sense,"[13] "density referent,"[14] and "elementary pulsation."[15] In the same example, the kánran articulates a variant of the Yorùbá *konkolo* pattern, commonly known as the "standard pattern"[16] or "time-line pattern," a term attributed to Kwabena Nketia.[17] Furthermore, the repetitive patterns of the omele instruments impart unto Yorùbá drumming the cyclic character for which West African drumming is generally known. In all the transcriptions, I represent the cycle that frames each piece with a number that matches the number of eighth-notes in a given span of omele patterns. Thus, the number 8 at the beginning of example 2.1 refers to the aggregate number of eighth-notes in the parts of kánran ìsááju, kánran àtèlé, gúdúgúdú, and aguda. This form of representation, which is adopted from Gerhard Kubik, only denotes the span of each cycle; it is not intended to suggest the stress patterns of European meters.[18] This form of representation underlines my preference for a continuous, unbarred narrative rather than a metrically constrained transcription.

As shown in all the examples, the cyclic character of the omele instruments contrasts strongly with the narrative sequences of the ìyáàlù, the lead drum. The strong analytical emphasis on the element of dance in West African drumming by scholars, itself strongly linked to the ubiquity of cyclic standard patterns, tends to divert attention away from the structural and aesthetic significance of the narrative sequences of the leading drum. The element of dance, though central to the conception and mediation of West African drumming, must be analyzed contextually, that is, as part of a wider framework of expression in which the circularity of standard patterns is offset by the linearity of the narrative sequences of the lead drum. My discussion here concentrates mainly on the techniques of the lead drummer. In this and subsequent examples, the ìyáàlù's part constantly acts as a foil to the cyclic patterns of the omele instruments, as illustrated in example 2.1, where the phrases of the ìyáàlù cumulatively outline expanding and contracting cycles that overlap and contrast with the cycles of the omele instruments.

Example 2.1 shows the ìyáàlù dùndún part as played by Ayantunde. Titled "Aroko Bódúndé," example 2.1 is an excerpt from an extended performance

Example 2.1. "Aroko Bọ́dúnde" (ìyáàlù and omele parts). Dùndún drumming
transcribed from author's own field recording.

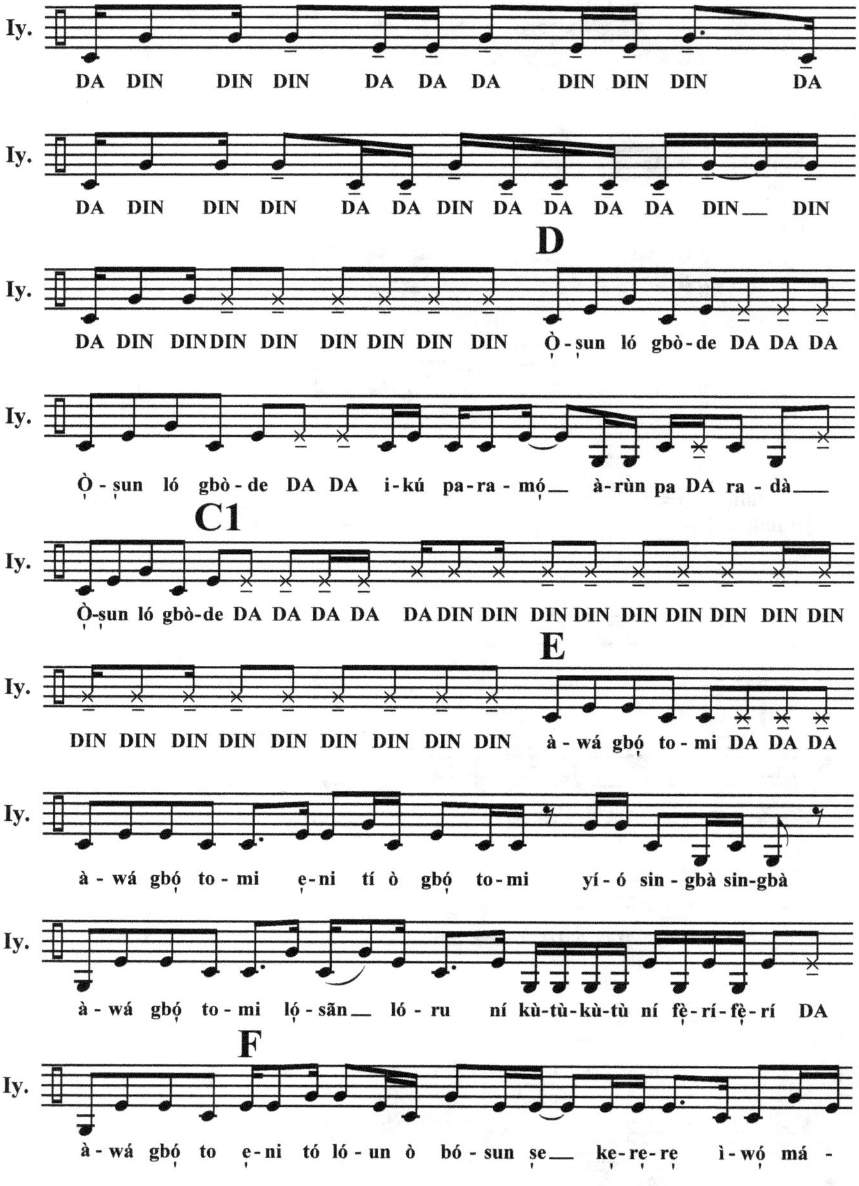

Example 2.1. *Continued.*

Example 2.1. *Continued.*

usually rendered a few days before the beginning of the Òṣun festival to remind people that the time of the festival is near.[19]

Aroko Bọ́dúndé: Praise for Òṣun

i. Aroko bọ́dúndé
Festival time is here
ii. Aroko aroko bọ́dúndé
Festival time is here
iii. Kó dìde, erugàlì kó dìde
Stand up, erugàlì (epithet for Òṣun)
iv. Òṣun ló gbòde
Òṣun is here
v. Ikú paramọ́, àrùn paradà
Death and sickness must go away
vi. Òṣun ló gbòde
Òṣun is here

vii. Àwá gbọ́ tomi
    We cherish the river (symbol of Ọ̀ṣun's power)
viii. Ẹni tí ò gbọ́ tomi yíó segbà segbà
    Disobedient people will be punished
ix. Àwá gbọ́ tomi
    We cherish the river
x. Lọ́sǎn, lóru, ní kùtùkùtù ní fẹ̀rífẹ̀rí
    In the afternoon, in the night, and at dawn
xi. Àwá gbọ́ tomi
    We cherish the river
xii. Ẹni tó lóun ò bÓṣun ṣe
    Whosoever does not honor Ọ̀ṣun
xiii. Kẹrẹrẹ ìwọ̀ má a wọ́ wọn bọ̀, kẹrẹrẹ
    Shall be consumed by the river, kẹrẹrẹ
xiv. Ìbáà ṣọkùnrin, ìbáà ṣobìnrin
    Whether a man or a woman
xv. Kẹrẹrẹ ìwọ̀ má a wọ́ wọn bọ̀, kẹrẹrẹ
    Shall be consumed by the river, kẹrẹrẹ

The opening phrase of the performance urges everyone to be well prepared for the Ọ̀ṣun festival, while most of the subsequent phrases are epithets and prayers in honor of the deity. For example, her healing and protective powers are acknowledged in line five; while, in subsequent lines, the drummer warns that terrible punishment awaits those who disobey the call or are disloyal to Ọ̀ṣun's injunctions. In addition, the drummer urges all indigenes of Òṣogbo to set aside this time of the year to honor the deity.[20]

Ìyáàlù Dùndún Drumming for Ọ̀ṣun

Many of the important performance strategies and musical features of Yorùbá dùndún drumming are highlighted in example 2.1, which is based on the Ọ̀ṣun praise chant discussed above. Although the part of the ìyáàlù and the underlying chant from which it is generated are shown in example 2.1 (like other examples in the chapter), it is important to note that the chant is not rendered vocally by any of the drummers in actual performance. It is left to the audience to figure out the speech content of drum patterns.

The part of the ìyáàlù in example 2.1 (CD track 1) comprises two main types of phrases: speech-based (lexical) phrases and purely musical (nonlexical) phrases. Nonlexical phrases are often referred to as "àlùjó" by Yorùbá drummers. They usually constitute the principal domain of improvisation, although improvisational phrases also may carry underlying texts. The word "àlùjó" as I mentioned earlier, translates literally as "dance-drumming" or "drumming for dance." It is used in connection with a mode of drumming that is deployed mainly to activate and support dance. Although there is an element of dance in virtually all types of Yorùbá drumming, àlùjó refers to drum performances that

are structured deliberately to facilitate robust dancing, especially as appropriate for social entertainment. Sule Ayantunde sometimes performs sacred texts,
such as those discussed in this chapter, in an àlùjó style. The word "àlùjó" is also
used in connection with specific nonlexical musical phrases, motives, or drum
strokes that cumulatively help to generate an àlùjó feel, and perform a range
of functions in the course of a performance. I have assigned two nonlexical
syllables, DA and DIN, to denote such patterns. These syllables are part of a
variety of mnemonic phrases that may be used by drummers for such patterns.[21]
DA-DIN phrases, especially when they occur within speech-based patterns, are
sometimes articulated with nonbouncing strokes, which give a more percussive accent. I have used a dash and a crossed notehead to differentiate DA-DIN
(or àlùjó) patterns, whether or not they have been articulated as nonbouncing
drum strokes. Àlùjó elements often "comment" on speech-based phrases, providing cadential or punctuating moments that accentuate their independence
from one another, thus enhancing the impact of the entire performance on the
listener.

Some of the speech-based musical patterns of ìyáàlù dùndún for Òṣun (labeled
as A, B, D, E, and F) are relatively independent utterances, thus enabling the
drummer to structure the piece with relative freedom. A major exception is the
phrase marked A, which generally functions as the opening and closing material. Contrasting with short àlùjó strokes and patterns (as found within phrases
like A, B, D, E, and F) are longer àlùjó phrases that help to heighten the element of dance and play a significant role in the structural unfolding of the
piece. An example of one of these longer phrases is phrase C, which functions
as a relatively extended transition between phrases A1 and D. In C1 it functions as a link between phrases D and E; in C2 it functions as a cadential device
that anticipates the end of the piece. In all of these instances, each sequence
of àlùjó patterns provides a brief period during which participating audience
members may reflect on the lexical meanings of the speech-based patterns that
appear immediately before. As cadential phrases and transitional moments,
àlùjó patterns in C, C1, and C2 also help to generate a coherent transition
from one phrase to another, functioning as moments of contemplation during
which the drummer ponders which phrase or set of phrases to play next. These
examples speak to the function of àlùjó phrases as performance-compositional
tools through which the drummer achieves structural coherence and sustains a
dynamic element of dance. The prominence of àlùjó material in this traditional
sacred piece draws attention once again to the role of the Yorùbá drummer
as a mediator through whom social and spiritual experiences are facilitated.
Here the dùndún drummer reinterprets the praising and appeasement of a
deity in an entertaining àlùjó style, generating an engaging performance. The
performance context of this excerpt is particularly conducive for the presentation of sacred texts within the context of social entertainment. Although focusing on a religious text, the piece is often performed as part of a town-wide

mobilization procession in preparation for the festival, a performance that is ultimately more social than sacred, as people sing and dance around the city with palpable excitement.

Ṣàngó Drumming

Ṣàngó, believed to have ruled the Yorùbá kingdom of Ọ̀yọ́ in the fifteenth century, later became deified as the deity of thunder and lightning, as oral history informs us. In his lifetime, he was known and feared as a ferocious king, said to emit fire from his mouth when he spoke. He waged numerous wars against neighboring communities but after a confrontation with two of his generals, Timi and Gbonka, whose loyalty he had doubted and whom he had wished dead, he was demoralized, and committed suicide. His subjects, wishing to remember him as a great king, agreed to conceal the real nature of his death. Like all the major Yorùbá Òrìṣà, Ṣàngó is now venerated through specific musical repertories dedicated to him. Ayantunde performed the omele patterns for Ṣàngó shown in example 2.2 in an àlùjó style.[22]

Apart from the use of nonlexical musical phrases, the àlùjó conception of the piece is expressed in the collection of omele patterns, which carry a strong element of dance. Omele instruments featured are the kánran ìṣááju and kánran àtẹ̀lé (small hourglass drums), the gúdúgúdú (pot-shaped drum) and the aguda (big hourglass drum). The kánran ìṣááju supplies a variant of the popular Yorùbá standard pattern (the konkolo), while the gúdúgúdú plays a pattern that is distinguished by the use of two pitch areas.[23] Although the aguda's part is similar to that of the gúdúgúdú, its every third stroke is played with the hand (represented in my transcription by the letter H), which helps to dampen the drum surface, thus varying the sound quality. The kánran àtẹ̀lé's pattern interlocks with that of the kánran ìṣááju, while the gudugugu and the aguda consistently play the smallest unit of durational movement in the groove, represented here as an eighth-note. All the four standard patterns provide the cyclic rhythmic foundation for the narrative of the ìyáàlù dùndún, the instrument which intones and elaborates on the praise chants of Ṣàngó, samples of which I transcribe and discuss below. These patterns accompany a distinctively fast and rigorous dance that captures his ferocious nature. In a Ṣàngó performance that I witnessed inside the Ọ̀ṣun sacred grove in Òṣogbo in July 2006, I observed that as the drumming increased in tempo and intensity, the dancer engaged in a series of invigorated dance steps with quick and sharp movements of both legs, and a rapid twisting of the dancer's robe. At some point in the performance, the lead drummer moved closer to the dancer and engaged in a sustained "dialogue" in which the dancer's "staccato-like" dance steps matched the very fast and pulsating patterns of the omele and ìyáàlù drums. The omele patterns provide the foundational groove for Ayantunde's drumming of the invocation

Example 2.2. "Olúkòso Obakòso" (ìyáàlù and omele parts). Dùndún drumming transcribed from author's own field recording.

Example 2.2. *Continued.*

and praise chant of Ṣàngó. As in the previous example, this chant, an excerpt from which is transcribed below, is not performed vocally by Ayantunde. It is rendered instrumentally.

The overarching theme of the excerpt is the fierce nature of Ṣàngó, who is described as having "the ferocious face of the tiger" and a "posterior that is as hot as the burning sun." The word "fire" features prominently in the chant, strengthening the portrayal of Ṣàngó's ferociousness. The drummer knows how temperamental Ṣàngó could be. He treads carefully as he does not want to become another victim of Ṣàngó's anger. "Do not severe my head from my body, I beg you in the name of God," the drummer pleads. For the drummer, who here represents the collective voice of Ṣàngó's devotees, this fiery Òrìṣà is a mystery that can neither be done away with nor be passively embraced. One must be on one's toes, as it were, to be a devotee of an Òrìṣà who is at once good-natured and ferocious, a dual personality that somehow recalls the character of Èṣù, the trickster deity of fate and human conduct. In spite of his ferociousness, Ṣàngó is also a generous deity whose willingness to provide for the needy is depicted in the statement that his "underwear is covered with cowry shells."[24] The drummed chant also recalls history, making reference to Ṣàngó's reign as an ancient king (the Aláàfin) of Ọ̀yọ́. As mentioned earlier, Ṣàngó was said to have committed suicide following the humiliation he suffered from two of his lieutenants. But in deifying Ṣàngó, his followers denied that he committed suicide, asserting that their king did not hang (Ọbakòso or Olúkòso). These words, which remind us of this history, recur prominently in this drummed chant.

Ojú Ẹkùn Iná: Praise-Chant for Ṣàngó

i.   Ojú ẹkùn Iná
       The tiger's face is ferocious

ii.   Ẹ̀hìn ẹkùn oòrùn ni
       Its posterior is as hot as the sun

iii.   Ọ̀jẹ́ jáfirin bẹ́mọ lórí
       Like the blacksmith's brass liquid that burns the head of a child

iv.   Olúkòso, Ọbakòso
       Our leader did not hang, the king did not hang

v.   Olúkòso ayáná abiná yọ lẹ́nu
       Olúkòso, the one who emits fire from the mouth

vi.   Oníbàntẹ́ owó jìnwìnnì
       The one with an underwear of cowry shells (money)

vii.   Ọbakòso
       The king did not hang

viii.   Má bẹ́ n lórí sọnù
       Please do not sever my head from my body

ix.   Mo forí ọba bẹ̀ ọ́
       I beg you in the name of God

x.   Ọ̀jẹ́ jáfirin bẹ́mọ lórí
       Like the blacksmith's brass liquid that burns the head of a child

xi.   Má bẹ́ n lórí sọnù
       Please do not sever my head from my body

xii.   Mo forí ọba bẹ̀ ọ́
       I beg you in the name of God

xiii.   Iná lójú, iná lẹ́nu
       The one with fire in his eyes and inside his mouth

xiv.   Iná lórùle e páànù
       With fire burning at the roof of his house

xv.   Ẹ̀éfín iná là á dá láyé
       While we make a smoke of fire here on earth

xvi.   Baba à mi ń dáná lájùlé ọ̀run
       My father (Ṣàngó) makes heavenly fires

xvii.   Pá tì pẹ̀ tì pẹ̀, àmàlà a Ṣàngó
       Pá tì pẹ̀ tì pẹ̀, the food of Ṣàngó

Ìyáàlù Dùndún Drumming for Ṣàngó

Ayantunde's performance of the iyáàlu part for Ṣàngó drumming (see ex. 2.2; CD track 2) is based on, but does not follow word for word, the Ṣàngó praise-chant discussed above. Example 2.2 begins with a nonlexical pattern, labeled A, which Ayantunde describes as Ṣàngó's àlùjó pattern.[25] This material reappears toward the end of the excerpt. Like the Òṣun piece discussed earlier, example 2.2 also features speech-based patterns. The structural importance of DA-DIN elements in the music is attested to in the ways in which they regenerate themselves. Thus, in addition to their "fill-in" role, as shown within phrases C and D, they are subjected to a process of variation (shown in phrases A1 and E) within which Ayantunde employed the syllables PA-TIPE-TIPE as a vocable for the àlùjó material. The use of àlùjó as a closing device in this example recalls a similar procedure in Òṣun drumming.

As shown in these examples, Ayantunde, rather than playing uninterrupted series of sacred texts, constantly incorporates àlùjó elements, a practice which helps to lend a playful mood to serious and sacred Yorùbá texts. And it is usually through such performances, especially those taking place at occasions like funeral and chieftaincy ceremonies, which lie outside strict traditional religious rituals and thus attract audiences of diverse social and religious demography, that nonadherents of traditional Yorùbá religion (including Christians and Muslims) become familiar with such sacred texts. The interpolation of àlùjó material within sacred texts and the interpenetration of speech-based drumming and nonlexical improvisation as shown in these examples constitute important adaptive performance strategies suited particularly to the dynamics of a modern society in which practices associated with Yorùbá traditional religion are becoming increasingly irrelevant to the cultural life of the majority of the people.

Bàtá Drumming: "Afaségbèjò" and "Mosákẹ́kẹ́"

Bàtá drummers employ performance practices that are basically similar to those of their dùndún counterparts.[26] Like their dùndún drummers, they often explore the interface between àlùjó and non-àlùjó phrases, and integrate social entertainment with sacred performance. In discussing selected examples of bàtá drumming here, I do not wish to rehash areas of similarities between the two drum traditions; rather, I concentrate on performance features that are unique to the bàtá ensemble. My discussion focuses on two examples of bàtá music. The first one, "Afaségbèjò," is a traditional piece that may be performed in rituals associated with Ṣàngó and Ògún. The folk poem on which it is based carries a strong moral lesson and has been made popular in modern social contexts by the famous jùjú musician Sunday Aladeniyi (a.k.a. Sunny Ade).[27] As shown in the text of this poem, transcribed below, it is a song of social control, with a thematic focus on irrational and foolish behavior. It is one of the many examples of Yorùbá "songs of abuse" that may be rendered to correct or ridicule a misbehaving person.

Afaṣẹ́gbèjò

i. Afaṣẹ́gbèjò ón tan ra rẹ̀ jẹ
    Only a fool tries to collect rainwater inside a net
ii. A wí wí wí wí, ẹ lẹ́ ò gbọ́
    You have ignored our advice
iii. A fọ̀ fọ̀ fọ̀ fọ̀, ẹ lẹ́ ò gbà
    You have disregarded wise counsel
iv. A gbélù sílẹ̀, a fẹnu wí
    We beat the drum, we spoke the message to no avail
v. Àpótí alákàrà ká bí ó wó
    The ruined basket of the bean seller (is what a fool deserves)
vi. On tí a ṣe lón fun wọ́n lára
    Our achievements make them feel uncomfortable
vii. Ìwà tí a wù lón bàwọ́n lẹ́rù
    Our disposition sends jitters down their spine
viii. Amúni ṣìwí amúni ṣìsọ
    Their demeanor is annoying
ix. Amúni tòkèlèbọmú ni baba wọn
    Their conduct is a big source of concern
x. Àbùkú kaláṣejù, ó tẹ́
    Shame is the lot of the person who lacks decorum

"Mosákẹ́kẹ́," the second example, is an àlùjó piece, which, although it is now generally associated with bàtá drummers, is said to have been created originally by an unknown dùndún group. Yemi Olaniyan, an ethnomusicologist and a dùndún drummer based at the Obafemi Awolowo University, Ile-Ife, explained to me that "Mosákẹ́kẹ́" was specially commissioned by some Yorùbá farmers in the late 1960s to celebrate an unexpectedly bountiful harvest. It has since become a popular piece among bàtá and dùndún drummers. Sule Ayantunde, however, believes it to be a traditional recreational piece that has been in existence for hundreds of years. He confirms that the piece has been a favorite among dùndún and bàtá drummers and may now be performed in a variety of contexts, including funeral and wedding ceremonies.

Mosákẹ́kẹ́: An Àlùjó for Bàtá

i. Mo sá kẹ́kẹ́, mo mú re gbó ifá gbandikan
    I went to the forest of divination, proudly displaying my facial kẹ́kẹ́ tribal marks gbandikan[28]
ii. Mo bàbàjà mo mú rè dí ọ̀pẹ gbandikan
    I went to a palm-tree plantation, proudly displaying my facial àbàjà tribal marks gbandikan
iii. Ọ̀pé mì tìtì mo ṣe bójò ló rọ̀ gbandikan
    The tree shook so forcefully I thought there was a heavy downpour gbandikan

iv. Òjò pagi lápá kan o dápá kan sí gbandikan
   One side of the tree was covered by rain while the other side was dry
   gbandikan

v. Òjò pa mí o má ṣe pòrẹ́ ẹ̀ mi gbandikan
   It is me, not my friend, that the rain should soak gbandikan

vi. Ìtàkùn tó sogbá ló sogbà ló selégéde gbandikan
   The calabash, the gourd, and the pumpkin all derive from similar
   roots gbandikan

vii. Tàtàburà gbà [a closing cadential phrase, imitating the sound of a
   gun]

My musical transcriptions of "Afaṣẹ́gbèjò" (ex. 2.3; CD track 3) and "Mosákẹ́kẹ́" (ex. 2.4; CD track 4), which derive from performances by Musibau Ayanlere's bàtá group in Ibadan, show only the parts of the leading drum (the ìyáàlù bàtá) and the basic pattern of the omele akọ. It can be observed that the omele akọ's part as played in the recorded versions of "Afaṣẹ́gbèjò" and "Mosákẹ́kẹ́" on the CD undergoes changes that are not reflected in my musical transcriptions. Furthermore, these bàtá examples, like those of the dùndún discussed earlier, derive from versions that were played phrase by phrase, with stops between them, to facilitate transcription. Also, the pitch lines used in the transcriptions denote tonal contours rather than absolute intervals. Although my main focus is on the part of the ìyáàlù bàtá, I have also provided the part of the omele ako in order to highlight the relationship between the two parts. In the two examples, the omele ako's part is played on two drums (the omele méjì) by a single drummer.[29] In "Mosákẹ́kẹ́," the omele akọ's ostinato pattern features a two-note chord, and differs, in its clearer tones, from the sounds produced on the larger skin (the ojú òjò) of the ìyáàlù bàtá, and those of the omele abo bàtá (not shown in the transcription).[30] In examples 2.3 and 2.4, the sounds produced on the two drumheads of the ìyáàlù bàtá (the ṣáṣá—the small head—and the ojú òjò—the big head) are represented in the two clefs below that of the omele akọ.

Example 2.3. "Afaṣẹ́gbèjò" (ìyáàlù and omele akọ parts). Bàtá drumming transcribed from author's own field recording.

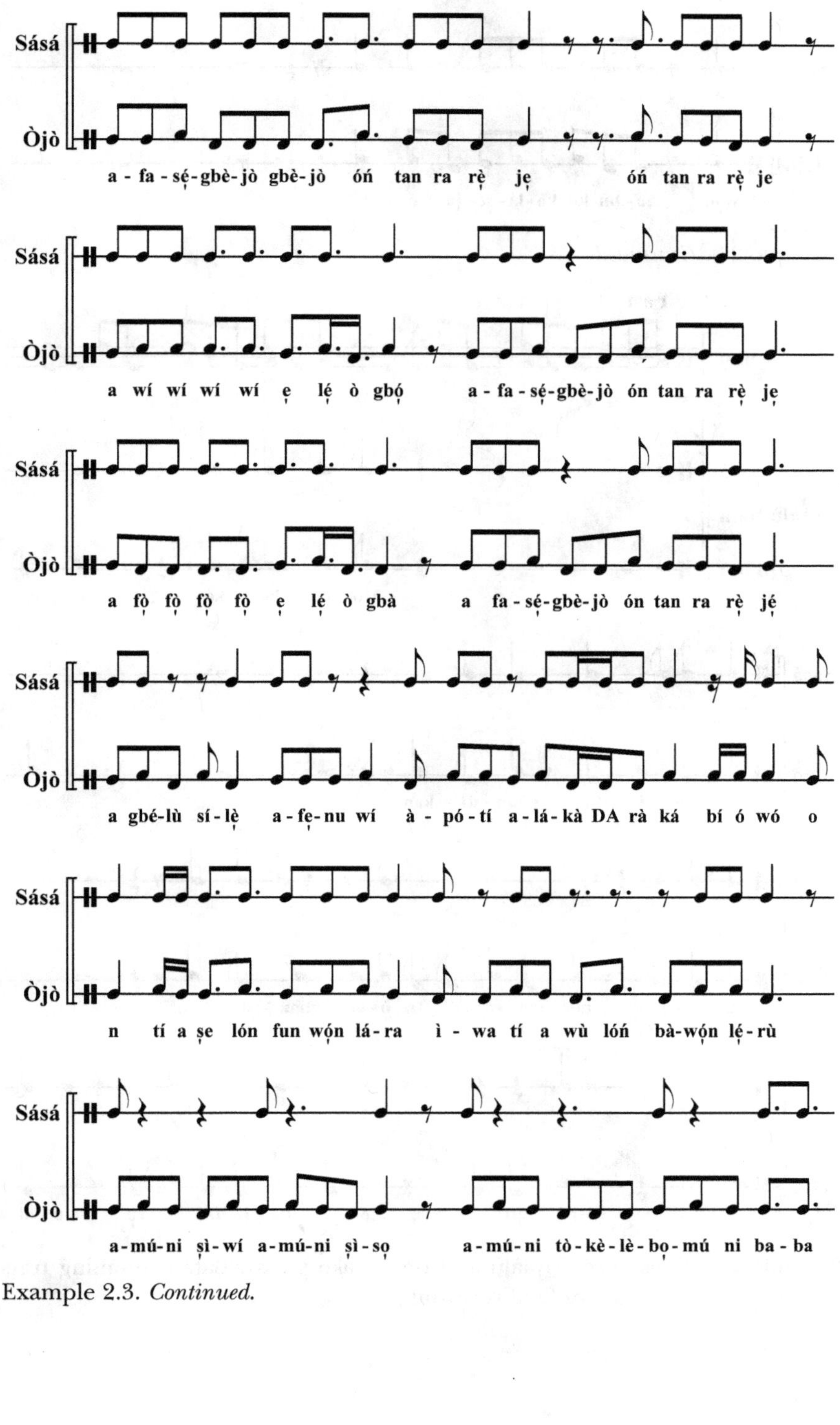

Example 2.3. *Continued.*

Example 2.3. *Concluded.*

Example 2.4. "Mọṣákẹ́kẹ́" (ìyáàlù and omele akọ parts). Bàtá drumming transcribed from author's own field recording.

Example 2.4. *Continued.*

As explained in chapter 1, the smaller drumhead (the ṣáṣá) of the ìyáàlù is usually played with the left hand, using a leather or plastic beater (bílálá), while the larger drumhead (the ojú òjò) is played with a bare right hand.[31] The monotone patterns produced on the ṣáṣá are relatively tonally distinct, and quite similar to those of the omele akọ. On the other hand, the tones of the ojú òjò (usually three) are barely distinct, and have to be generated through a variety of techniques, as described in chapter 1. As shown in example 2.4, only two of the three vague tones of the big drumhead of the ìyáàlù bàtá are mostly played in "Mosákẹ́kẹ́." In "Afasẹ́gbèjò," however, all three tones are used prominently, as can be observed in example 2.3. But even when all three tones are played by the drummer, they are not sufficient to accommodate the quite extensive tonal range of the Yorùbá language. As Phillips has explained, a pitch vocabulary of five notes, not three as often suggested, is needed to convey the various glides and tonal inflections that characterize the Yorùbá speech.[32] The three tones used in example 2.3 thus do not clearly articulate the tonal inflections of their underlying Yorùbá text.

As these examples show, although the ojú òjò of the ìyáàlù could be made to generate three vague tonal levels, many modern-day drummers tend to do away with at least one of the tones every now and then in the course of a performance. Indeed some bàtá master drummers often seem to abandon the principle of tonal imitation altogether in performance and play only speech rhythms. In example 2.4 there is no correlation between the tonal contours of the words Òjò pa gi lápá kan o dá pá kan sí and the drum strokes that the drummer generates for the phrase. A similar lack of tonal correlation exists toward the end of example 2.4, where the tonal orientation of the sentence Ìtakùn tó so gbá ló selégbédé is almost totally abandoned. There is no doubt that some bàtá drummers are more proficient than others in their ability to imitate Yorùbá speech. By contrast, even the least talented dùndún drummers are able to make their instrument "talk" and even "sing."

The relative lack of tonal clarity in bàtá drums is further compounded by the fact that the monotone patterns played on the ṣáṣá head of ìyáàlù bàtá often do stress rhythmic support rather than aligning with or complementing the tonal patterns of the ojú òjò. Thus, although the pitches (both vague and distinct) that could be generated on the ojú òjò and ṣáṣá of the ìyáàlù and the omele abo amount to a fairly varied pool of tonal resources, they are distributed among different instruments, and the different skin surfaces and are not always tuned to imitate the melodic contours of Yorùbá words.[33]

Unlike the performances of most dùndún master drummers, which generally clearly explore both the tonal and rhythmic features of Yorùbá texts, correspondences between linguistic and musical patterns in bàtá drumming are often identifiable by the average listener mainly in terms of rhythmic correlations. Thus although, in principle, bàtá and dùndún drummers both incorporate nonlexical and speech-based phrases, the relative lack of tonal clarity and the limited tonal resources of the bàtá often render the two types of material indistinguishable from one another. While performances of popular pieces such as "Mosákẹ́kẹ́" may be more easily identified by listeners, it is often very challenging for listeners to understand the speech meanings of bàtá performances that are less familiar, or to comprehend spontaneous "speech" interjections played in the course of a performance.[34] In such situations, the capability of the average listener to comprehend the shift from àlùjó to lexical or speech-based patterns becomes considerably challenging.[35]

Villepastour, relying on a scheme compiled by Muraina Oyelami,[36] has discussed the principles governing how "Yorùbá speech is mapped onto the bàtá"; that is, how different types of Yorùbá vowels are assigned specific types of drum strokes on the ìyáàlù bàtá and omele abo bàtá.[37] Oyelami's scheme indicates that the allocation of drum strokes is generally dictated by the need to reflect the linguistic intonation and the "intrinsic intensity" levels of vowels.[38]

Although consideration for the tonal inflections of vowels as indicated in Oyelami's scheme is an important feature of bàtá drumming, this is not always the case, as can be observed in my own examples, which show that the tonal levels of vowels are often ignored and even contradicted in the melodic contour of drum strokes.

Regarding the issue of "intrinsic intensity," I must state that while variations in intensity are common in Yorùbá drumming generally, I was not, in my extensive work with bàtá drummers, able to observe any consistent approach to the articulation of vowels based on this principle. The use of the ṣáṣá is, as illustrated in my own examples, often informed by rhythmic and tonal considerations rather than a systematic approach to differentiating between vowels with high and low intensities. This lack of consistency is corroborated by Villepastour's observation that the "the ṣáṣá is frequently left out when one would expect it on an intense vowel (again, violating Oyelami's guidelines), with the overall effect of accentuating speech tone contour."[39] Given the high degree of deviation from Oyelami's scheme, it would seem that further research involving multiple bàtá ensembles has to be conducted before any solid conclusions could be drawn regarding the significance of the issue of intensity in the practice of bàtá drumming. Indeed, I would like to suggest that, given the primacy of tone over intensity in the articulation of speech in Yorùbá language, the issue of intensity may be of marginal significance to how Yorùbá drummers and their audiences conceive and mediate the Yorùbá drum language within the context of a musical performance.

Yorùbá Drumming Is Contemplative Performance

The various musical examples of dùndún and bàtá drumming discussed above illustrate salient features of Yorùbá drumming, while drawing attention to the differences between the two arts. Yorùbá drumming illustrates the interplay between "agency" and "structure" in the sense that sacred musical materials, which derive from ancient repertoires, are often reworked according to the dynamics of the occasion at hand and at the discretion of the drummer. Such a performance technique is demonstrated in the rapprochement between the standard patterns of the omele, which sometimes signify the identities of ancient deities, and the part of the ìyáàlù, which typically integrates new musical material with ancient religious texts through improvisation. Yorùbá drummers often exercise significant freedom and creativity in the art of reinterpreting indigenous Yorùbá religious texts and musical idioms to generate a form of social entertainment that caters to the aesthetic tastes of modern-day audiences, many of whom have embraced the new religions of Christianity and Islam. As I have demonstrated above, the use of àlùjó material is critical to the effectiveness of this performance technique.

As my examples have also shown, the dùndún's strong visibility in contemporary musical settings is grounded ultimately in the capability of dùndún ensembles to generate an expansive mode of performance in which speech surrogacy is important, but not paramount. Analyzing the linguistic qualities of bàtá and dùndún, though helpful, merely scratches the surface of the matter. One must probe into the realm of musical performance to fully understand why dùndún enjoys greater popularity over bàtá. The dùndún's enormous tonal capability is demonstrated not merely in its ability to imitate the tonal levels of Yorùbá speech. It lies in the drum's capacity to articulate a variety of tonal registers in a manner that is linguistically comprehensible and musically appealing. Tonal shifts are the tools through which Yorùbá drummers achieve their musical and oratorical effectiveness. The examples presented here show how a dùndún drummer turns speech phrases into melodic patterns and alternates between speech and "song" with ease and clarity—teasing, amusing, entertaining, educating, and engaging the audience.

The visibility of àlùjó as a form of social entertainment is consistent with and representative of the desire of Yorùbá drummers to survive in a fast-changing society. It is important to remember that religious contexts provided perhaps the most important basis for traditional Yorùbá drumming in the precolonial era. Making this tradition relevant in modern Yorùbá societies has entailed the generation of a mode of drumming that adapts to an increasingly secularized environment. Àlùjó drumming provides a most important tool in the process of adapting a predominantly sacred tradition to the social needs of modern Yorùbá society. This performance strategy is most strongly illustrated in the examples in which sacred religious texts are presented within performances that are also offered as social entertainment. In such performances, drummers reorder the texts, breaking them into different units and combining these units with newly improvised material to generate new phrases. The use of àlùjó also helps to defy the limiting impact of language on musical improvisation. Although linguistic communication constitutes a creative resource for drummers, nonlexical patterns are particularly amenable to improvisational explorations. They provide a liberating temporal space within which the individual agency of a drummer is fully activated in the process of reinterpreting ancient religious texts.

The use of àlùjó is even more significant when viewed in terms of its implication in the social history of Yorùbá drumming. The reinterpretation of ancient sacred texts as àlùjó music (and through the use of àlùjó elements) to cater to the needs of an increasingly secular Yorùbá society demonstrates the central thesis of "practice theory," a concept linked to Marx's dialectical idea about social history, in which "the reproduction of a structure becomes its transformation."[40]

Àlùjó drumming is the vehicle through which ancient Yorùbá sacred music is simultaneously reproduced and transformed: in it resides a concordance of continuity and change.

My discussion above demonstrates the value of Yorùbá drumming as a form of contemplative musical experience: both for the drummer, who must engage in a deep process of reflection as he weaves text and tone to build up his performance, and for the listener, who must engage in a sustained process of reflective listening as he or she ponders musical and poetic narratives. The poetry, the religious philosophy, and the process and style of musical organization displayed in all the examples depict a performance tradition that addresses the mind perhaps more than it exercises the body. In Yorùbá culture, to dance or listen to Yorùbá drumming without understanding the "utterances" of the drums is considered a sign of intellectual and artistic deficiency.[41] The narratives of the ìyáàlù player often represent a literary discourse, and to understand it requires the possession of cultural capital. To not understand or be totally sure of when a performance has shifted from speech-based drumming to nonlexical àlùjó drumming is to miss the contemplative dimension of Yorùbá drumming. Although bàtá drummers also do engage in these two types of discourse, modern-day audiences with little or no familiarity with its complex mode of communication generally find it very challenging to comprehend the rapprochement of the two modes in bàtá drumming.

Chapter Three

Songs of the King's Wives

Gendered and Social Identities in Yorùbá Vocal Performance

Women and Gender in Music

Resonating strongly in my discussions in chapters 1 and 2 is the notion that men dominate Yorùbá drumming. There is an equally strong notion that women are the masters of song and chant performance. As in many cultures around the world, female musicians perform a range of functions, from cultural preservation,[1] and performing for wealthy patrons[2] to complicated functions such as inter-gender "mediation of antagonism"[3] and the performance of catharsis in a patriarchal society.[4]

As has been clearly demonstrated by Karin Barber, women are the most adept performers of the Yorùbá oríkì, or praise-chants.[5] They are the principal musical orators in the traditional Yorùbá public sphere, especially at annual festivals, where they function as historians and pundits, mobilizing support for traditional institutions by praising royalty, tracing genealogical lines, and providing insights into the body politic of their communities. But while it is true that Yorùbá women are the masters of vocal traditions, they may also provide drum accompaniment for their performances. The idea that Yorùbá women are forbidden to play the drum and rarely play other musical instruments has been reiterated in studies that focus on drumming traditions from the Ọ̀yọ́ region (the area in which most studies of Yorùbá music have been done); but evidence from the Èkìtì region suggests that this is not universally true in Yorùbáland.[6] My discussions in this chapter and the next focus on two all-female musical traditions, both of which, in different ways, deconstruct the assumption that the drum is a symbol of male superiority in Yorùbáland. Focusing on these two examples, I examine how music is performed to articulate the identity of women as powerful players in the social and political life of a remote Yorùbá community in Èkìtì.

Kelly Askew's study of Tanzanian Taarab music provides a good model for investigating African performance traditions in terms of their content and form, and how they speak to the social conditions of the people who perform them.[7] In that study, Askew harmonizes a wide range of analytical perspectives that draw on Victor Turner's "agonistic paradigm of social drama,"[8] the processual dimension of performance,[9] the "concern for form and politics of context,"[10] and the significance of performance as "text."[11] She proposes an integrated theory that factors in the form, the content, and the dialogical dimensions of African performances, because it is at the intersection of these elements that their "performativity," that is, their "nonfinite, emergent and contingent" nature, lies.[12] In my study of the music of Emùré-Èkìtì women in this and the next chapters, I adopt Askew's integrative approach by examining specific performances as enacted in their immediate physical context and in terms of their social significance in the larger society. I devote considerable attention to how musical form and content and the creative process are reflective of social relations within, and affirm the identity of, specific groups.

The two traditions studied here are *orin Olorì* (music of the king's wives)[13] and *Aírégbé* (songs of female chiefs), two related musical ensembles in Emùré-Èkìtì. Emùré-Èkìtì, an ancient Yorùbá town with a population of about ninety thousand people, is located in the southern part of Èkìtì, one of Nigeria's thirty-six states.[14] It comprises four major streets, namely Idamududu, Ogbontioro, Òkè Emùré, and Odò Emùré. Orin Olorì is performed during the annual new yam festival (Ọdún Ìjẹṣu) that marks the beginning of the harvest season, and provides the opportunity for the symbolic tasting of the season's first yams by the *Elémùré* (the king of the town).[15] As in such events all over Yorùbáland, this festival provides an opportunity for members of the community to celebrate a common ancestry, pay homage to the king, and reaffirm their loyalty to him.

The Aírégbé festival, also an annual event, is largely exclusive to women, although it is presided over by the male king. In its original form, the festival was part of an extended initiation ceremony for pubescent girls who were made to go through a period of confinement during which they received education about motherhood and matrimonial responsibilities, before taking part in a graduation ceremony at which male suitors identified their future wives. The young girls were camped under the tutelage of adult women who held chieftaincy titles in the town. Today, however, this festival has changed. Camping and the circumcision of the young girls have been abandoned. Aírégbé is today celebrated annually as a performance event by female chiefs with a few young girls in attendance. The festival now exists mainly to empower women, honor the king, and as a symbolic representation of its historical antecedents. In addition, Emùré-Èkìtì girls who take part in the festival are now generally considered too young to marry and are thus not paraded for male suitors.

The female chiefs, who see themselves as guardians and vanguards of traditional female institutions in the town, have taken it upon themselves to ensure that the values which are inscribed in Aírégbé are preserved even though the rites of circumcision are no longer practiced. Chief Morenike Awopetu, the *Iyalode* of Emùré (head of all Emùré women), explained to me that but for her efforts, the Aírégbé tradition would today be a thing of the past. For the past thirty years, she has ensured that the event is commemorated annually as a song and dance event by all female chiefs in the town. In its present form, therefore, Aírégbé has become a rallying point and a symbol of identity for female chiefs who have now constituted themselves into a musical ensemble, performing Aírégbé songs. As a distinct all-female performance, Aírégbé music is comparable to orin Olorì, a musical tradition exclusive to another group of women, the numerous wives of the king.[16] It is also important to note that songs deriving from the old Aírégbé festival as well as newly composed ones with a variety of themes are now performed by these titled women at occasions such as marriage, chieftaincy, and coronation ceremonies. Although my discussion here focuses on Emùré, I draw on examples from other parts of Yorùbáland as a means of relating my discussion to broader perspectives about gender and performance in Yorùbá society. I explore how the status of Emùré-Èkìtì women is defined, inscribed and redefined through the organization and structure of musical performance.

I was drawn to the Èkìtì community for a number of reasons. I grew up in this part of Yorùbáland and have watched performances by female instrumental ensemble groups since I was a little boy. Until recently, I took it for granted that women played drums, because it was a common occurrence in my (somewhat remote) hometown of Ìkọlé-Èkìtì.[17] For although British influences in Èkìtì date as far back as the late nineteenth century, the colonial influence was not as strong here as it was in Yorùbá towns that are closer to the seaport, like Lagos, Ìbàdàn, and Abẹokuta. The remote location of Èkìtì provided a barrier behind which older cultural practices flourished with minimum external interference. It is noteworthy that Èkìtì is one of the few Yorùbá ethnic communities today in which women play drums and maintain a highly visible presence at public performances involving the entire community. As a background to my study of Olorì and Aírégbé musical traditions, I begin with a brief discussion on the significance of gender in Yorùbá performance.

Gender in Yorùbá Performance

In *The Invention of Women*, Oyeronke Oyewumi challenges Western assumptions about gender and how such assumptions have been imposed on the analysis of social relations in Africa and made to influence the production of intellectual knowledge about the continent. She argues that biological determinism, as it informs the construction of power and social relations on the basis of sex categories, is irrelevant to the traditional African culture, if precontact Yorùbá culture is indicative. According to her, the biological categories of man and woman

(ọkùnrin and obìnrin) do not automatically translate into distinct social categories. She argues that in traditional Yorùbá societies, social categories, rather than
being tied to sex categories, are traditionally determined by other factors, notably seniority of age.[18] Oyewumi's position rejects a European narrative about
the notion of gender as a master organizing principle that speaks to "biological
sex differentiation" and "culturally conceived notions of gender and prestige
systems that accord value to one gender over the other."[19]

Oyewumi's position has, however, been strongly challenged by a number of
scholars of Yorùbá culture, most especially by Lorand Matory, who draws close
links between words and ideas that have gendered implications and the exercise of authority by Yorùbá priests. He observes, for example, that "shrine ico-
nography, the initiations, and the spirit possession performances of the Ṣàngó[20]
and Yemọja priesthoods of Ọ̀yọ́ North employ representations of these gendered
and nongendered arrangements and combine those representations in powerful mixed metaphors, in a way that makes the priests' ritual assertions about
the proper order of authority in society seem inevitable and inexorable to the
people seeking the god's help."[21] For Matory, the words akọ (male) and abo
(female) are "categories of relational gender, structured by the gendered conventions of marriage." Thus, although the two words are not strictly isomorphic
to the constructions of "man" and "woman," they always operate in relationship
to one another. In all cases involving these words—whether pairings between a
priest and devotees in which the priest is the husband (an ọkọ), or as male and
female initiates who are regarded as ìyàwó (wife) in cultic frameworks, or even
in matrimonial settings in which a junior wife becomes an "ìyàwó" to boys and
girls born before she married into the family—the relationship between "ọkọ"
and "ìyàwó" is indicative of a gendered conception in which power "flows asym-
metrically" from "ọkọ" to "ìyàwó." Matory concludes that "the ọkọ-ìyàwó relationship is therefore not reducible to a mere anatomical contrast between men and
women."[22] As Ellen Koskoff has observed, however, gender divisions need not
necessarily reflect the superiority of one gender over the other, since there are
instances in which "men and women are perceived not in a conceptual framework of dichotomous opposition, but rather in terms of complementarity, and
where control is more or less shared."[23]

Olajubu's discussion of gender in Yorùbá societies stresses complementarity rather than asymmetry, and argues that gendered social classification was
indeed present in "precontact" Yorùbá society. She observes that "men and
women were expected to perform certain roles, though boundaries for such
prescription remained fluid."[24] Olajubu also explains that gender cults pervade religious spheres, where sacred cults are often organized along gender
lines. Two notable examples are the orò cult, which is exclusive to men, and
the ìyá a mi cult, which is exclusive to women. Each of these is imbued with
different but equally significant modes of power. The orò cult is "an association of men invested with the authority to execute judgment in the society,"

while the ìyá a mi cult is "concerned about the sustenance of the ritual powers on which the Yorùbá polity was rested."[25] Central to the position of Olajubu is the notion of a harmonizing relationship between man and woman. Although there is a concept of gender in Yorùbá society, it does not always translate into an asymmetric conception of power or into a form of patrimony which disadvantages women. The gendered allocation of cultic power in which different groups and ideas are reconciled to facilitate spiritual harmony is reflective of the interdependence of male and female powers, "neither of which is less potent."[26]

Koskoff has categorized musical performances in terms of how they may reflect on inter-gender relations. These include: "performance that confirms and maintains the established social/sexual arrangement; performance that *appears* to maintain established norms in order to protect other, more relevant values; performance that protests, yet maintains" established norms, and "performance that challenges and threatens (the) established order."[27] While the first three categories of performances are quite common in traditional Yorùbá societies, it is rare to find those that challenge established institutions in a fundamental manner, although rituals and performances may target individual misdemeanor and award temporary punishment to erring members.[28] The predominance of the first three categories of performances is indicative of the nature of the relationship between individuals and society in traditional Yorùbá societies and indeed of the intergender harmony that exists in such societies. Thus, although the organization of musical events in Yorùbá culture does indeed reflect the allocation of musical roles on the basis of biological differences, gendered allocation of musical roles does not necessarily suggest male superiority or translate into an advantage for the male.

Barber's analysis of Yorùbá traditional praise-poetry epithets, oríkì, for example, shows that Yorùbá women have traditionally exerted dominant roles in the performance and transmission of this genre. She explains that female performers dominate and are the masters of the oral performance of the Yorùbá oríkì, playing crucial roles in performing it within sacred contexts. According to Barber, "Women have been important in the cults at least partly because it is they who control the vital channels of communication with the Òrìsà through their mastery of oríkì. Rather than being the subjects of 'praise' which puts big men in the limelight, they actually operate the 'praising' mechanism by which the flow of spiritual forces is directed and through which, ultimately, the multiple personalities of the òrìsà are constituted."[29] This dominant status of women in oríkì performance and their role in channeling the "flow of spiritual forces" toward configuring and activating the power of Òrìsa are indicative of the force of power and authority ascribed to women in traditional Yorùbá societies. Women seem to have lost this visibility in modern performances, notably in neotraditional Yorùbá popular music bands, in which they are often marginalized to the fringe of the arena as background singers and dancers, a point to which I return later.

Contrasting with the dominant role of women in indigenous ritual vocal performance is the assumed dominance of men in instrumental music.[30] Today, it is generally assumed that men are the ones to play drums in traditional Yorùbá music as well as in modern popular music bands.[31] But although the male domination of instrumental music in modern popular music tends to translate into social and economic advantage for men over women, the situation is different in traditional contexts where instrument playing does not automatically translate into a social advantage for men. In the Òṣun festival, which I describe briefly below, male drummers do not constitute the primary actors or the focus of attention, in spite of the critical nature of their role.

Spatial Dimensions of Gender and Power in the Òṣun Festival Performance

In addition to her identity as the deity of healing and fertility, Òṣun is regarded as a guarantor of economic prosperity and a protector in times of war. In many Yorùbá societies, Òṣun is appeased and celebrated during annual festivals that involve the participation of all and sundry.[32] The annual festival held in the town of Òṣogbo in Western Nigeria has become perhaps the most important of such festivals, attracting participants from within and outside Nigeria.[33] What is particularly significant for the purpose of my discussion here is how the physical space of the festival, the Odò Òṣun[34] (the Òṣun sacred grove), and the activities within it illustrate the complementary sharing of power by women and men. During the festival, the Odò Òṣun is demarcated into two spaces, each of which represents a specific domain of power and authority. The first space is the main Òṣun shrine, where the votary maid (arugbá)[35] and the Òṣun chief priestess (Ìyá Òṣun) retire to, and where important sacred rituals are performed by the chief priestess and other devotees. The second space is the open area adjacent to the shrine, which is defined by a constructed canopy. This is where the king (the Àtáója) and his chiefs, as well as modern political office holders, are seated during the festival. The political authority of the king is clearly displayed in this second space as traditional chiefs and members of the town take turns to pay homage to him. But at some point during the festival, the king must leave his seat and proceed to the shrine, amidst drumming and dancing, to confer and pray with the chief priestess and other devotees.

The protocol demanding that the king should leave his seat to go to the shrine is a demonstration of the complementary relationship between political and spiritual authority. The mandatory "journey" of the king to the shrine is symbolic of the dynamics of interaction between these two domains of authority. The Àtáója's political authority is enabled by spiritually powerful women whose

Figure 3.1. Ọ̀ṣun Òṣogbo shrine inside the Ọ̀ṣun grove, domain of the Ìyá Ọ̀ṣun and the Arugbá. Òṣogbo, 2007, photo by author.

actions and voices activate and embody the divine power of Ọ̀ṣun. Although the king exerts political power in the day-to-day affairs of the town, the source of his authority lies in the sacred powers of women, who exert spiritual power. The relational dynamics between female spiritual authority and male political power are neither peculiar to Òṣogbo nor isomorphic to the religious doctrine of a female deity. Margaret and John Drewal have observed the same complementarity in the rituals associated with the *gèlèdé* mask of another Yorùbá ethnic group, the Ìjẹ̀bú people of Ògùn state. The gèlèdé masquerades "represent a highly visible, artistic expression of a pan-Yorùbá belief: that women, primarily elderly women, possess certain extraordinary power equal to or greater than that of the gods and ancestors, a view that is reflected in praises acknowledging them as "our mother," "the gods of society," and the "owners of the world." Margaret and John Drewal further observed that "with this power the "mothers" can be either beneficent or destructive. They can bring health, wealth, and fertility to the land and its people, or they can bring disaster—epidemic, drought, pestilence."[36] In a similar vein, Andrew Apter, in his study of ritual worship in Ayédé-Èkìtì, stresses the spiritual power of women, explaining that

Figure 3.2. The King's canopy at the Ọ̀ṣun Ọ̀ṣogbo Festival. Ọ̀ṣogbo, 2007, photo by author.

the invocation of feminine power is often used to "enhance or consume the power of the king" of the town.[37]

Male kings are aware of the potency of feminine power, and the tragic consequences of undermining the authority of women. The spiritual enablement (or curtailment) of male political power by women provides an important reflection on how power is conceived in the traditional Yorùbá society, and is often manifest in the conception and organization of musical performances. For example, although the role of male drummers is undeniably critical to the success of the annual Ọ̀ṣun festival, and although drumming facilitates communication with spiritual beings, instrumental accompaniment is generally subordinate to the singing and dancing of female devotees who occupy the front line in the act of appeasing Ọ̀ṣun. Indeed, the role of drummers, including that of the lead drummer, is to enhance rather than to lead the act of worship. As important as their roles are, the activities of drummers are subject to the dictates of female devotees who lead in the act of worship. Although the performance practices that I have described above do not in anyway represent all known Yorùbá musical traditions, they shed light on the leadership roles that women often play,

Figure 3.3. Worshippers by the Ọ̀ṣun riverside inside the Ọ̀ṣun grove. Òṣogbo, 2007, photo by author.

as illustrated in my discussion of Olorì and Aírégbé groups below. In order to contextualize my discussion of these two local ensembles within the multiethnic structure of the Yorùbá society, I begin with some introductory comments on Èkìtì music.

Èkìtì Music in Yorùbá Culture

As mentioned earlier, the discussion in this chapter focuses on the music of Emùré-Èkìtì in the Èkìtì state. Established in 1996, the Èkìtì state has a population of about three million people spread over sixteen local government areas. The Èkìtì people constitute one of the many ethnic groups in Yorùbáland. Since its emergence as a state within the Nigerian federation, Èkìtì has witnessed a fast pace of infrastructural development, notably in the areas of road construction, housing development, telecommunications, and in the construction of new housing and office schemes for newly created government ministries. Commercial activities have also increased steadily, especially in Adó-Èkìtì, the state capital, which now boasts two universities, a federal polytechnic, banks, and big hotels. The creation of the Èkìtì state has led to an appreciation of the area as a relatively homogeneous independent cultural entity, a state of affairs which contrasts with its marginalization when it was governed as part of a much bigger pan-Yorùbá Western region. But there is a marked contrast between the expanding cosmopolitan landscape of Adó-Èkìtì, the state capital, and the rural life of a small town like Emùré-Èkìtì.

The relative neglect of Èkìtì in scholarly work on Yorùbá music is partly due to the remote location of the area and the political hegemony of Ọ̀yọ́-Yorùbá, which I discussed in the introduction and in chapter 1. Most of the early anthropologists and ethnomusicologists of Yorùbá music located their studies in more easily accessible areas such as Ọ̀yọ́, Ìbàdàn, and Òṣogbo in the central Ọ̀yọ́ region. Much of what is known about Yorùbá music through scholarly literature has thus been confined largely to the musical traditions of these other Yorùbá communities. The hinterland groups, like the Èkìtì, Oǹdó, Ọ̀wọ̀, Àkókó, and Ìjẹ̀ṣà, have received little attention. It is also interesting to note that the only widely known published study on Èkìtì, the one by Anthony King,[38] focused not on Èkìtì music as such but rather on a drum ensemble tradition of Ọ̀yọ́ settlers in Èkìtì.[39]

Èkìtì musical traditions, in spite of their close affinities to those of other Yorùbá ethnic groups, are typified by a host of stylistic and cultural elements that tend to deviate from some of the more well-known features of Yorùbá music. For example, it is not generally known that Yorùbá membrane drums include those made from clay pots, such as the àpúrì (pot drums) made in the town of Òkèmèsí-Èkìtì. Furthermore, the Èkìtì and Ìjẹ̀ṣà vocal traditions often use cadential harmonies in seconds, a performance device not widely found outside of this area (the general presumption is that Yorùbá music is characterized mainly by harmonic thirds).[40] Given its relative insulation from European Christian influences (Christianity did not begin to attract significant interest in Èkìtì until the beginning of the twentieth century), it is plausible to suggest that the musical practices of this area are much more reflective of precolonial Yorùbá musical traditions than are those of communities in Ọ̀yọ́ or Lagos, areas in which Christianity has been influential as far back as mid-nineteenth century. Islamic influences are also much less visible in Èkìtì music than they are in the musical traditions of the Ọ̀yọ́ region, an area which fell to the Fulani Islamic Jihadists in the nineteenth century. Today, many Ọ̀yọ́-Yorùbá kings, including the Aláàfin of Ọ̀yọ́, the Àtáója of Òṣogbo, the Tìmì of Ẹdẹ, and the Ṣòun of Ògbómọ̀ṣọ́ are Muslims. The Yorùbá talking drum, the dùndún, whose origins have been traced to the Islamic Middle East and North Africa, functions powerfully as the symbol of royal authority in the palaces of these Ọ̀yọ́ kings, but is a lot less visible in the Èkìtì region. Although the dùndún drum is now beginning to gain popularity in Èkìtì, the region is not regarded as a primary area of dùndún drumming.[41]

Linguistic factors also account for considerable differences between the musical traditions of Èkìtì and those of other Yorùbá ethnic groups. Although both are dialects of the same Yorùbá language, Èkìtì and Ọ̀yọ́ are distinct from one another in terms of linguistic tone and vocabulary. Given the close connection between language and music in many parts of West Africa, it should not be surprising that the musical styles of these two areas differ to a certain extent, in spite of the fact that they share certain features of Yorùbá music. Most Yorùbá people are capable of distinguishing between Èkìtì music and Ọ̀yọ́ music, and it is not uncommon for schoolteachers and their pupils to prefer the performance of songs and dances from Èkìtì and other hinterland groups as Yorùbá "cultural dances" over those of the more cosmopolitan area of Ọ̀yọ́. This reflects a general tendency to view traditional Èkìtì music as more ancient than that of Ọ̀yọ́. The two musical traditions that I discuss in this chapter and in chapter 4 illustrate the ways in which Èkìtì music deviates from some of the well-known assumptions about Yorùbá music, notably in terms of the role and status of women, performance practices, and compositional style.

Olorì and Aírégbé Music

There are interesting contrasts and similarities between Olorì music and Aírégbé music. As I mentioned earlier, Olorì music is performed only by the numerous wives of the king of Emùré, while Aírégbé is performed mainly by women who hold chieftaincy titles. Olorì ensembles are found in the palaces of many Ekiti kings; I have yet to hear about any such ensemble in the Ọ̀yọ́-Yorùbá region. In addition, although Olorì music features the use of àgèrè (a single-membrane barrel-shaped drum), Aírégbé is performed without instrumental accompaniment. Emùré female chiefs, by virtue of their high social status, are not expected to play the drum. It is also important to note that most of the female chiefs are advanced in age compared to Olorì women. But in spite of the differences between these two performance traditions, they are related: both are all-female performances, and performances of both may now take place within the same event, although the two traditions have different and distinct musical repertoires. Also, queens who are also chiefs may perform both categories of music.

In July 2007, I watched the Aírégbé festival in the town. The king had died a few months before the festival, and, pending the coronation of a new king, the event was presided over by a female regent. (Although women do not become kings in Èkìtì, the institutional provision for the appointment of female regents provides the female gender an opportunity to have a shot at leadership, if only for a short while.) Female regents in Èkìtì rule during the time when competition for ascendancy to the throne often becomes tough

Figure 3.4. Female drummer with àgèrè drum of the orin Olorì ensemble, Emùré-Èkìtì. Emùré-Èkìtì, 2007, photo by author.

and even deadly. Tact, diplomacy, and courage are qualities that are called for at such critical transitional moments. Although the 2007 event that I watched was an Aírégbé festival, featuring the performance of female chiefs, members of the Olorì ensemble also performed at the event. The chief hostess was the female regent adorned in male attire, holding a horsetail in her hand and wearing ankle- and neck-beads, two important symbols of Yorùbá royal authority. The female chiefs also dressed ceremoniously, clutching horsetails and wearing beads around their ankles, as expected of all female title-holders in the town.

The festival began with the Olorì women singing and dancing to the accompaniment of àgèrè drums. About forty-five minutes later, the chiefs took over, singing Aírégbé songs. The transition from Olorì to Aírégbé was marked by the cessation of drumming and the introduction of new, more structurally complex songs. The regent was seated most of the time but got up occasionally to dance and to show appreciation to the performers by pasting wads of money on their foreheads. Two features of the festival are of particular significance: the presence of a female regent who dressed like a man and assumed the power of a

Figure 3.5. The regent of Emùré-Èkìtì, watching a performance of the Olorì Ensemble. Emùré-Èkìtì, 2007, photo by author.

male king; and the role-switching of some performers who criss-crossed social boundaries, appearing first as queens (in Olorì music), and later as titled chiefs in Aírégbé.

The relationship between the two groups of performers is indicative of the fact that women in traditional Emùré society do not constitute a monolithic social group. They belong, at different times in their lives, to one of three groups—newly initiated girls, wives, and chiefs—depending upon their age, experience, and seniority. In festival situations, each of these three social categories is assigned a musical role that is commensurate with its status. New initiates may be said to be musically marginalized, singing only a recurring responsorial phrase; Olorì (queens) render more substantial musical performances; and the chiefs engage in the most sophisticated musical performances, as I will demonstrate in chapter 4. This stratification of musical performance levels corroborates Oyewumi's argument, cited earlier, about the importance of age in the ascription of social status in traditional Yorùbá societies. Many of the women who are now titled chiefs were once ordinary citizens or royal wives

Figure 3.6. Chief Morenike Awopetu, the Ìyálóde of Emùré-Èkìtì (*middle*), with some of the other female chiefs. Emùré-Èkìtì, 2007, photo by author.

whose elevation to the status of a chief derives from personal achievement in some sphere of life, whether in business, education, or politics. The complementary relationship between Olorì and Aírégbé ensembles represents a musical illustration of the dynamics of intragender stratification and social mobility in Emùré-Èkìtì.

The Olorì Ensemble in the Private Sphere

In addition to public outings, Olorì music is performed at female-only meetings held weekly within the palace grounds. At such meetings, the women discuss issues that directly affect them as a group and map out strategies to overcome the challenges that they face. In recent times, for example, they have focused on how to combat the scourge of HIV/AIDS by taking the campaign to public places like the church and the marketplace. In addition to such critical examples, Olorì meetings also deal with mundane issues like quarrels and disputes involving members of the group. The women have also recently constituted themselves into a cooperative society that gives loans to needy members. Celebrations marking important events like the weddings or college graduations of the women's children, funerals of relatives, or the award of a chieftaincy title are also planned at these weekly meetings. At every meeting, monies are contributed to the collective purse to facilitate loans as well as for the purpose of celebrating landmark achievements. At each of these meetings, Olorì songs are sung to the accompaniment of àgèrè drumming. The leader of the group explained to me that Olorì music is performed during their meetings "because the music belongs to us." Singing helps them bond with one another and facilitates group reflection on personal experiences and collective struggles. In none of my interactions with members of this group did I get any sense that they were using music to set themselves up as a gendered group opposed to the reign of their male king or to the men in the town. The performance of a unique set of songs by the women represents only a desire to mark their status as queens and thus set themselves apart from other women. Music is used to reinforce their status as a relatively privileged social group within the community. Music is performed by the group to demarcate a social space and a social identity, to facilitate a desire to work together, promote mutual interests, share experiences, and work out solutions that they face as a group of people who are (or once were) married to the most powerful men in their community. The use of music by the women thus performs two important functions: to self-identify as a social category in the society and to reinforce a larger sense of collective identity amongst the Emùré people. That sense of collective identity is often symbolized in the power of their king, as shown in the song texts discussed below.

Olorì Songs

A study of selected Olorì songs clearly reveals a recurring emphasis on the preeminence of the Elémùré as a divine leader whose power should not be questioned. Many of the songs refer to the king as a master who must be obeyed. In a song titled "Abẹ I Kọṣẹ Orí," for example, the women compare themselves to the barber's clipper, which must not "refuse the task of shaving." Other symbols employed in the song include the àdìrò (cooking stand), which "must perform the task of cooking." The song ends with the statement that a servant does not refuse the errand of his master, and that they [the women] will be going to the palace to honor the king with a special performance.

Abẹ I Kọṣẹ Orí

i.   Abẹ I Kọṣẹ Orí
The clipper does not refuse the task of shaving the head

ii.   Àdìrò mọ̀ ọ kọṣu àsìsè
      The cooking stand does not refuse the task of cooking a piece of
      yam
iii. Ọ́n mọ̀n i kọṣẹ́ ọlúa ọni
      A servant does not refuse the errand of her/his master
iv.   A mà a bíré ra dókè àọ̀fin ò
      We shall go to the palace with our musical ensemble
v.   Òní lamọ̀ a molorì àyìyẹ̀
      Today, we shall know who truly is a queen

Asked whether this song is derogatory to the status of women by referring to them as "servants," the women replied with a categorical no, an answer that draws attention to the dual role of Olorì women as "wives" and as "queens." In Yorùbá culture, the title Olorì (queen) is an official status that goes with the responsibility of supporting the king in the act of leading the town. Oral information records numerous stories about powerful ancient Yorùbá kings who failed and fell because they did not listen to the counsel of their queens, who are charged with the enormous responsibility of providing advice to the king, especially in situations where the loyalty of members of the king's council is suspect. The case of Ṣàngó, king of the old Ọ̀yọ́ kingdom, readily comes to mind. Ṣàngó, who later became deified as the deity of thunder and lightening, had fallen victim to his own ego, and faced rebellion from two of his war generals—Timi and Gbonka. Ṣàngó ignored the counsel of Ọya, his Olorì, to tread carefully; a mistake that led to tragic consequences and marked his downfall.

The use of the words "servant" and "master" in the song transcribed above here relates more directly to the status of the singers as queens than to their position as wives. Olorì indeed consider themselves as public servants. They are servants not of their husbands, but of the king, in their official capacity as counselors. All Yorùbá subjects, regardless of their gender or position, are servants to their king. Such a line of duty becomes even more imperative for those (like chiefs and queens) who hold recognized positions of responsibility. It is important to note that not all wives do rise to the elevated position of the king's counselors as Olorì. But all are eligible and are therefore potential candidates for that exalted position. In addition to affirming their loyalty to the king, the women also assert their identity as a social group within the community by directing attention to the unique nature of their musical performance. Hence they sing in the last line that the true identity of an Olorì will be revealed in the performance slated to be held in the palace.

In another song, "Dìde Dìde Olorì," they urge all queens to rise up and honor the call of the ọwá, another name for the king. This song describes the unique importance of Olorì music in Emùré as one of the main musical traditions performed during the new yam festival, an event marking the beginning of the harvest season. In its patriotic theme, this song is contextually and thematically similar to the previous one. The women affirm their loyalty to the king in their role as public servants rather than as wives.

Dìde Dìde

i. Dìde dìde o òpólorì ìn mò dìde o
   Rise, all queens
ii. Ọmọkùnrin ù rólé
   Men, too, should please join
iii. Aya ukú ẹkún lá mọ̀ dìde o
   All women, rise and obey
iv. Ọwá rán ni ápè mí ò á tó o
   The call of the king

Similar sentiments are conveyed in "Aṣọ Uyì," a song in which the women enjoin all queens to honor the king by putting on their ceremonial dresses. The song also adds that the beautiful sight of their own appearance befits the honorable presence of their king. Honor thus begets honor. The element of self-praise is a pointer to the women's sense of self-confidence, a quality that easily came across each time I watched them perform. In spite of the formidable economic challenges of surviving in Nigeria, many of the women were enthusiastic about their roles in their community. On many occasions they expressed confidence in their ability to support the king and sustain the vital political institutions of their community, an act which is also self-empowering.

Aṣọ Uyì

i. Aṣọ uyì ni ìn múró
   We must dress decently
ii. Ùè uyì ni ìn wọ̀
   And move in dignity
iii. Ọwá rán ni yá pè á ò
   The king has sent for us
iv. Aya oyè wo mò ṣere.
   Thank you for the honor

In a song titled "Òpó Ulé Elémùré" (Pillars of Elémùré's palace), they sing about the importance of the market as the locus of economic activity and suggest that women are the controllers of the major commercial activities in the town.

Òpó Ulé Elémùré

i. Òpó ulé Elémùré
   Pillar of the palace of Elémùré
ii. Ará ulé ọlọ́jà lorè,
   The dwellers of the marketplace

iii.   Òpó mọ́mọ̀ yọsẹ̀ lábẹ́ Òrìṣà,
       The pillar must not collapse under the deity
iv.   Mà a ṣe tèmiyè lójú aṣeni
       I will succeed in spite of my enemies

The theme of economic power is linked to that of group identity and how they, as a group, contribute to the process of empowering and sustaining traditional institutions. In the song, they describe themselves as the "pillar" of Emùré-Èkìtì. The king is likened to a deity (Òrìṣà) for whom the women act as a source of support. They urge that this source of support, the "pillar," must not be allowed to collapse. This is followed by a reference to the market. Markets in traditional Yorùbáland are the main centers of rural commerce, and are organized and dominated by women. As in many parts of Yorùbáland, Emùré women are the ones who do most of the harvesting and take farm produce to the market to sell. They also engage in trading activities that take them to big commercial towns like Òṣogbo, Àkúré, Ìbàdàn, where they buy necessary items such as shoes, clothes, candles, matches, and soap, none of which are produced locally. To a large extent therefore, the economic life of Emùré-Èkìtì is dominated by women. The complementary relationship between female economic power and the political authority of the Yorùbá male king is spatially illustrated in the fact that the market is usually located adjacent to the king's palace. The song ends with a line that powerfully affirms the determination of the women to succeed in spite of the ever-present challenges of life.

Olorì songs are generally short and repetitive, employing what may be described as the pentatonic scale, and operating within a tonal span that rarely exceeds an octave. The songs in examples 3.1, 3.2 and 3.3 are typical in that they rarely exceed five measures in musical transcription. The soloist's call and the chorus's response are identical. The call sections are not framed by any extemporization. In their short lengths, and in the use of the same phrase by both solo and chorus, these songs fall within the category of Yorùbá songs associated with dance performance. Yet they carry important messages. The linguistic and melodic contours generally follow the same direction, as can be observed by comparing the tone-marked texts of the transcriptions of the lyrics provided above and the melodic patterns shown in examples 3.1, 3.2 and 3.3. Although minor differences do occur in different performances of the songs, either when performed by different people or by the same group on different occasions, such differences are usually marginal and of little structural significance. These songs contrast very vividly with the songs of the female chiefs, which display a much more complex structure, a feature which homologically reflects the higher political status of Emùré-Èkìtì female chiefs.

Example 3.1. "Abẹ́ I Kọṣẹ́ Orí," song of the king's wives, transcribed from author's own field recording.

Example 3.2. "Dìde Dìde," song of the king's wives, transcribed from author's own field recording.

Example 3.3. "Àrà Laṣọ Èyàn," song of the king's wives, transcribed from author's own field recording.

Musical Privileging of the Female Voice

Female ensembles, such as the Olorì ensemble, are rarely found in the Ọ̀yọ́-Yorùbá region, where the playing of drums is often dominated by men and the role of women is restricted to singing and dancing. In some localities, female musical groups are exclusively associated with specific types of musical instruments.[42] The prominence of Olorì ensembles in Èkìtì highlights the relative political, social, and economic strength of women in the region. The strong visibility of Olorì and Aírégbé, notably in their attachment to the two most important festivals of the town, highlights the critical importance of the role of women in the sustenance of the social, sacred, and political institutions of Emùré-Èkìtì. Olorì songs clearly emphasize the role of women as principal actors in the social conversation that takes place during important festivals such as the New Yam and the Aírégbé. Such festivals, which in traditional Yorùbá societies bring the king, his chiefs, and all members of the community together, represent the main public forum at which the contours of social status and political power are illuminated.

The drummers in Olorì ensembles, unlike the male drummers in the Òyó region, are neither professionally trained nor do they come from àyàn drumming families. The two female drummers whom I interviewed explained to me that they picked up drumming specifically for the purpose of performing as part of the Olorì ensemble. The musical complexity that marks the performances of male drummers is conspicuously absent in their performances. While there is a temptation to interpret this as reflecting a lack of proficiency or virtuosity on the part of these female drummers, it is far more instructive to relate their drumming patterns to the simple structure of the music that they accompany. The graceful nature of the dances and the powerful songs that the drummers accompany call for a rhythmic accompaniment that is devoid of the intricate narratives of the Yorùbá male master drummer. Further, the emphasis on the human voice helps to fashion a performance strategy in which singers and songs, rather than drummers, enjoy a greater visibility. This aesthetic preference for singing is even more pronounced in the Aírégbé performance of the female chiefs, in which drumming is completely dropped. The musical privileging of the female voice is quite intentional: the women could invite men to accompany them, as do women's groups in many Yorùbá communities. But the Emùré women prefer to take charge of the dancing, the drumming, the singing, the rehearsals, and the coordination of their ensemble themselves.

Thus Olorì performance provides a cultural space within which the agency of female members is completely unhindered and unencumbered by the presence and intervention of men. In addition to this is the fact that Olorì music, complete with àgèrè drumming, is performed at Olorì weekly meetings, where issues that are exclusive to the group are discussed. The performance of the music at such meetings no doubt helps to reinforce a strong sense of identity and group solidarity. But more importantly, the music, in its role as a symbol of female empowerment, speaks to the determination of the women to engage issues and problems that are peculiar to their members without interference by men. For although the music is performed at public occasions to entertain other members of the society and to honor the king, its performance at the female-only meetings helps to demarcate an exclusive social space.

As evident in their texts, Olorì songs do not challenge and are not in any way subversive of the authority of the king. Thus, although the organizational structure of the Olorì ensemble is inherently deconstructive of gender assumptions about musical practice in Yorùbáland, the private use of the ensemble is strategic only in terms of a quest to create a parallel domain of influence within which women can take on the gender-specific challenges of their community.[43] This is particularly significant, given the fact that the majority of the members of Olorì are the widows of past kings who, although they are designated (symbolically) as wives of the reigning king, tend to be more socially vulnerable because of their status as widows. For such women, the Olorì group provides a space of support in addition to helping to neutralize, if only temporarily, the hierarchical division that exists between them and the real wives of the reigning king. Olorì and Aírégbé performances of Emùré-Èkìtì women illustrate the use of music to identify cultural cohorts and articulate "shared habits (which) bind people into social groups according to specific aspects of the self (gender, class, age, occupation, interests, etc).["44] I explore the relationship between musical performance and group formation further in the next chapter by analyzing a specific example of Aírégbé music.

Chapter Four

The Aírégbé Song Tradition of Yorùbá Female Chiefs

Ethnomusicologists working in Africa often focus on the strategies displayed in the course of a public performance while ignoring the creative process and the decisions that lead to it. This practice assumes, wrongly, that traditional African public musical performances derive from ancient repertoires that hardly change, and thus can be easily reenacted with little or no preparation. Kwasi Ampene, in his study of *nnwonkoro*, a female song tradition of Akan women of Ghana, draws attention to this fallacy when he observes that "not much is known about techniques and processes of musical composition in preliterate societies."[1] While it is true that a public performance represents an important arena for creative decisions ("composition-in-performance,")[2] and provides an important context for understanding the nature of African musical performance, it is important to note that deliberate and deliberative compositional activities and rehearsals often precede a public performance. Regarding this issue, Alan Merriam observed that African musicians do practice "composition, recognize it as a distinct process, and are in a number of cases quite able to discuss it."[3] The process of composing a new musical performance in Africa is often communal, rather than individual. George Dor defines communal creativity as "a creative activity, whether performance or composition, in which members of a particular community come together to collectively express their communal ethos." According to him, "membership of a particular group" involved in this activity "may be inclusive or exclusive." Commenting on an example of communal creativity in Ghana, he observes that joint ownership of, and the process of composing, songs represent an important index of group identity among the Anlo-Ewe people.[4] Capturing the very intentional process of this creative act as rendered at specific moments offers considerable reward to the goal of understanding how music constitutes a form of social action in African societies. As Christopher Waterman has explained, the social significance of a musical performance derives not just from the content of the performance but also from the conceptual, contextual, social, and behavioral elements that guide its production process. According to him:

Whether the researcher's ultimate aim is to approach social reality through the arts, or to approach the arts through their social content, the procedure must be the same. In either case, the arts cannot be "read" without both comprehending their nature as aesthetic constructs with their own principles and conventions, and locating them in the specific social universe which is the ground of their existence. . . . The point at which the two dimensions meet is in the *production* of the arts: not just in its material but also in its ideational aspects. We need to ask by whom and by what means, in what circumstances, under what constraints, in whose interests and in accordance with what conventions, these arts are produced.[5]

My discussion in this chapter probes into the creative and performance features of Aírégbé music, the song tradition of Emùré-Èkìtì female chiefs whose ethnographic contexts I discussed in chapter 3. In analyzing a selected example here, I am interested in how the process of creating and performing a song, the musical structure and the song texts of a performance contribute to the process of defining and articulating the identity of a social group within a larger village community. In chapter 3 I explained that the organization of female groups in Emùré-Èkìtì reflects a hierarchical structure at the top of which are female chiefs. The social clout of Emùré female chiefs is reflected in the creative process through which they compose new songs. Compared with orin Olorì, examples of which I discussed in chapter 3, Aírégbé songs reflect a much more elaborate and deliberate process of creativity. The collaborative and dialogical process of working out new songs draws attention to how Emùré female chiefs mediate social and political events of their community and define their status through musical creativity and performance. Communality and negotiation are the two critical words that define the compositional process of Aírégbé songs. My description below focuses on a specific piece, capturing its structural procedure and the ethnographic context from which it is derived, as enacted during one of my many visits to Emùré.

"You Caught Us Unawares"

My first contact with Emùré female chiefs, the performers of Aírégbé songs, took place in 2006 when I embarked on a preliminary investigation. Although I was not able to witness any musical performance during that first visit, I was given a video recording of a previous Aírégbé festival. I was fascinated by the songs, the dances, and the entire festival as captured in the video recording. In 2007, I traveled back to Emùré to watch the festival, which was rather modest in scope that year because the king had died just a few months earlier.[6] In the course of watching the festival, I realized that many of the songs that were performed on that day were different from the ones that I had watched on video.

In May 2008, during another field trip to the town, the widow of the deceased king informed me that new songs were usually composed for new events, even though a rich repertoire already existed.[7] I did not realize the full import of this information until a few days later, when I met the entire group. My original plan had been to go through the texts of the songs that I had recorded and transcribed from the previous year, with a view to ascertaining the accuracy of my transcriptions. To my surprise, however, many members of the group were more interested in performing new songs than going through those recorded from the previous year. Some of the women explained that they could not remember some of the old songs, the texts of which I had read out loud to them, while others said they were not present when the songs were performed. They would have worked specifically on those songs if they had known that they were the ones that I wanted. They explained that they were "caught unawares" by my request regarding the "old songs," that they had worked out many new ones since my last visit, and would rather perform such new ones than spend time trying to figure out the texts of those of the previous year.

Interestingly however, the process of "remembering" the new songs was not a straightforward matter. Rather than simply singing their "new" songs, the women spent considerable time recomposing them. They began to put their heads together, right in my presence, to work out the new songs, which, as I later found out, combine some well-known phrases with completely new ones. The process of crafting and reworking songs was sometimes contentious. They disagreed, agreed, rejected some phrases, adjusted phrases here and there, shared jokes, laughed, and paused now and then, all in the process of "remembering" a new performance. They told me that one of the songs they were putting together was based on one that they had performed for the installation ceremony of their new king earlier in the year. After about forty-five minutes of this collective process of composition and recomposition, they told me they were ready to perform a final version of a song entitled "Ọba Kọ Yẹ Á," which I discuss and analyze below.

Ègbè and Èṣà in Song Performance: Musical Form as Social Action

The creative process and the formative elements of Aírégbé songs resonate beyond the boundaries of musical performance to constitute a form of social action. As I have earlier mentioned, the songs are marked by a structural process that is more elaborate than that of Olorì songs, a feature which parallels the higher social status of Emùré chiefs as an elite group of women renowned for their wealth of knowledge and wisdom, an attribute that the Yorùbá believe comes with age.

Emùré female chiefs employ two key words—*ègbè* and èṣà[8]—to describe the form and the process of creating their songs. *Ègbè*, as used by the women, refers to the recurring theme of a song, while èṣà refers to the intervening material between different statements of ègbè, through which the performance is propelled and developed. The women explain that ègbè usually occurs right at the beginning of a song as an opening musical theme, together with its lyrics. It also recurs at important moments within a performance. As a recurring phrase, it establishes and reiterates the key thematic material upon which an entire piece is built. On the other hand, èṣà is the "flesh and body" of the piece. It is the part of the performance where the full details of a piece are worked out, negotiated, and developed to generate a full performance.

I observed that the group spent considerable amount of time negotiating the basic form of ègbè, and an even longer time working out the èṣà sections of their song. Thus, although ègbè and èṣà are musical material, they emerge from and are symbolic of a process of communal composition that is defined by intense negotiation, argument, debate, fun-poking, and even sometimes, mildly unfriendly exchanges. In its dynamic form, this creative process thus imitates the day to day routine of social interaction, evoking the tension, debate, and conflict of ordinary life. In this regard, Aírégbé singing reenacts social reality and constitutes a symbolic medium for articulating and resolving intragroup debate. Indeed the notions of conflict and resolution are homologically suggested in the socio-musical concepts of ègbè and èṣà. Ègbè means "to support" or "to agree." In Aírégbé performance, ègbè, in addition to serving the purpose of musical emphasis, functions as a symbol of agreement and unity among the performers. Èṣà, like ègbè, also represents a musical activity and denotes a process of social interaction that informs the creation of a new song. Èṣà, which literally could mean "to choose," refers to the rigorous creative process through which an entire performance is realized. Since the process of musical development could traverse an almost infinite number of pathways, it is not surprising that the act of negotiating the èṣà sections of a song is most daunting, because different ideas have to be rejected or harmonized in the process of arriving at specific socially grounded musical decisions. The final shape of an entire performance is ultimately defined by the continuous engagement between these two creative elements. My analysis of the texts and the musical form of "Ọba Kọ Yẹ Á," which now follows, further illuminates the social and musical dimensions of Aírégbé music.

Ọba Kọ Yẹ Á: Song Texts as Narratives of Identity

Compared with Olorì songs, Aírégbé songs reflect greater philosophical depth and deeper insights into the history and culture of Emùré-Èkìtì. My discussion of the lyrics of "Ọba Kọ Yẹ Á" as a composite of five different thematic categories is informed mainly by the explanations provided by the Emùré-Èkìtì female chiefs who composed and performed the piece. Each section is dominated by a particular theme, as follows: praise for Elémùré, social mobilization, self-praise, historical connections, and corporate prayer. But I should also mention that these categories are not mutually exclusive, because multiple themes do feature in a single section while some phrases are repeated in different sections. The first section of the performance (see text below) introduces the thematic focus of the ègbè sections, praise for Elémùré.

Section One: Praise for Elémùré

In this section the women sing about the power and political appeal of their king, a quality conveyed through a reference to the magnificence of his palace. The song also discusses the royal authority of Elémùré by making reference to the large crowd of people that regularly converge to accord him honor. The phrase "mountain top" refers to the public sphere where Emùré people have gathered in the past to pay homage to their king. The women sing that the inner chamber of Elémùré's palace is beautifully adorned, and urge their listeners to go visit and behold the magnificence of the palace. It is important to note that a Yorùbá king's chamber (àkòdì) is not normally accessible to ordinary citizens. Unlike the gbàgede, the space right in front of the palace where the king addresses the general populace, the inner chamber is accessible only to those who hold important positions in the community, mainly chiefs. In singing about the beauty of the king's chamber, these female chiefs flaunt their privileged position, with the unique advantage of unhindered access to the king's private chamber. The flaunting of the women's social capital is a recurring theme in Aírégbé song performances.

Ọba Kọ Yẹ Á

I.	*Ọba Kọ Yẹ Á: The King Who Is Glorious*
i.	Ọba kọ yẹ á wọ̀ a dàbọ̀ bá ò
	May our glorious king live long
ii.	Mòkemùré o ẹ̀ṣọ́ orúta mọ̀ sẹ iyè
	Behold the greatness and the beauty of the mountain-top king
iii.	In mọ̀ dakòdì
	Please visit his dwelling place
iv.	Ọní bá ti dáọ̀fin rẹ̀ ọ́gbemu regun ke
	His palace is great to behold

Section Two: Social Mobilization

Having established the central theme of the song, the singers proceed to mobilize all Emùré people to pray for and support the king. Three categories of people are mentioned: youth, women, and the elite male group known as *gbàmọ,* which consists of young men specially trained to protect the king.[9] Each of these groups is called upon to pray for the king so that his reign will continue to bring peace and prosperity. The king, a source of pride to the town, deserves the prayers of everyone. As an integral and privileged part of the ruling elite, the female chiefs advance the cause of Emùré royal authority and thus help sustain a system and an institution in which they have a great stake, and which they consider paramount to the survival of their community. The performance progresses with more eulogy for the king when the singers describe the king as a ferocious lion that cannot be seen by the "ordinary eye."

Ọba Kọ Yẹ Á

II.	*Kete Ọ̀dọ́ Emùré: All Emùré Youth*
i.	Kete ọ̀dọ́ kè i lúlé Elémùré
	All the youth of Elémùré's place
ii.	Ìn jí a yá nọọ́ àdúrà sọ́wálúayé[10] bàbá Àṣàbí
	Let us pray for Owálúayé, the father of Àṣàbí
iii.	Kete obìnrin kè i lúlé Elémùré
	All the women of Emùré
iv.	Ìn jí a yá nọọ́ àdúrà sọ́wálúayé bàbá Àṣàbí
	Let us pray for Owálúayé, the father of Àṣàbí
v.	Mi kó gbàmọ a ìn yá múra kan mò a bọ
	All members of gbàmọ [traditional male elite]
vi.	Kán a yá nọọ́ àdúrà sọ́wálúayé bàbá Àṣàbí
	Let us pray for Owálúayé, the father of Àṣàbí

Section Three: Self-Praise

In the third section of the song the singers digress from their focus on the king to sing about themselves and their performance. They inform their listeners that the restrained but graceful nature of their performance befits their status as chiefs. In focusing further on their performance, they make references to two items of their costume: ankle-beads and colorful attire, both of which are integral to the multidimensional nature of their performance: the sounds of the beads appeal to the ear, and the beauty of their costumes to the eye. The beads, in addition to indicating their status as chiefs, function as body idiophones, which sound in sympathy with the movements of the dancer. The singers also compare their voices to that of the nightingale. Such instances of self-reflexivity within a performance are quite idiomatic of Yorùbá performances, serving as a device for drawing attention to the personalities of the performers. Barber and Waterman, citing a similar performance technique among Yorùbá fújì and oríkì performers, have explained that Yorùbá performers often "spread and imprint their image on everything," while "advertising themselves."[11] By digressing from royal praise to self-praise, self-recognition, and self-advertisement, Emùré female chiefs seize the unique opportunity of a public performance to draw attention to their status as important social actors within their community.

Ọba Kọ Yẹ Á

III. *Se L'amo a Mo Jíjo: Yes, We Can Dance*
A ti í rúà é rí bọ́ ni á tì a mọ̀ jíjó
Some may think we cannot dance
E la mọ̀ a mọ̀ jíjó, ṣe la mọ̀ a mẹ̀gẹ̀;
But we can; we can even do complicated dance steps
Se la mọ̀ a pòtéré erin lúà komọ̀ a ríre alájòkó Ìjàn
We can sing very well too; like the nightingale of Ìjàn (a town nearby)
Sisírìgún mẹ̀ pọdún í jẹ làrì ṣorò
Sisírìgún [a local plant] never dies

Section Four: Historical and Royal Connections

The fourth section explores a wider cultural terrain by making references to other Yorùbá kings. Couched in the Yorùbá "attributive-epithet" style,[12] but employing the song mode (orin) rather than the chant mode (oríkì or ìwí),[13] the women sing about kings who have important historical ties to their own king. In doing this, they sing key words that highlight important attributes of each of the kings. The list of kings includes the Ọlọ́wọ̀ (king of Òwọ̀),[14] the Èwí (king of Adó-Èkìtì),[15] and the Ẹlẹ́kọ̀lé (king of Ìkọ̀lé).[16] They pray for the Ẹlẹ́kọ̀lé, and hail the Ọlọ́wọ̀ for his enormous wealth. In praising the Ọlọ́wọ̀, they comment about his "garden of beads."[17] They also sing that the Elémùré is fit and able to "stand" amongst these other powerful "crowned" kings.[18] Their king is a "ferocious man whose fiery eyes cannot be beheld by the ordinary eye." He "bestows royal authority on his daughters and controls a large forest of riches."

The mentioning of these kings highlights important historical facts. For example, Emùré people believe that Òwọ̀ is their ancestral home, that is, the town from which their ancestors migrated to their present settlement hundreds of years ago. These few examples indicate the depth of historical and cultural knowledge often displayed by the women in their songs. "Ọba Kọ Yẹ Á" articulates different levels of identity: the women sing about themselves, about Emùré-Èkìtì, and about a wider Yorùbá community, comprising of a variety of kings heading multiple villages, towns, and ethnicities.

Ọba Kọ Yẹ Á

IV. *Iyùn Kàn Mejì: Royal Beads*
Iyùn kàn mejì á délé Ọlọ́wọ̀ asùnlọ́lá
There are two beads for the king of Owo, the man who is surrounded by a garden of beads
Iyùn kàn mejì á délé ọba Èwí òtú
There are two beads for the Èwí, king of Adó-Èkìtì
Ẹlẹ́kọ̀lé ò júmi kí ọ wo mọ̀ a dàbọ̀bá
Ẹlẹ́kọ̀lé, king of Ìkọ̀lé-Èkìtì, may you live long
Iyùn kàn mejì á délé Elémùré ri ọ̀fin

There are two beads for Elémùré
Elémùré rìn òfin í sọmọ rẹ̀ lóyè olúgbó ọwá re màayò yún
Elémùré, the ferocious king whose fiery eyes cannot be beheld by the
"ordinary eye"[19]
He bestows royal authority on his daughters and controls a large
forest of riches
Iró mẹ yọ̀ọ̀ jíjó kíi mọ́ mọ̀ ró sẹ̀wẹ́lẹ́ o
The jingles attached to the dancing feet cannot but sound
Aṣọ́ mẹ̀ yọ̀ọ̀ dáró kíi mọ́ mọ́ gbo ire
A dyed cloth cannot but shine

Section Five: Corporate Prayer

In the fifth section of the performance, the women pray that their king shall not die. Wealth in Yorùbá culture is not defined strictly in terms of material or monetary possession. A person's worth or wealth is also measured in terms of the multitude of relations and friends that he or she can lay claim to. This community-based concept of wealth is what Waterman has described as an "agglutinative" concept of honor.[20] The king represents a big treasure for his subjects. All are thus enjoined to pray for him. The prayer for God's protection and long life is rendered in a manner that can be personalized by everyone. Drawing figuratively on the life of "sisírìgún," a local perennial plant that resurfaces every year, the women pray that they and their king will live from year to year to witness great events every new season.

Ọba Kọ Yẹ Á

V.   *Sisírìgún Mẹ̀ Pọdún Í Jẹ: May We Live to Celebrate Again*
Sisírìgún mẹ̀ pọdún í jẹ làrì ṣorò
Sisírìgún never dies
Orí jẹ́ mi íbọ̀ mọ̀ mà ti ṣodún nǐ mà a ṣàmọ́dún
May I live to celebrate every year
A mọ̀ dakòdì
We have visited his dwelling place
Ọní bá ti dáòfin rẹ̀ ọ́gbemu regun ke
His palace is great to behold

Thematic Development and Structural Process

It is instructive at this stage to briefly examine how the socially grounded concepts of èṣà and ègbè are musically configured in "Ọba Kọ Yẹ Á."[21] How do the structural and performance features of the music reflect and reinforce the values that bind Emùré chiefs together as members of a distinct social group? Kofi Agawu has explained that to register African music as text is to foreground "its essence as a performed art" and as "complex messages based on specific

cultural codes." Such an analytical approach actually helps to draw attention
to the immediacy and processual quality of a performance. Analyzing a specific performance as I have done in this chapter helps us to focus on individual and group creativity, on individual and collective agency, and on how
compositions are created in specific contexts and reflect "specific moments of
intentionality."[22]

"Ọba Kọ Yẹ Á" begins with a melodic material that recurs continuously and
functions as its principal theme (ègbè, theme A, see ex. 4.1; CD track 5). Each
appearance of theme A is set to this text:

Ọba kọ yẹ á wọ a dàbọ bá ò
Mòkemùré o ẹṣọ orúta mọ sẹ iyè
In mọ dakòdì
Ọní bá ti dáọ̀fin rẹ̀ ọ́gbemu regun ke

The various appearances of this material are separated by episodic sections,
ẹṣà, each of which develops the song further in terms of the text and the melody.
Theme A is set to words which praise and pray for the king, a message which
pervades the song. Theme C, for example, continues the prayer-praise element
of theme A, urging the youth, the women, and the elite of Emùré (gbàmọ) to pay
homage to and pray for the king. The focus on the king, as conveyed in these
opening melodic phrases, pervades the song.

Theme C (see ex. 4.1), however, also performs an important musical function. For while the previous phrases end mostly on G, the tonic of the song's
pentatonic scale, theme C helps to open up the piece, so to speak, by generating a series of melodic sequences each of which ends on B, the third degree of
the pentatonic scale, set to the syllable "bi" in the word babasàbi. By virtue of its
length, its melodic sequences, and its emphasis on higher notes of the scale,
theme C helps to generate a sense of intensity and excitement, a feeling which
was palpable each time the women performed this song. Following theme C,
the piece progresses through a number of phrases that lead ultimately back to
theme A, which heralds the second cycle of the performance, as can be observed
in table 4.1.

The second cycle combines themes A and B with four additional ones (D,
E, F, and G). Themes A, B, D, E, and F are retained in the third cycle, while a
new one (H) appears there. This cycle also features a series of call-and-response
exchanges, hand-claps and a more interactive and energized rendition.
Thereafter the performance returns once again to an abridged version of ègbè.
Thus, as can be observed in table 4.1, each new cycle begins with a recall of previously heard materials before exploring new ones, thus generating a cumulative
procedure that guarantees a judicious balance between repetition and variation,
two vital indices of a good musical performance. The cumulative progression of
the song, as defined by an increasingly varied thematic character, is marked by a
progressive expansion of the temporal span of each successive cycle, beginning

Example 4.1. "Ọba Ko Yẹ Á," transcribed from author's own field recording.

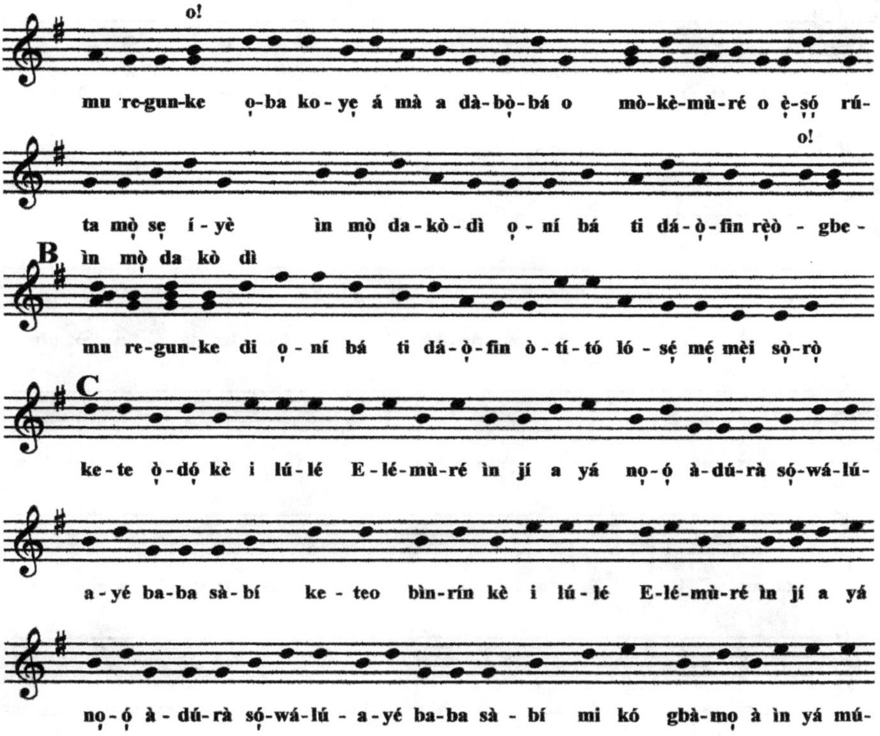

Example 4.1. *Continued.*

ta mò sẹ í - yè   ìn mò da - kò - dì   ọ - ní bá   ti dá - ọ̀ - fin rẹ̀ò gbe -

mu re - gun - ke   ọ - ba ko   yẹ á mà a   dà - bò - bá o   mò - kè - mù - ré o   ẹ̀ só ___ rú -

tà mò sẹ í - yè   ọn mò da - kò - dì   ọ - ní bá   ba dá - ọ̀ - fin rẹ̀ò gbe -
o!

mu re - gun - ke   ọ - ba ko   yẹ á mò a   dà - bò - bá o   mò - kè - mù - ré o   ẹ̀ - só rú -

ta mò sẹ í - yè   ìn mò da - kò - dì   ọ - ní bá   ti dá - ọ̀ - fin rẹ̀ò gbe -

mu re - gun - ke   ọ - ba ko   yẹ á mò a   dà - bò - bá o   mò - kè - mù - ré o   ẹ̀ - só ___ rú -

ta mò sẹ í - yè   ìn mò da - kò - dì   ọ - ní bá   ba dá - ọ̀ - fin - rẹ̀ò gbe -
o!

mu re - gun - ke   ọ - ba ko   yẹ á mà a   dà - bò - bá o   mò - kè - mù - ré o   ẹ̀ - só rú -
o!

ta mò sẹ í - yè   ìn mò da - kò - dì   ọ - ní bá   ba dá - ọ̀ - fin - rẹ̀ò   gbe -

B ìn mò da kò dì

mu re - gun - ke   dì - ọ - ní bá   ba dá ọ̀ - fin   ò - tí - tọ́ ló   sẹ mẹ́ mèì sò - rò

Example 4.1. *Continued.*

D

è-rò á o e-rín ti yí-pa-ra-dà dòì-sá-jú   mi ó kù a ò-tú e̩-gbé̩

E

o-ló-yè lo̩-ro̩-gba o   a ti í rú-à é rí bó̩ ni á tì a mò̩-jí-jó

F

e la mò̩ a mò-jí-jó i - s̩e la mò̩ a mè̩-gè̩   s̩e la mò̩ a pò-té-ré e-

G

rin lú- à ko-mò̩ a rí-re   a-lá-jò-kó Ì-jàn   sí - sí-rì-gún mè po̩-dún í je̩

lá-rì s̩o-rò o-rí jé-mi   í-bò̩ mo̩ mà ti s̩o-dún-ùn - ní mà a s̩ù-mó̩-dún   o

A

mo mò̩ da-kò-dì o̩-ní bá   ba dá-ò̩-fin rè̩ò-gbe - mu re-gun-ke   o̩-ba ko-

ye̩ á mà a dà-bò̩-bá o   mò-kè-mù-ré o è̩-s̩ó̩   rú - ta mò̩ s̩e í-yè

ìn mò̩ da-kò-dì o̩-ní bá   ti dá-ò̩-fin rè̩ò-gbe - mu re-gun-ke   o̩-ba ko-

ye̩ á mà a dà-bò̩-bá o   mò-kè-mù-ré o è̩-s̩ó̩___   rú - ta mò̩ s̩e í-yè

o!

ìn mò̩ da-kò-dì o̩-ní bá   ba dá-ò̩ fin rè̩ò-gbe - mu re-gun-ke   o-ba ko̩

Example 4.1. *Continued.*

yẹ á mà a dà-bọ-bá o   mò-kè-mù-ré o ẹ-sọ́   rú - ta mọ̀ se í-yè

B ìn mò da kò dì

ìn mọ̀ da-kò-dì ọ-ní bá   ti dá-ọ̀ fin rẹ̀ò-gbe - mu re-gun-ke dì ọ-ní bá

D

ti dá-ọ̀-fin ò-tí-tọ́-ló-sẹ mẹ́ mèi sọ̀-rọ̀   è-rò a ò e-rín ti yí-

pa-ra-dàò dòì-sá-jú   mí o kù á ò-tú ẹ-gbẹ́ o-ló-yè lọ̀-rọ̀ gbào

E

a ti í rú-à é rí bọ́ ni á tì a mọ̀-jí-jó   sẹ la mò a mọ̀-jí-jó o

F

sẹ la mọ̀ a mẹ̀-gẹ̀   sẹ la mọ̀ a pò-té-ré e - rin lu à ko-mọ̀ a rí-re

H

a lá jò kó Ì-jàn I - ró mẹ̀ yọ-ọ̀ ji-jó kí-i mó mò ró sẹ̀-wẹ́-lé o a-

só mẹ̀ yọ ọ̀ dá-ró kì mó mò-gbó ì-rè   i - yùn kàn a rà-kó-kó___ki-yùn

kàn a rà-kùn-gbá I - ró mẹ̀ yọ-ọ̀ ji-jó kí i mó mò ró sẹ̀-wẹ́-lé o a-

só mẹ̀ yọ ọ̀ dá-ró kì mó mò-gbó ì-rè   i - yùn kàn me-jì a dé-lé ọ-ló-

Example 4.1. *Continued.*

wò à-sùn-lọ́-lá I - ró mè yo - ò ji - jó kí ì mọ́ mọ̀ ró sẹ̀-wẹ́-lẹ́ o a -

sọ́ mẹ̀ yọ́ ọ̀ dá-ró ki mó mò-gbó ì-rè i - yùn kàn me-jì a dé-lé ọ-ba

è-wí ò-tù I - ró mẹ̀ yọ-ọ̀ ji-jó kí i mọ́ mọ̀ ró sẹ̀ wẹ́-lẹ́ o a -

sọ́ mẹ̀ yọ́ ọ̀ dá-ró ki mó mò-gbó ì - rè Ẹ - lẹ́-kò-lé ò jú-mi kí ọ wọ

mòa dà-bọ̀-bá I - ró mẹ̀ yọ-ọ̀ ji-jó kí i mó mò ró sẹ̀-wẹ́-lẹ́ o a -

sọ́ mẹ̀ yọ́ ọ̀ dá-ró ki mó-mò gbó ì - rè i - yùn kàn me-jì a dé-lé

lé-mù ré rì ọ̀-fin I - ró mẹ̀ yọ-ọ̀ ji-jó kí i mó mò ró sẹ̀-wẹ́-lẹ́ o a -

sọ́ mẹ̀ yo ò dá-ró ki mọ́ mò gbó ì - rè Ẹ - lé - mù-ré rìn ò-fin í sọ-

mọ rẹ̀ lò-yè o-lú-gbó ọ - wá rè-mà - yò-yun I - ró mẹ̀ yọ-ọ̀ ji-jó kí i mó

mò ró sẹ̀-wẹ́ - lẹ́ o a - sọ́ mẹ̀ ya à dá-ró ki mọ́ mọ̀-gbó ì-rè si -

Example 4.1. *Continued.*

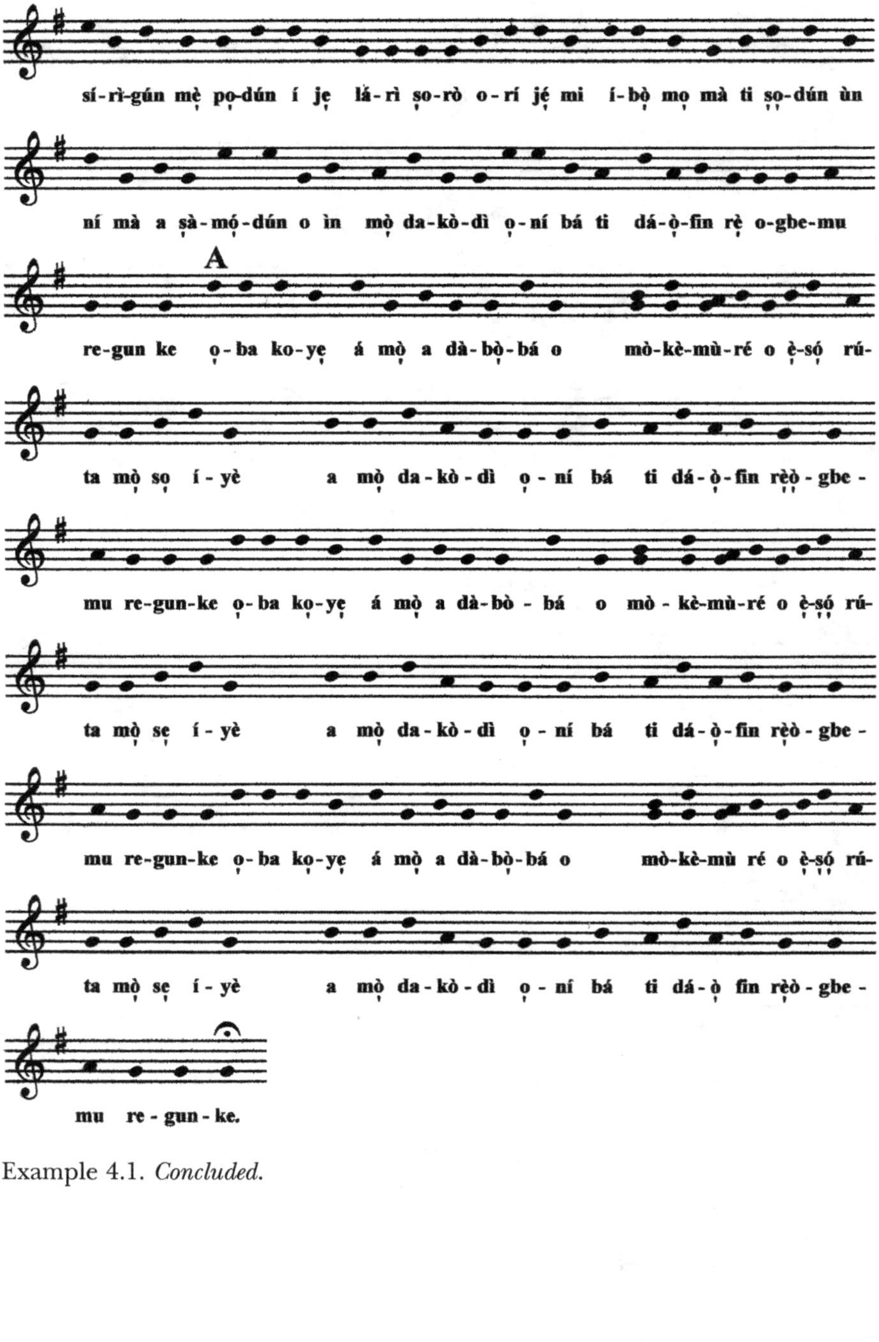

Example 4.1. *Concluded.*

Table 4.1. "Ọba kọ Yẹ Á." *ẹ̀gbè* and *ẹ̀ṣà* in musical form

Sectional layout	Themes	Song-text	Translation	Cyclic progression	Linear progression	Role of ẹ̀ṣà and ẹ̀gbè
First ẹ̀gbè	A	*Ọba kọ yẹ á*	Glorious king	Cycle one	A	Ègbè-dominated
First transition	B	*Ìn mọ̀ dakodi*	Behold his palace			
First ẹ̀ṣà	C	*Kete ọdọ/kete obìnrìn / Mi kó gbàmọ*	Pray for the king		B	
Second ẹ̀gbè	A	*Ọba kọ yẹ á*	Glorious king	Cycle two	A	
Second transition	B	*Ìn mọ̀ dakodi*	Behold his palace			
Second ẹ̀ṣà	D, E, F & G.	i. *Èrò á ò erin ti yí ṭaradà* ii. *Ati it rua eri* iii. *Ṣe la mọ a ṭòtèré* iv. *Sisìngún*	The lion (the king) is transformed; yes we can dance; we praise king; prayers for long life		C	Ẹ̀ṣà-dominated

Table 4.1. Continued

Sectional layout	Themes	Song-text	Translation	Cyclic progression	Linear progression	Role of èṣà and ègbè
Third ègbè	A	*Ọba kọ yẹ á*	Glorious king	Cycle three	A	
Third transition	B	*Ìn mọ dakòdi*	Behold his palace			
Third èṣà	D, E, F & H	i. *Èrò á ò erín ti yí paradà* ii. *Ati ti rua eri* iii. *Ṣe la mọ a pòtèrè* iv. *Iró mọ yaà jíjó* (Chains of responsorial phrases)	The lion (the king) is transformed; yes we can dance; we praise king.		D	
Concluding ègbè	A	*Ọba kọ yẹ á*		Cycle four	A	Ègbè

from the first cycle to the third one. The only exception is the very final cycle, which is shorter because it consists of only one main thematic material, theme A (the ègbè), which provides a conclusion to the performance. The dynamic nature of successive cycles imparts a sense of linearity to the song, as can be observed in table 4.1, which shows that the singing of new phrases helps to generate new sections and move the piece forward. This is particularly noticeable in how alternations of ègbè and èṣà sections help to structure the piece, as can be observed in the last column of table 4.1. While ègbè sections frame the piece, the middle section, which functions as an extensive development, is dominated by èṣà phrases.

Tonality and Language

This song, like many Yorùbá songs, employs a pentatonic scale, although the occasional appearances of the pitch note F♯ help to push the song beyond the prevailing pentatonic scale, as illustrated in the section of the piece where the words "erín ti yí paradà" are sung (see theme D). It is important to note that such deviations occur in sections of the piece in which the performance approaches a chant mode. Further, the melodic character of the song is defined by the use of vocal ornaments and glides which lend to the entire performance a distinct vocal color not easily captured in musical transcription but clearly audible in the recording.

Another striking feature of this song is the fact that melodic contours often do not follow the linguistic contours of the Yorùbá speech. This particular feature challenges the general assumption that Yorùbá vocal music is defined consistently by a parity of movement between the contours of vocal melody and those of the Yorùbá words to which they are set. The melodic phrase to which the text "Ìn mò dakòdì ọní bá" is set often conflicts with the tonal contour of the words. The preponderance of this form of text-singing in this and other performances by Emùré women derives from the fact that song categories within the Aírégbé song tradition are often defined by a preexisting melodic formula, an *a priori* framework, into which new texts are worked. The use of a preexisting melodic formula occurs on different structural levels. First, all new compositions are defined by the use of an essentially pentatonic scale structure." Second, Aírégbé songs often are composed of melodic patterns that recur, albeit with some variations, irrespective of the changes in the text to which they are set. This technique can be observed by comparing the melodic pattern of "Ọba Kọ Yẹ Á" to another song, "Atáyérọ," example 4.2. Indeed example 4.2 is sometimes interpolated into "Ọba Kọ Yẹ Á," a practice that can be explained by the fact that theme A (of ex. 4.1) and the melody of example 4.2 are quite similar. They are motivically related, share similar contour patterns, and are based on the same anhemitonic pentatonic scale.

Example 4.2. "Atáyé Rọ," transcribed from author's own field recording.

The use of an *a priori* melodic scheme in this manner suggests the privileging of musical form over linguistic texts, and speaks to the existence of a distinct musical genre, anchored on a melodic protostructure that provides a framework for the creation of new performances. Instances of deviation of melodic contours from the tonal inflections of words are thus quite substantial, as can be observed by comparing melodic contours with the diacritical marks of their texts as shown in example 4.1. Many Aírégbé songs have a melodic character that remains identifiable even when texts change. This is because words are often made to fit into a preexisting melodic scheme. Emùré women provide an ethnographic support for this observation through their statement that "orin aírégbé lụṣìmọ̀," that is, "Aírégbé songs are unique in their character and are easily identifiable."[23]

The relative independence of musical form from language is also reflected in the fact that the various phrases that comprise the piece can be analyzed within a four-section musical form, framed by ègbè sections. In other words, the overall musical form of the song seems to suggest an interpretation independent of the sequential pattern and the thematic flow of the lyrics. I pointed this out to the women, wondering whether they were aware of this lack of perfect synchrony between the progression of the lyrics and the four-part form of the song. Several of the women responded that what mattered most to them in the structuring of their performance was to constantly alternate ègbè with ẹ̀ṣà. They explained that a good performance must constantly return to ègbè to be enjoyable, and that "too much of ẹ̀ṣà is tasteless." This response clearly shows that consideration for musical coherence plays a significant role in the process of working out and performing Aírégbé songs, in addition to the meaning of the words. Other features of the piece that challenge certain assumptions about Yorùbá vocal music include the presence of sporadic harmonies, and the singing of extended, legato melodic phrases. Contrary to some commonly expressed views, not all African songs are short, fragmentary and percussive.[24]

As this brief analysis shows, the total outline of this performance is framed by a cumulative outline in which previous texts and melodies are recalled and varied, while new ones are continuously introduced. The recurrences of the opening material within episodes that function as developmental sections help to generate a sense of coherence and sustain a process of structural unfolding framed by an increasing energy level. It is also interesting to note that the structure of "Ọba Kọ Yẹ Á" departs from the more widely discussed ubiquitous short call-and-response phrases of African songs. Although call-and-response exchanges feature in it, the entire song is defined by a long-range structural process that departs from the minimalist call-and-response exchanges characteristic of the Olorì songs discussed in the last chapter.

Age, Chieftaincy and Social Status in Musical Performance

As illustrated in "Ọba Kọ Yẹ Á," Aírégbé songs, in conveying important cultural and historical facts about the Emùré community and their neighbors, function as an important medium for performing "local and supralocal histories" and a distinct historical mode of "memory production."[25] The relatively elaborate musical form of Aírégbé songs, and the considerable wealth of cultural knowledge displayed in the creation of "Ọba Kọ Yẹ Á" are indicative of the status of Emùré female chiefs as a distinct elite group of people with considerable cultural and political authority. Indeed there is no other musical ensemble in Emùré, male or female, that commands the same respect and social recognition as the Aírégbé song group. There is a sense in which the creative process and the performance and stylistic features of this song provide important dimensions about how music contributes to the process of identity formation. Timothy Rice once asked whether such a process is defined by "performativity, symbolization or boundary formation."[26] The high degree of cultural knowledge and structural sophistication displayed in Aírégbé songs is commensurate with the social status and the relatively advanced age of the genre's performers. Compared with the music of the king's wives (Olorì), the songs of the more elderly Emùré female chiefs reflect a much more invigorated musical process and an organic musical form. There is a strong sense in which Aírégbé songs, which as we have seen are imbued with a great element of performativity, help to create an exclusive social boundary within which the identity of Emùré-Èkìtì females chiefs is located and defined.

The women are in effect performing their age and status in their songs. Furthermore, the communal creative approach through which they work out new pieces and the ways in which the boundaries of composition are negotiated, varied and revised, are performance strategies that are agency-driven. New texts are worked out, while preexisting melodic formulas are subjected to variations in the course of generating new performance material. The structural complexity of Aírégbé derives from a cultural capital that speaks to the experience, age, and social status of the female chiefs who perform the songs. One of the issues that I will be pondering in the next chapter is how the features of the traditional Yorùbá vocal practices discussed in chapter 3 and the present chapter are retained, reinterpreted, or undermined in the music of Yorùbá composers of church music, a relatively new Yorùbá musical idiom linked strongly to the work of European musicians and church missionaries in Nigeria.

Chapter Five

Yorùbá Music in the Christian Liturgy

Notation, Performance, and Identity

"Firstly, strict adherence to the characteristics of Yorùbá music . . . ; and secondly, study of the methods of development of European music of a certain type and adaptation of them to our need."
—Phillips, *Yoruba Music*, 17

Composing for a New Religion

This chapter focuses on Yorùbá church music, a relatively new musical genre whose origins date back mainly to the early decades of the twentieth century. Yorùbá church music departs from indigenous, precolonial Yorùbá musical practices in two important ways. First, the music is integral to the liturgy of a new religion; and second, it is often written down in staff notation or in solfège, thus departing from the oral tradition of indigenous music. As the first Western-influenced musical tradition in Yorùbáland, it provides the major plank for the development of new musical genres and practices. The integration of Yorùbá music into Christian worship presents interesting perspectives about the process and manner of identity construction through musical expression during the colonial era. That process depended largely on the activities of a few Western-educated Yorùbá Christians who were motivated by the need to create a new style of Christian music that, unlike the imported European type, was suited to the tastes and cultural background of Yorùbá worshippers. The resultant musical compositions, which reflected the elitist background of the musicians who pioneered the new tradition, were culturally marginal to traditional Yorùbá musical practices and were alien to the average Yorùbá person. It must be noted that many of the early Christian churches were located in the Ọ̀yọ́ region and in the adjoining areas of Abẹ́òkúta, Lagos, and Badagry. Thus the Christian music reflects a strong influence of the Ọ̀yọ́-Yorùbá culture, notably in its exclusive use of the Ọ̀yọ́ dialect. Even more notable is the fact that the Right Reverend Samuel Ajayi Crowther, the first African bishop and the man who translated the Bible from English into Yorùbá, hailed from the town of Ọ̀ṣoògùn, near Ọ̀yọ́. His translation employed the Ọ̀yọ́ dialect and provided the Yorùbá texts to which early Yorùbá church musicians set their music. Considering the fact that language is at the root of cultural and social identity, and the strong relationship between language and music, it is not difficult to understand why virtually all known compositions by Yorùbá pioneer composers of church music have a distinct Ọ̀yọ́-Yorùbá character. The activities of the pioneers of Yorùbá church music draw attention to how the habits and preferences of a few known individual agents can become widely shared and have a long-term impact on the social and cultural life of a given community. Thomas Turino stresses this fact when he explains that cultural "habits have specific histories, create material effects, and over time gain relative stability. They are real, existing forces at the level of both the individual and society."[1] In the case of Yorùbá church music, the "existing forces" were the elitist background of the composers and the cultural hegemony of the Ọ̀yọ́-Yorùbá region.

My discussion in this chapter explores these issues by focusing on representative musicians and their works. Given the historical nature of the subject, my methodology in this chapter departs substantially from the strong ethnographic orientation of all the other chapters of this book. My discussion and conclusions derive largely from published historical sources, and are informed by a study of musical scores. But I also draw on discussions with some of the musicians as well as on my personal experience of musical events and religious services in many Yorùbá churches over the past thirty years.[2] My discussion of Yorùbá church music is in two chapters. In the present one I focus on the activities of pioneer elite and literate Yorùbá composers and choirmasters of the early twentieth century who initiated the use of Western staff notation and solfège in composing or adapting Yorùbá songs. In addition to composing and arranging songs, such Western-educated Yorùbá musicians taught Western hymns and church anthems to illiterate Yorùbá Christians, who mediated these influences in various ways.[3] In the next chapter I discuss how Yorùbá Africanist churches, the *Aládùrà* (prayer bands), which emerged much later in the twentieth century, moved away from the musical liturgy of the early Yorùbá church to develop neotraditional musical forms that ministered powerfully to the social and economic needs of members. As in the other chapters, I accord attention to the role of key individuals as agents of transformation by providing relevant biographical sketches, by paying attention to their views, and by analyzing selected examples of their compositions. But first, I present a brief historical background.[4]

European Music and Christianity in Yorùbáland

The activities of foreign missionaries in Lagos and its environs in the nineteenth century set the pattern for the spread of Christianity and Western Church music in other Yorùbá towns. The Church Missionary Society (CMS), the largest missionary group of the time, established its first mission in Badagry, near Lagos, in 1845. This was followed by the establishment of another branch in Abẹ́òkúta, in 1846. The Methodist Church established its own branch in Badagry, in 1842; the Baptists, in Ìjàyè, in 1853. In 1867 the Catholic established its mission Lagos. The establishment of Christian missions was paralleled by a concomitant settlement of foreign nationals, notably in Lagos and its environs. Many of the foreign nationals had come to Lagos as traders, colonial officials, and missionaries.

By the end of the nineteenth century there was already a sizeable Christian population in a number of Yorùbá cities, including Lagos, Ìbàdàn, and Abẹ́òkúta. At this point, only Western music was employed during Christian worship services. European classical music was also performed for special occasions inside the church, and concerts were performed in missionary schools like the Lagos Anglican Grammar School, established in 1859, and the Lagos CMS (Church Missionary Society) Female Institute, founded in 1872. As Lynn Leonard has noted, a very high standard of European classical music was maintained in these schools.[5] For example, Robert Coker, the music teacher at the CMS Female Institute, was nicknamed the "Mozart of West Africa" because of his versatility as a composer and performer of Western classical music. Trained in Germany, Coker was the first Nigerian to study Western classical music to a professional level in Europe. He, together with another musician, Dr. Nathaniel King, contributed greatly to the promotion of Western music in missionary schools in nineteenth-century Lagos. In addition to introducing many Yorùbá people to Western music through their teaching work, these two musicians organised regular concerts at which both local and expatriate musicians performed together. Also active in the process of popularizing European music in Nigeria were philanthropic societies such as The Academy and The Philharmonic, which organized European-type concerts in aid of newly established schools in Lagos.[6] The works of composers like G. F. Handel, J. S. Bach, W. A. Mozart, Felix Mendelssohn, and Josef Haydn featured prominently at such concerts.[7]

Yorùbá Identity in the Christian Church

Toward the end of the nineteenth century, Nigerian worshippers began to press for the ordination of indigenous pastors and the use of traditional music in the church. Yorùbá Christians desired that their Christian faith be sung in "culturally appropriate ways."[8] Their agitation produced significant results: by the beginning of the twentieth century, locally trained musicians had begun to compose their own hymns for use in the church. The newly composed hymns, though often accompanied by the organ, often followed indigenous Yorùbá forms, notably in the use of call-and-response patterns and melodies which reflect the tonal inflections of their Yorùbá texts. Further, Yorùbá folk songs, which had earlier been banned because of their alleged pagan associations, were adapted for use in the church.

The emergence of new syncretic compositions constituted a significant musical development. The composers of the first generation of Yorùbá musicians to receive musical training from European teachers and missionaries adapted European elements, notably tonal harmony, into their music. The activities of these semiprofessional church musicians provided the foundation for the emergence of a second generation of Nigerian composers who, with the benefit of professional training in Europe and the United states, pioneered a new tradition of art music.[9] This generation made increasing use of Yorùbá music in the church.

For musical as well as textual reasons, it was desirable to use Yorùbá melodies as vehicles for Christian lyrics.[10] In the Yorùbá hymn book of the first generation, Western hymns had simply been translated into Yorùbá.[11] This resulted in tonal distortions, wrong pronunciations, and wrong meanings of the Yorùbá texts. The emerging Yorùbá composers of the second generation decided to address this problem by writing new songs in which the inflectional patterns of the Yorùbá words are retained. Newly composed songs were used alongside Baptist, Anglican, and Methodist hymns and chants. In their bid to completely Africanize Christian worship, some more radical Nigerian Christians demanded that the use of European hymns and chants be discontinued altogether.[12] Many subsequently opted out of European churches to form new Africanist congregations where they hoped they would be able to achieve the ultimate objective of fully Africanizing the Christian liturgy.[13] As I explain in chapter 6, the formation of these Africanist churches opened up a new trajectory for the development of Yorùbá church music.

Pioneers of Yorùbá Church Music

Pioneering composers and performers of notation-based Yorùbá music in the first half of the twentieth century included Emmanuel Sowande,[14] Rev. J. J. Ransome-Kuti,[15] Rev. T. Ola Olude, T. K. E. Phillips,[16] and Akin George.[17] Also prominent were Dayo Dedẹkẹ, Olaolu Omideyi, and G. B Oriere. It was Ekundayo Phillips, however, who made the greatest contribution to the growth of the Yorùbá Christian musical liturgy. Born in 1884, Phillips received organ lessons as a child from his uncle, the Reverend Johnson, before proceeding to Trinity College in London in 1911 to study music. On his return to Nigeria a few years later, he was appointed organist and choirmaster at the Christ's Church,

'So long, farewell ! till We meet again'
(T K E Phillips, after the 'Musical Offering' Service).

Figure 5.1. Ekundayo Phillips. Lagos, ca. 1964. Reproduced with permission from Michael Olatunji.

Lagos, a post he held until 1962. As expected of a professionally trained musician, his compositions are not restricted to simple hymnals, folksong arrangements and responses, as is the case with the works of most of his contemporaries. For example, his composition *Samuel* (for soloists, chorus, and organ) is the first Nigerian oratorio. Phillips's contribution to the study of Yorùbá music was acknowledged when, in 1964, he was awarded a honorary doctorate degree in music by the University of Nigeria, Nsukka. By the time of his death in 1969, he had established himself as the most respected authority on Yorùbá church music.

In 1953, Phillips published a pioneering ethnographically based study that explains important stylistic features of Yorùbá music as well as the procedures through which he believed Yorùbá music could be "developed" for use in the Christian church.[18] Phillips's study is particularly significant because it is conceived as a minitreatise on composition for Yorùbá composers. His guidelines influenced not only his own colleagues but also the next generation of Nigerian composers and performers, including Fela Sowande, Ayo Bankole, and Sam Akpabot, all of whom he trained. Surprisingly, however, studies which attempt to assess the significance of Phillips's views on Yorùbá music are few.[19] Such an assessment is a crucial first step toward an understanding of the relationship between Yorùbá church music and traditional Yorùbá vocal music (elements of which I discussed in chapters 3 and 4). The new type of music that was developed by Phillips and his contemporaries was conceived to advance the cause of a Yorùbá identity in the imported Christian church in the early decades of the twentieth century.

Ekundayo Phillips on Yorùbá Music

Tonal Qualities of Yorùbá Language

To represent the tonal character of the Yorùbá language, Phillips employs a European-derived three-line staff, each line of which represents a principal tone of the Yorùbá language. To represent the glides and subtle shades of tones that are articulated when the language is spoken, Phillips uses the spaces above the three lines. The result is a notation which indicates the range of tonal movement in Yorùbá speech. Linguistic intervals less than a tone apart are represented by a "line-to-space," or "subsidiary" progression, intervals a full tone or more apart by a "line-to-line" or "principal" tonal movement. The tones and their subsidiaries are not fixed, and may change with each speech rendition or even in the course of a single sentence. Phillips speculates that the interaction between such principal and subsidiary tones provides the roots from which singing in Yorùbá society developed. According to him, principal and subsidiary tonal movements highlight the inherent musicality of the Yorùbá language, and provide the basis for the prominence of a traditional pentatonic scale in which the highest tone is an octave above the lowest.

Transition from Speech to Music

In explaining the progression from Yorùbá speech to Yorùbá song, Phillips identifies different types of speech utterances, namely: normal speech, impassioned speech, and chanting. "Impassioned speech" occurs as an expression of "excitement, strong emotion or passion." Like normal speech, impassioned speech exists as part of daily utterances. But unlike normal speech, it is accompanied by significant emotion and an attendant heightening of speech pitch. It is still speech, though, and remains within the domain of spoken utterance rather than that of musical performance. Sites of impassioned speech include intense arguments, expressions of anger, and other situations in which there may be some kind of emotional outburst. Chanting, as a form of expression, is closest to singing. Phillips also explains that chanting is rarely performed in daily life. It often features in rituals, as part of traditional Yorùbá sacred festivals, or as special greetings and praise-epithets (oríkì). Chanting is characterised by the use of poetry, and it carries a strong element of performance. It involves much more tonal angularity than is found in ordinary speech. Phillips illustrates his discussion with examples from food sellers and hawkers of goods who advertise their wares in utterances that navigate the fluid terrains of speech, recitative, and song. Outlining his speculative theory about this speech-music trajectory, he explains: "It must have been that when Impassioned Speech came into being, it was practised as a useful medium of expression, superior to ordinary speech. Then it was discovered, either by accident, or by natural stress, as harmonies are produced by pressure in a wind instrument, that something better could be produced, and so, musical tones began to come in occasionally, until finally, recitatives were fully developed, first only imperfectly—something like Recitative Secco, and later as real music, something like Recitative Stromentato."[20]

Phillips's hypothetical explanation follows the probability-driven origin theories of certain Western musicologists of the early twentieth century, for example, Percy Scholes and George Grove.[21] Phillips explains that impassioned speech and recitatives provide the "missing link" between Yorùbá speech and Yorùbá melody. Drawing on a comparison between Yorùbá music and European music, he goes on to suggest that the Yorùbá traditional recitative (like oríkì) represents an African variety of an old European tradition. Phillips states that Yorùbá music has a lot in common with a supposedly older European musical tradition and explains that twentieth-century Yorùbá music is comparable to European music of the medieval period. Yorùbá musicians should therefore feel free to employ the harmonic resources that are characteristic of medieval European music to "develop" Yorùbá music. One such feature is the pentatonic scale.

The Pentatonic Scale

Phillips observes that the pentatonic scale is common to both Yorùbá music, and European medieval music of roughly from the tenth to the fifteenth centuries. According to him, European music began with the use of the pentatonic scale before progressing to the seven-note mode of the medieval period and, much later, major and minor scales. Phillips further explains that the use of the entire chromatic scale in twentieth-century atonal music was the climax of the historical evolution of European music toward a progressively richer vocabulary of tones. By comparison, Phillips explains that Yorùbá music has only managed to evolve to the level of the pentatonic scale. In isolated cases, it is possible to find the use of more than the five regular pitches of the scale in a song. Such "strange notes" are, however, merely incidental and not in any way organic to the construction of songs. According to Phillips, "Yorùbá have no succession of tones yet. They have only the pentatonic scale to their credit; although at times, some strange notes creep into their songs which might be regarded as the result of an instinctive feeling after variety and extension by means of embellishment."[22]

The Significance of Phillips's Work

It is important to locate Phillips's views on music and musical development within the context of the prevailing colonial environment in Nigeria between 1900 and 1960, the period when he was active as a composer, researcher, and performer. His concept of development is reflective of the general thinking of both the colonizer and the colonized during the period. The apparent objective of colonization, as explained by the colonizing countries, was to bring "development" to the "Dark Continent" of Africa. It was a concept that permeated social, political, religious, and cultural spheres of life. The desire of "advanced" countries to share their cultural and intellectual traditions with the so-called underdeveloped countries was projected as a mission to develop humanity at a global level. This notion clearly influenced the works of Phillips, and indeed represented the foundation on which his views on musical composition rested. Phillips believed that European music offered great potential for the development of Yorùbá music. Attesting to the dominance of the development-oriented nationalism of the colonial era, Phillips has observed that "Nigerians are undergoing their training under the English and, in the connection, one of the concerns of all those who have the interest of this country at heart is whether or not we are developing on national lines in various directions."[23]

We know that economic interests, rather than altruism, constituted the main basis for European colonial intervention in Africa. In Nigeria, the concept of development was employed by the British to justify their colonial presence, and was embraced by many indigenous professionals, including teachers, priests, politicians, and musicians, whose work was associated with the imported Christian church. Phillips's approach to the issue of development, though largely influenced by the larger political ideology of the times, reveals a sustained attempt to reconcile imposed political and cultural ideas with cherished indigenous musical values. Phillips wanted to preserve the folk character of Yorùbá music while adopting European style elements that he considered compatible with it. According to him, history "has clearly shown that most of the nations that had ever risen to great heights owed much to the accumulated knowledge of the nations that existed before them. Think of the Jews and the Egyptians, the English and the Romans, the Japanese and the English. . . . Whilst advantage has been taken of the accumulated knowledge of the centuries of development of European music, its application has been subject to the control of the rules and idioms of Yorùbá music as expounded."[24]

Phillips's writings and musical compositions thus reflect a philosophy defined by a desire to develop traditional Yorùbá forms through the use of borrowed but compatible resources. It is instructive to see how these ideas manifest in his compositions, and have influenced the works of other Yorùbá church musicians and composers.

Following the Phillips Model: Ọlaolu Omideyi and Dayọ Dedẹkẹ

Both Ọlaolu Omideyi and Dayọ Dedẹkẹ belonged to the group of professionally trained musicians who were active in the church and influenced by Phillips's ideas on Yorùbá music. Born in 1923, Dedẹkẹ studied music under the Reverend I. O. Kuti in Abẹ́òkúta before proceeding to the Trinity College of Music, London, to study singing, conducting, and composition. In 1963 Dedẹkẹ published *Má Gbàgbé Ilé*, a collection of original compositions and arrangements.[25] From 1970 to 1989 Dedẹkẹ was the diocesan organist and choirmaster for the Anglican Ẹ̀gbá Diocese in Ògùn State. One of his responsibilities was to coordinate the musical program of the whole diocese, especially during the Synod. His duties also included training choirmasters and organists in schools and churches within the diocese.[26] Dedẹkẹ worked tirelessly to promote Yorùbá church music through all these activities till his death in 1992.

Omideyi, who died on January 1, 2003, at the age of eighty-five, was remarkable for working with and training local organists and choirmasters, as well as choirs. Born in 1918 in Ìbàdàn, he attended Ìbàdàn Grammar School and Igbóbì College (secondary school) in Lagos. In interviews in 1984 and 1999, he explained to me that it was his father, himself a church musician and priest, who introduced him to the Anglican church music. After his secondary education, he went to the Pratt School of Music, Lagos, where he obtained a Fellowship diploma in 1945.[27] On the completion of his training at Pratt School, Omideyi was appointed organist and choirmaster at the African Salem Church, Lagos, although he continued to take organ lessons with Ezekiel Adebiyi, organist at the St. Jude's Church, Ebutte

Meta, Lagos. Thus, by the time Omideyi proceeded to the Royal College of Music, London in 1954, he was already fairly grounded in the theory and practice of European classical music. He graduated from the Royal College with a diploma in organ studies. On his return to Nigeria, he held several positions, including head of music and music research at the Nigerian Broadcasting Corporation; organist and master of the music at the St James' Cathedral, Ìbàdàn; and Provost of the now defunct Nigerian Ecumenical School of Church Music, also in Ìbàdàn. He was also the President of the Association for the Promotion of Church Music in Nigeria until his death. In these various roles, Omideyi worked very actively toward the promotion of Yorùbá church music as theorized and prescribed by Phillips. I now analyze selected categories of works by Phillips, G. B. Oriere, I. F. Ayelaagbe, Dayo Dedẹkẹ, and Christopher Ayodele.

Yorùbá Hymns and Chants

Phillips's *Vesicles and Responses,*[28] published in 1926, sets the stylistic tone for Yorùbá church music, and provides a model for the works of the more recent generation of composers.[29] Hymns, canticles and chants by Yorùbá composers are generally set to the accompaniment of the organ or the harmonium and, in a few cases, to that of traditional percussion instruments, especially drums, gongs, and rattles. A striking feature of many of the songs is the use of the pentatonic scale, which is commonly featured in traditional Yorùbá music. Running through the music is a text-setting approach that is sensitive to the tonal demands of the Yorùbá language. Phillips emphasized the importance of text setting in the preface to his work:

> The growing practice of chanting the Vesicles and Responses wherever English service is held (in Nigeria) has led to some enthusiasts to try the experiment in Yorùbá with lamentable results too well known to need dwelling upon. Owing to the nature of Yorùbá language, any attempt to sing these short sentences to the usual Ferial or Festal setting or any other must always be unsatisfactory and meaningless. It was in order to nip this obnoxious practice in the bud, and to supply a felt want, that I composed these settings in the tones natural to the (Yorùbá) language.[30]

In Phillips's work, measure lines are avoided "in order to emphasise the idea of the free rhythmic nature of the (Yorùbá) language, and to avoid any fixed measured time." He makes use of pentatonic scales, with occasional pitches outside the established scales.[31] The pentatonic character of the melodic parts is often obscured, however, by the largely diatonic character of the accompaniment, as can be observed in example 5.1. Melisma, generally absent in Yorùbá traditional music, is also avoided in Phillips's settings, which remain standards in the musical liturgy of Yorùbá Anglican churches to this day. Phillips's tone-setting approach remains a model for generations of Yorùbá composers of church music, as shown in many of the examples discussed below.

Example 5.1. Excerpt from Vesicles and Responses by Ekundayo Phillips. Reproduced with permission from Michael Olatunji.

Yorùbá Lyrics Anthems

These compositions are generally written in solfège, usually by and for Yorùbá musicians who lack professional training in music.[32] Like the chant discussed above, the melodic contours in the lyrics anthem follow the tonal inflections of Yorùbá speech. Commonly employed forms include the developing strophic form, in which the melody of each stanza is slightly adjusted to reflect the tonal inflections of certain words, and the through-composed form.[33]

One of the most prolific composers of the lyrics anthem was G. B. Oriere, who until the early 1970s was organist and choirmaster at the St. Stephens Cathedral,

Ondó. He compiled his first set of compositions in 1959, and his second in 1968. The two compilations feature a total of 120 compositions that explore a host of biblical, moral, and social themes. They include songs for Christmas, the Passion, and the Ascension, as well as for marriage and funeral ceremonies. Oriere's songs were popular in the 1960s and 1970s among organists and choirmasters with limited skills because of their simple, generally strophic form.[34] The pentatonic songs are designed for congregational singing and are usually accompanied by the organ and traditional drums, both parts of which are to be improvised.[35] To ensure that tonal inflections of the Yorùbá texts are reflected in his melodies, Oriere uses slightly different words, usually but not always with identical inflectional contours, for different stanzas, while not losing sight of the need to maintain thematic coherence across the different stanzas. Oriere's "Ọ̀kàn Tó Rẹ̀" (The weary heart), transcribed from solfège to staff notation (ex. 5. 2), illustrates many of these features.

Example 5.2. "Ọkàn Tó Rẹ̀" by G. Oriere, transcribed by author.

Not all lyrics anthems employ the strophic form. Some, especially those rendered as "special numbers" on special occasions such as the Harvest, Easter, and Christmas, feature relatively elaborate forms. This category of songs, which may be composed by a choirmaster-organist or a gifted chorister, dates back to the early part of the twentieth century, and is still performed in Yorùbá-Anglican churches today.[36]

Virtually all orthodox and Africanist denominations in Western Nigeria have some variety of this tradition. Some of the more popular examples are the C. A. C. lyrics anthem, the Anglican lyrics anthem, and the ECWA (Ìgbàjà) lyrics anthem.[37]

As in the previous examples, the contours of through-composed melodies are tied strongly to their Yorùbá texts. These anthems, as expected, are usually longer than strophic songs. "Àjòdùn Yùngbàyùngbà" (A song of celebration) by I. F. Aiyelaagbe, example 5.3, illustrates the features of lyric anthems. It has a fantasia-like structure whose first section, measures 1–16, has three parts: the opening part: (measures 1–8); a middle part (measures 9–14); and a varied repetition of the opening part (measures 15 and 16). The second section (measures 19 to the end) deviates into call-and-response phrases in which the soloist's part, unlike that of the chorus, continually changes. This second section, with its call-and-response patterns, provides a striking contrast to the first.

Example 5.3. "Àjòdún Yùngbàyùngbà" by I. Ayelaagbe, transcribed by author.

Example 5.3. *Continued.*

The Works of Dedẹkẹ

Unlike lyrics anthems, Dedẹkẹ's compositions and arrangements are written using European staff notation. Some are written for solo voice (or many voices in unison), while others are part-songs for two to four voices. Dedẹkẹ's *Má Gbàgbé Ilé* consists of Yorùbá folk songs that have been specially arranged for Christian worship, songs by other composers arranged by Dedẹkẹ, and his own original compositions. In all cases he provides keyboard accompaniment parts as well as percussion parts for a set of three drums. For songs in $\frac{3}{4}$ and $\frac{2}{4}$, two different sets of Yorùbá-derived rhythmic accompaniment are provided (see exx. 5.4 and 5.5). Dedẹkẹ's harmonic style is generally diatonic, with only occasional use of the secondary dominant. The use of parallel harmonies enables Dedẹkẹ to write parts that continuously reflect the rise and fall of the inflection of Yorùbá words. On some occasions, however, especially when he writes for up to four parts, the lowest part does not move in parallel motion with the three upper parts because the use of parallel movement tends to become problematic in a four-part harmony if dissonant harmonic relationships are to be avoided. For example, while the three upper parts of the song "Olúṣẹ́gun" (The victorious Jesus), example 5.6 (CD track 6), move in parallel motions, the bass line moves independently. Realising the implication of this for the tonal inflections of the Yorùbá words, the basses are instructed to hum. Dedẹkẹ's balancing of linguistic and musical considerations echoes Phillips's works, although he does not limit his harmonic choices to those of medieval European music, as recommended by Phillips. (In CD track 6, the choir exercised some freedom in its interpretation of Dedeke's music.)

Example 5.4. Drum patterns for songs by Dayo Dedeke in $\frac{3}{4}$ and $\frac{6}{8}$.

Example 5.5. Drum patterns for songs by Dayo Dedeke in $\frac{2}{4}$ and $\frac{4}{4}$.

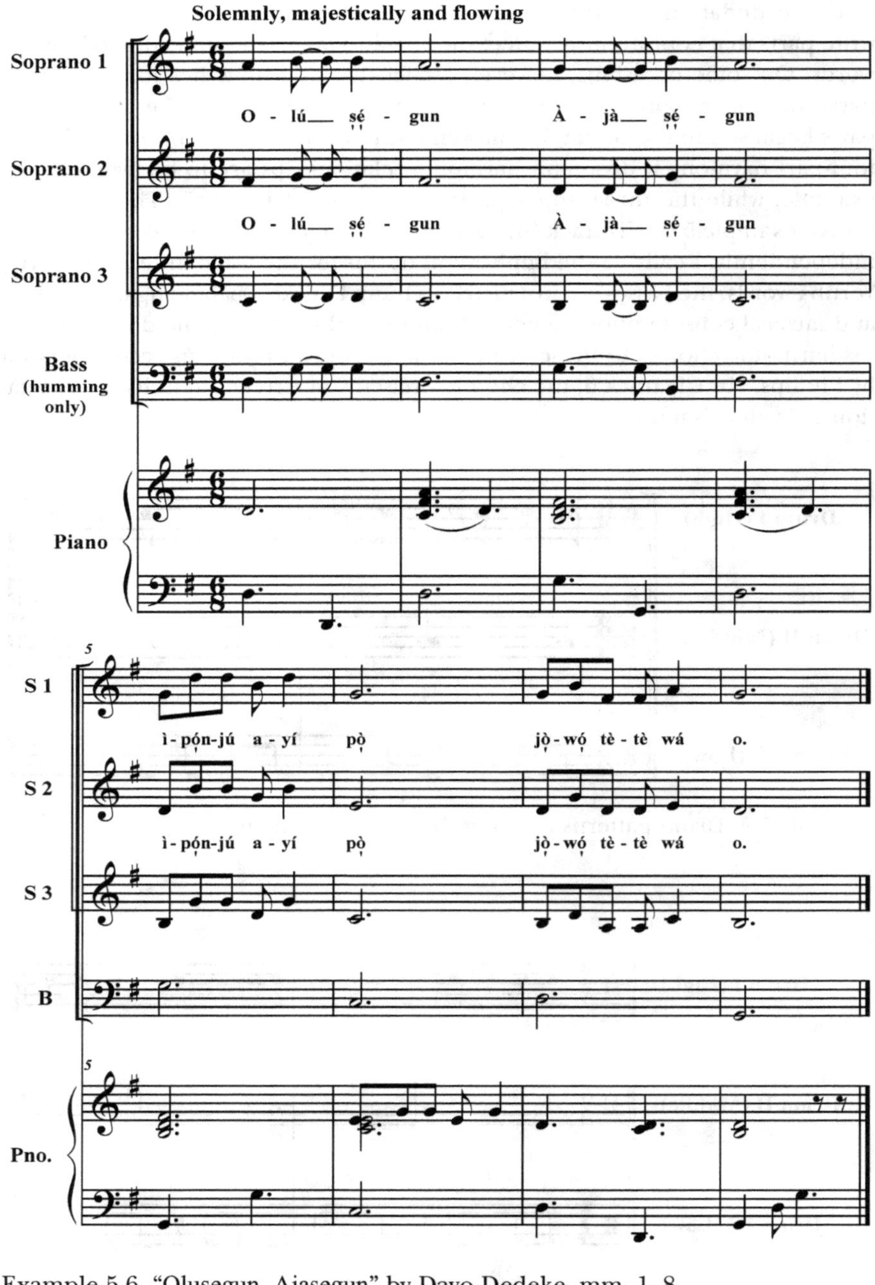

Example 5.6. "Oluṣẹgun, Ajaṣẹgun" by Dayo Dedeke, mm. 1–8.

Dedękę's approach to form often reflects a very simple synthesis of African and European forms. Further, his works employ simple harmonies and piano accompaniments. Dedeke's works thus fall outside the category of lyrics anthems. Yet, they lack the more explorative character of art anthems discussed below. Strophic and ternary forms, which dominate his works, are often saturated with call-and-response patterns. For example, "Kérésìmesì Odún Dé" (It's Christmas-time), example 5.7 (CD track 7), features call-and-response patterns interlocked with ternary form. In section A (measures 1–10), the call-and-response pattern is employed to create a ternary sub-division: a (mm. 1–6), b (mm. 7 and 8) and a' (mm. 9 and 10). Section B (mm. 11–28) consists of various calls and responses. The third section, a repetition of A, brings back the ternary subdivision (table 5.1).

Table 5.1 "Kérésìmesì Odún Dé" by Dedękę: Outline of form

	A	B	A
Subsection:	(a b a')	(call-and-response)	(a b a')
Measures:	1–10	11–28	1–10 (repeated)

The role of the organ/piano accompaniment in Dedękę's compositions sometimes goes beyond being merely supportive. Naturally, in solo and unison songs such as "A Tún Pàdé" (Till we meet again), example 5.8, the organ/piano provides harmonic support.[38]

Example 5.7. "Keresimesi Ǫdun De" by Dayo Dedeke, mm. 1–10.

Example 5.7. *Continued.*

Example 5.8. "A Tun Pade" by Dayo Dedeke, mm. 1–8.

Example 5.8. *Continued.*

Yorùbá Church Art Anthem

More sophisticated compositional skills are displayed in the works of academically trained Yorùbá composers of church music such as Ekundayo Phillips, Ayo Bankole, Yemi Olaniyan, Christopher Ayodele, Ayo Ogunranti, and myself.[39] Reconciling traditional Yorùbá and Western elements is a pervading compositional concern in the works of these composers. Constructing a multipart vocal work in which all melodic contours follow the inflectional patterns of the Yorùbá texts can be quite challenging, as we have seen even in simple works like those of Dedẹkẹ. In "Èmi Yíó Gbĕ Ojú Mi Sókè Wonnì" (I will lift up mine eyes), a Yorùbá setting of Psalm 121 by T. K. E. Phillips, this compositional challenge is met with good craftsmanship. In this work, Phillips employs a host of text-friendly features, including unisons, sequences, parallel harmonies and imitative procedures, as can be observed in the opening measures of example 5.9 (CD track 8). Musical interest is generated through the use of modulations, and a pitch-building approach which combines European and Yorùbá procedures. Also, the formal character of the anthem outlines an episodic structure in which each new text is set to a new melody, a process which continues till the very last measures of the piece. The formal outline of the piece is thus generated by the prosodic form of the text.

The opening pentatonic melody is set to diatonic harmonies in the home key of G major. In m. 16, the music moves to the key of C major, and the baritone solo part affirms a pentatonic scale. The influence of modal procedures in the piece becomes more pronounced from m. 24, when the chorus enters. In m. 39, for example, the passage progresses with an imitative process that culminates in a cadential resolution in the Aeolian mode. The piece ends with a triumphant "Amen" in the opening key of G major. As this brief description shows, the use of modal procedures, the Yorùbá language, and logogenic (word-born) melodies

Example 5.9. "Emi O Gbe Oju Mi Soke" by Ekundayo Philips, mm. 1–12. Reproduced with permission from Michael Olatunji.

Example 5.9. *Continued.*

speak to a desire to affirm a recognizable Yorùbá identity in spite of Western influences.

The influence of Phillips resonates strongly in "Olúwa Lo Lùṣọ́ Àgùntàn Mi" (The Lord is my shepherd) for SATB and organ, a Yorùbá setting of Psalm 23 by Christopher Ayodele, one of Nigeria's leading organists and choirmasters. Like Phillips's works, this song (ex. 5.10; CD track 9) employs the pentatonic scale, and is set to the tonal harmonies of the organ. Unisons and parallel harmonies, both of which are well suited to logogenic melodies, are also employed. The work does not feature any modulation; it employs a structural procedure in which new lines of the text tend to generate new melodies, with the result that new melodic phrases are continuously invented. Unlike "Èmi Yíó Gbĕ Ojú Mi Sókè Wonnì," however, Ayodele's composition ends with a return of the opening section.

Ayodele's piece also differs from those of Phillips in one major way: logogenic part-writing is sometimes abandoned, especially in sections in which harmonic parts move in contrary motion. Logogenic melodies are, for example, abandoned immediately after the soprano announcement of the opening theme. Here, although the soprano part follows the speech pattern of the Yorùbá text, all the remaining parts move independently of speech patterns. Ayodele explained to me that, in spite of the lack of correspondence between the contours of melody and those of the Yorùbá texts in this section, a good Yorùbá listener should be able to understand the meaning of the texts as reflected in the soprano part. Such discrepancies between text and tone are, as I explained in chapter 4, not unusual even in indigenous Yorùbá music where, as in Ayodele's piece, considerations of linguistic meaning may be temporarily abandoned for a purely musical reason.

Example 5.10. "Oluwa Lo Luṣọ Agutan Mi" by Christopher Ayodele, mm. 1–8. Reproduced with permission from Christopher Ayodele.

Elitism and the Challenge of Representation

The musical compositions discussed here illustrate the ways in which the first generation of Yorùbá church musicians sought to create a culturally relevant musical repertoire. In all the works, melodic and (at times) harmonic procedures reflect traditional features of Yorùbá music, notably, the use of the pentatonic scale, text-generated melodies, and parallel harmonies. But in spite of the efforts of these pioneer musicians to represent a Yorùbá identity in the church, the elitist framing of their works is indicative of the cultural and class identities of the people who attended Yorùbá Anglican churches in the early twentieth century, especially in places like Abẹ́òkúta, Ìbàdàn, and Lagos. The use of notation, the incorporation of European stylistic and structural templates, the use of Western musical instruments, the writing of works conceived in the Western classical tradition by these composers are reflections of that elitism; because of it, their works represent only a narrow slice of Yorùbá musical identity. In spite of the rhetoric about representing a Yorùbá identity, what we perceive in the works of these musicians is a representation of the interests of the members of an emerging elitist social cohort who had been trained primarily within the British educational and cultural system. The sustenance of that system in Nigeria was critical to the flowering of their careers. The Yorùbá identity that they sought to promote through their works was not a collective one; rather, it was defined and shaped by the pro-Western and elitist orientation of their experience. In generating a completely new tradition of music, these pioneers illustrate the ways in which the actions of "individuals [may] have intended and unintended consequences that undermine the stability" of the music of a society.[40] Through their works, these composers helped to support the status quo: they promoted the cultural interests of the British colonial power and reinforced the prevailing cultural hegemony of Ọ̀yọ́-Yorùbá. The elitism of their music would later provoke a countercultural movement in the music of the Yorùbá Africanist church—the Aládǔrà (Christian prayer bands), the topic of the next chapter.

Chapter Six

Yorùbá Music in Christian Worship

The Aládùrà Church

The use of sacred music as a form of therapy is a performance practice that has only just begun to attract the attention of Africanist ethnomusicologists. In a study conducted among the Tumbuka people of northern Malawi, for example, Stephen Friedson focuses on how sacred musical performances in which prophets, spirit mediums, and patients constitute a community of worshippers and engage in an interactive musical activity function as a medium for attaining social, physical, and spiritual healing.[1] Musical sounds and dance in such contexts provide the nexus for attaining spiritual and "cultural truth," and function as a medium through which members of a religious community work together to seek solutions to, and overcome or cope with, various challenges of life.[2] Carol Muller discusses how female congregational members of the ibandla lamaNazaretha (the Church of Nazarite) explored the religious grounds of Shembe's Africanist church and the cultural forms of music and dance to create a space of safety and comfort—an oasis, so to speak—within the turbulent political and social environment of apartheid South Africa. For these women, music and dance performances combining Western and traditional Zulu elements provided a liberating medium for gaining back a sense of freedom that was suppressed in the "context of everyday struggle, violation and violence" in South Africa.[3]

Participation in such religious and cultural forms helped to engender a sense of freedom and security, and provided a "respite from the common experience of pain and fragmentation." The "narrative discourses on the miraculous," expressed within the ambience of religious song, dance, dream, and narrative, constituted a "means of claiming cultural truth, because the state was increasingly rendering other domains—the political and economic—inaccessible" to native South Africans.[4] The performance elements of song, drumming, and dance as realized within the context of an African-mediated form of Christianity constituted a "privileged operational zone" and a temporary escape from the hegemonic and socially oppressive environment of apartheid South Africa.[5] With reference to Foucault, Muller explains that the performance and religious activities of the women of the ibandla lamaNazaretha illustrate a situation whereby "expressive domains elaborate on the nature of social experience and (function as) a "technology for self-disclosure."[6] Muller's study is motivated by the objective to "represent Nazarite members in terms of individual agency in a context of everyday struggle" of life.[7] Also describing the social significance of music in the African Christian church, Roberta King has observed that "how one sings is how one believes" and that music in the African church often represents a means of "processing life" and, "with the wedding of appropriate musical style and verbal text, forms a collaborative facilitation of social processes and cognitive understanding."[8]

My discussion in this chapter focuses on the Celestial Church of Christ (CCC), one of the Yorùbá Africanist Churches in Nigeria often collectively referred to as the "Aládŭrà" (prayer bands). The music of this church constitutes a remarkable development away from the predominantly European models of the early Christian church in Nigeria, which I discussed in chapter 5. Rather than serving merely to enhance religious worship, musical performance in the CCC is more socially connected to the day-to-day challenges of life that the members of the church face, and contrasts with the elitism and aloofness of the early Yorùbá church. For the many socially marginalized members of the congregation who have suffered a loss of self-esteem and who struggle daily to survive the harsh social and economic terrain of a city like Lagos, the empowering role of religious musical performance cannot be overemphasized. My discussion of the social functions of the music of the CCC is based on an extended study of its flagship choir, the Central Choir (CC), which has, since its formation in 1989, developed into a strong community. In line with the social vision of their Church, members of the CC have explored Christian religious singing as a means for self-preservation and survival.

A Brief History of the Aládŭrà Church Movement in Nigeria

The phrase African Instituted Churches (AIC) refers to multiple Christian denominations formed by individuals and groups of African worshippers who, in their desire for a Christian mode of worship in which there is a strong reflection of African practices and a strong emphasis on spiritual revelation, opted out or were pushed out of the European orthodox churches.[9] The history of this religious movement in Nigeria has been well documented in the works of Peel, Adegboyega, Omoyajowo, Olupona, and Oduro.[10] The Aládŭrà, whose origins date back to the early 1920s, and are also often referred to as "white-garment" churches because of their white uniform, "assert their Christian authenticity through an overarching symbolic structure of blended Christianity and Yorùbá rituals."[11] By interpreting Christianity through the prism of Yorùbá ritual and religious practices, the

Aládǔrà movement simultaneously affirms Christian and African identities.[12] The Aládǔrà practice the biblical teachings on the Baptism of the Holy Spirit, speaking in tongues, prophecies, and other forms of spiritual revelation.[13] They also engage in extensive and rigorous prayer sessions supported by fasting.

In the early decades of the last century, Aládǔrà denominations were known for their radical posture toward evangelism, and for taking their mission well beyond the confines of the church to township streets and villages, confronting adherents of traditional Yorùbá religion who were seen by them as engaging in pagan practices. The Aládǔrà are opposed to the Anglican practice of infant baptism, and insist that baptism should be administered only to those who are mature enough to take a decision about committing their lives to Christian living.

The Yorùbá Aládǔrà movement started as a breakaway group from the Saint Saviors Church, an Anglican church in the Yorùbá town of Ìjèbú-Òde, in 1921. Initially a subgroup of worshippers within the church, they eventually transformed into an independent denomination under the name Christ Apostolic Church. Today, the church has branches throughout Nigeria as well as internationally, in cities like New York and London. Many other churches have branched out of the original Aládǔrà group, including the Eternal Sacred Order of Cherubim and Seraphim, founded by Moses Orimolade in 1925, and The Church of the Lord (Aládǔrà), formed by Josiah Ositelu in 1930.

The Celestial Church of Christ (CCC) was founded by Samuel Bilehou Oschoffa in Toffin, Republic of Benin, following what has been described as a divine call. Although the CCC had little or no affiliation with any of the other Aládǔrà denominations in Nigeria, it also emphasizes spiritual revelation and the incorporation of Yorùbá cultural practices.

The Celestial Church of Christ

A Yorùbá carpenter, Reverend Samuel Bilehou Joseph Oschoffa belonged to the group of charismatic leaders who brought their African cultural background to bear upon their interpretation of the Bible.[14] Rev. Oschoffa was born in Port Novo, Benin Republic, in May 1909, into a family in which Christian and traditional religious practices were both observed. Although his father was a Christian of the Methodist denomination, his mother was a follower of traditional Yorùbá religion. The young Samuel chose to embrace Christianity and attended Catholic and Baptist churches before forming his own church in 1947 in his hometown. Rev. Oschoffa conceived of the CCC as the "final rescue vessel" that must be boarded by the faithful. Although the church was brought from the Republic of Benin to Nigeria in 1951 and formally incorporated there seven years later, the CCC did not begin to attract a large membership in the country until the early 1970s. By the early 1980s, the CCC, with a following of over half a million, had become one of the largest Aládǔrà Churches in Nigeria. The spread of the CCC

Figure 6.1. Inside the Central Choir Parish Church of the CCC, Ìbàfò. Lagos, 2011, photo by author.

in Nigeria, especially among the Yorùbá people, has indeed been phenomenal. Headquartered at Makòko in Ògùn State, Nigeria, it has parishes in cities across Yorùbáland, including Lagos, Ìbàdàn, Abéòkúta, Oǹdó, Àkúrẹ́, Adó-Èkìtì, Òṣogbo, and Iléṣà. The CCC has broken into many factions since the death of its founder in 1985, but all the new groups tend to retain the same doctrinal and worship practices that obtained in their parent groups.

Some anthropologists have identified striking similarities between the religious doctrine of the CCC and that of Yorùbá traditional religion. Christoph Henning, Müller E. Klaus and Ute Ritz-Müller have, for example, observed that "the beliefs of the CCC are based on those of the Yorùbá culture, according to which the world consists of heaven (orun), the residence of spiritual beings, and earth (aye), the home of mankind."[15] For although the CCC is proud to tout its credentials as a Christian religion, many of the saints and angels in the Bible seem to be characterized in a manner that reflects the hierarchical structure of indigenous Yorùbá religion. For example, most Celestial prayers are initiated with a formulaic recitation that goes: "Jehovah, Jesus Christ, Holy Michael our Captain."[16]

Recounting his first moment of spiritual encounter, Rev. Oschoffa said that on May 23, 1947, he heard a distinct voice proclaiming "the mercy of Jesus Christ."[17] Rev. Oschoffa had another encounter four months later, on September 29, an experience narrated as follows:

> While I was praying with friends in my house there came upon me a ray of brilliant light similar to the headlights of a car. At its rear stood a winged being with a body like fire and whose tiny eyes flew towards me. The ray of light became increasingly shorter, until the being came to stand a yard in front of me. Thereupon it spoke: "God has conferred upon you a mission to preach to the world. Many Christians who are troubled or in need of help still seek the counsel of fetish priests and other dark powers. They die believing themselves to be Christians, although they have long ceased to be, since Satan has put his mark on them. Therefore they cannot meet Christ after their death. God has assigned you to preach to the world and to warn the people. In order that they shall believe you and listen to you and follow you, you will perform healing miracles in the name of Jesus Christ. These deeds will bear witness to the fact that God has sent you."[18]

Oshoffa's testimony points to his church's mission, a religious function that must have accounted for the rapid growth of the church. The CCC has since its formation continued to minister to the spiritual and material needs of its numerous members, especially with reference to the challenge of coping with the harsh economic and social conditions of life in Nigeria. In spite of its relatively widespread membership outside Nigeria, the population of the CCC is predominantly Yorùbá. This is not surprising, giving the fact that the founder of the church was a Yorùbá; that the doctrine of the church is strongly rooted in the Yorùbá culture; and that most of the church's branches are located in Western Nigeria. As expected, music plays an important role in the liturgy of the CCC.

Music in Celestial Worship: An Ethnographic Account

My discussion begins with a description of a typical worship service in Akure, the capital city of Ondo State, in which the CCC has become an influential Christian denomination. The service that I describe below took place at the Celestial Church of Christ, Agunloye Parish, Akure, in June 2007.

Opening Hymns and Purification

This Sunday worship service starts at 10:00 a.m. with a solemn processional hymn, which ushers in the clergy and the choir. Male and female members of the congregation sit in different wings of the church, as it is customary in the CCC, with the males occupying the right wing, and the females the left, all facing the altar. The opening hymn is Jerimoyamah, a song said to have been "received" (that is composed through divine inspiration) by Rev. Oschoffa; it is regarded as one of the most "spiritual" of all the worship songs used in the church. The solemn mood of the service continues after the Yorùbá reading of Psalm 24 ("The Earth Is the Lord's") and the singing of more hymns and chants. The first prayer (*ìyàsímímọ̀*—purification) and the second one (*ìdúpẹ́*—thanksgiving) follow. A hymn, "Nîbo La Ó Dúró De Jésù?" (How will Jesus meet us?), set to an Anglican Church tune, follows after these two prayers. Three more prayers are led by three elders: the first prayer, led by a male, asks for the power of the Holy Spirit to descend; the second, by a female, asks for protection and victory; the third, by another man, petitions for blessings and progress.

Special Prayers, Punctuated with Chanting

Another hymn precedes the next set of prayers, led by another set of elders, including the "shepherd" (the most senior pastor and head of parish). After these prayers, all the members of the congregation, as well as the pastors and choristers, stand or kneel down facing the alter chanting the Gloria (in the Anglican style). This is followed by the shouting of the sevenfold Halleluiah, a worship activity distinctive of the CCC. Two Bible passages, one each from the Old and the New Testaments, are read. Each passage is rounded off by the singing of the Gloria. At this point, I am invited to read the New Testament part of the two readings as a prelude to a long sermon by Wole Adetiran, the director of the Celestial Church Central Choir, who is visiting this parish with his choir. I notice that hymn books are not used, although the church does have a printed hymnal. Singing from memory recalls Yorùbá oral-based performances and contrasts with the regular use of the hymnal in orthodox denominations like the Anglican and the Baptist. Adetiran's sermon is enlivened by renditions by members of the visiting Central Choir, which he conducts from the pulpit.

Mood Change: Yorùbá Praise in Christian Worship

The atmosphere in the church changes significantly following the end of the sermon. The solemn atmosphere that had pervaded the worship service up to this point changes to a highly celebrative mood. Up until this point in the worship service, only the organ (a keyboard) was used to accompany singing. Now, there is a celebratory congregational song of praise, to accompany the collection of offerings and tithes, which features drumming, dance, and call-and-response singing.

A special thanksgiving offering is held for the choir because today marks the annual choir anniversary. All members of the church, except the priests, lead singers, and instrumentalists, recess out of the church and then process back for thanksgiving, dancing and singing. The thanksgiving procession is led by a man carrying a big container into which members put their offerings, mainly cash, but also such items as candles, honey, and sugar.[19] A male song leader, supported by three other singers (one male and two females), leads the congregation during the thanksgiving. But at some point during the thanksgiving, a man, who was later described as the choir leader for the church but had sat away from the choir stall throughout the service, spontaneously takes over as the song leader. He chants in praise of God, using traditional Yorùbá praise epithet words like Ọbáńgíjì (Almighty), Ọlọ́wọ́gbọgbọrọ (the one whose hands are long and powerful), and Alèwílèṣe (the one who fulfills his promises). At this point in the service, the musicians are in complete control of proceedings, and the pastors seem pleased with the situation. They voluntarily and temporarily relinquish the leadership of the worship service to the musicians, all of whom seem overtaken by the power of music worship.

Closing the Service

An elderly woman is asked by the shepherd to round off the thanksgiving section of the service with a prayer. This is followed by the reciting of Our Lord's Prayer, the Gloria, and a final prayer by the shepherd. Members of the congregation shout four rounds of the sevenfold Halleluiah, facing each of the four corners of the church for each round. To bring back the solemn mood of the opening part of the service, the opening song is repeated as the recessional hymn. But the service is not yet over. Members, with hands raised heavenward, render the sevenfold Halleluia again outside the sanctuary before going back into the church to offer final, individual prayers of thanksgiving and protection. They kneel down and touch the ground with their foreheads, thus ending the service with a well-known indigenous Yorùbá gesture of worship.

Communal Feast

Following the end of the service, church members retire to the old church building, which now serves as an auditorium, for a "love feast." Such feasting has come to mark the Celestial congregation as a fellowship of people who see themselves as members of the same family. Dining and living together within the premises of the church are important modes of fellowship that one finds in virtually every parish of the CCC. Apart from the main sanctuary, each parish typically houses a number of buildings, including the residence of the shepherd and chalets for members who have been instructed through spiritual revelations to live within the premises of the church for a specified period of time and for a variety of reasons, including healing, counseling, praying, and fasting. The phenomenal growth of the church in Nigeria and in the Republic of Benin, especially in the 1970s and 1980s, can be attributed to the ways in which the church has been able to minister to the social and the spiritual needs of its members.

The account presented above reveals a progression from a short solemn opening—during which Protestant-style hymnals and chants feature prominently—to a celebrative section in which Yorùbá songs, dance, and drumming dominate. The thanksgiving part, which includes a dance procession from the premises of the church toward the altar inside, constitutes the high point of the service and recalls indigenous Yorùbá religious processions such as those performed during annual traditional festivals.[20] Other Yorùbá-derived rituals displayed include the touching of the ground with forehead (ìforíbalè) and the raising of supplicating hands heavenward. Also revealed in this account is the fact that vestiges of the colonial musical liturgy, mainly in form of hymns and chants, remain in the Africanist church, in spite of the dominance of neotraditional Yorùbá performance. What is displayed in the worship service therefore amounts to a syncretic religious experience in which European-derived Christian religious activities are reworked in a manner that suits the unique social and cultural experiences of Yorùbá worshippers. Thus, in spite of the desire of the pioneer leaders of the Aládǔrà to completely Africanize their church, Western worship elements remain.

The communal feasting that takes place after the service underlines a most fundamental aspect of the CCC doctrine, which is to supplement spiritual blessing with a support system that caters for the material and social well-being of its members. The organization of musical activities in the church is attuned to the objective of providing communal support for one another and creating moments and spaces of respite from the harsh realities of life in Nigeria. This "welfare evangelism" provides the doctrinal foundation for the ways in which religious singing in the CCC functions to praise and worship God, to mitigate social hardships, and enhance the self-esteem of its members. In exploring the role of music in this regard, I will now discuss the activities of the Central Choir (CC), a group which meets every weekend for all-night musical rehearsals that double as worship sessions. I discuss how the venue and time of this weekly event as well as the activities that take place there constitute a "privileged operational zone" and a sanctuary for members of the church.

The Central Choir as a Bonded Community

The central choir was established in 1987 by Oluwole Adetiran, who has been its musical director ever since. As the flagship choir of the church, the CC has the mandate to facilitate the training of instrumentalists, choirmasters, and choristers for parishes scattered nationwide, and to develop a musical tradition that aligns with the mission of the church as described above. To meet these objectives, Adetiran collaborates with local choirmasters in the various parishes to form zonal and state branches of the CC. Each branch is led by a musical director and a choirmaster. In addition to providing the forum for training musicians, the CC performs at important events of the church such as annual general meetings held at the national headquarters in Makoko in Ògùn State, Nigeria. The CC also performs at events like funerals, weddings, church dedications, and celebrations of the harvest, especially when these involve the participation of the national leaders of the church.

Based primarily in Lagos, the CC meets every weekend, rehearsing overnight from Friday evening till Saturday morning, giving performances during the day on Saturday and ministering during the Sunday service in any of the many parishes in Lagos. Up until 2003, the CC held its rehearsals at different locations within the Lagos metropolis, rotating among a number of parishes. All this changed however in 2004, when Adetiran acquired a piece of land in Ìbàfọ̀, a suburb of Lagos, and built a new parish.[21] In addition to hosting the weekly rehearsals of the CC, the Ìbàfọ̀ parish has since grown into a full church populated almost exclusively by members of the Central Choir, and appropriately named the Central Choir Parish. The establishment of this parish highlights how religious devotion and musical activity in the CCC collapse into one, feeding off one another. More importantly, the Central Choir Parish represents a physical space and a tangible evidence of how musical performance and religious worship combine to provide a space of sanctuary for its members. The CC has been transformed from a model choir—a role that it continues to perform—into an exclusive group of people for which choral singing is more than just a musical experience. With membership drawn largely from the slum areas of Lagos, and from the underprivileged strata of the society, the CC and its weekly meetings constitute a "home" away from the chaotic and challenging conditions of life that are experienced on a daily basis by many of its members.

Choir rehearsals are still held at the same time, from Friday evening till dawn. But rather than departing for their various homes on Saturday mornings, many members simply stay within the church premises for the weekend's ministering engagements. Many extend their stay till Sunday to attend the church service. This arrangement ensures that many members stay together as a community right from Friday evening till Sunday afternoon, when they depart for their homes to prepare for another hectic week of life in Lagos.

Oluwole Adetiran as Agent of Transformation

Oluwole Adetiran, the man who started the Central Choir of the CCC, shares a strikingly similar religious and musical background with the pastor and founder of the CCC, the late Rev. Oshoffa. Like Oschoffa, Adetiran, now in his early sixties, has a Protestant Christian background (Baptist in the case of Adetiran, Methodist in the case of Rev. Oschoffa), and was at various times a member of other major orthodox Christian denominations in Nigeria. Born in Ìgbájọ in Ọ̀ṣun state, Adetiran had his elementary education at the Baptist Missionary School in the town and grew up under the very strong influence of his mother, who was the choirmistress for the local Baptist Church.

On the completion of his primary education in 1961, Adetiran went to Ìbàdàn, Yorùbá's second-largest city and home to a rich tradition of Protestant church music. Since the early part of the twentieth century, Ìbàdàn has been a hub of activity for Christian church music in its various ramifications in Nigeria. It is, for example, home to prominent Anglican churches such as Saint Paul's Anglican Church, Màpó; Saint Stephen's Anglican Church, Ináléndé; and Saint James's Cathedral, Òke Bólà. Adetiran featured prominently in the musical activities of many of these churches before joining the CCC. He was, for example, a chorister at the First Baptist Church, Ìdí-Ìkán, and maintained a close relationship with the late I. F. Aiyelaagbe, who was the principal organist for the Saint Stephens Anglican Church for many years. From 1968 to 1972, Adetiran worked as a sales assistant at the Benevolent Bookshop and Musical Instruments Store in Amúnigún, Ìbàdàn, an enterprise which imported and sold electronic pedal organs to churches all over Nigeria from the 1960s to the 1980s. While working at the bookshop, he met many organists, watched them perform, and took lessons from them.

In 1974, he proceeded to the Baptist Teachers College, Ede, for his secondary education. In 1976, he took up a teaching post at a primary school in the nearby city of Abẹòkúta, a place generally regarded as the citadel of Protestant church music in Nigeria and home to Nigeria's first church, Saint Peter's Anglican Church, built in 1844. Adetiran returned to Ìbàdàn in 1978 and joined the CCC Mọkọlá parish, a move which marked the beginning of a remarkable musical career. Not unexpectedly, he joined the choir and began to play an active role in the musical activities of the church, singing as well as playing both organ and guitar. He had by that time begun to see himself as a professional musician with a special calling for church music. Like most aspiring church musicians of the time, he proceeded to the University of Nigeria, Nsukka (UNN) in the Eastern part of the country, to study music. As the only institution in Nigeria to offer a degree in music, UNN attracted students of diverse denominational and cultural backgrounds from various parts of the country.[22] The university also provided an opportunity for its students to engage in a variety of musical activities, including concerts of classical music, traditional African drumming, and modern popular music. In addition to his academic work, Adetiran helped to start a parish of the CCC on campus, leading both as a priest and the musical director.

On graduating from Nsukka in 1983, he took up an appointment as a music lecturer at Ibadan Polytechnic, in the city where he had started his training as a musician many years earlier. In 1987, following consultations between him and the leadership of the Celestial Church of Christ, he was appointed the Director of the Central Choir. Adetiran, who recently retired from his lectureship position after rising through the ranks to become head of the music department and dean of the faculty of business and communication studies, now devotes his entire time to directing the CCC Central Choir, living right within the church premises.

The Repertoire of the Central Choir

The musical repertoire of the CC is representative of the songs that are used in the CCC worship services. The variety of the repertoire, a sample of which is provided in table 6.1, is reflective of the multiple denominational backgrounds of Rev. Oshoffa and Oluwole Adetiran, and speaks to how musical styles from different denominations have been incorporated into the musical liturgy of the church, an issue which I return to later. The songs shown in table 6.1 belong to five distinct categories, namely Yorùbá folksongs, highlife songs, songs adapted from American popular and gospel music, hymns, and Yorùbá anthems. The eclectic nature of the music of the CCC is in sharp contrast to the more uniform character of the music of the older orthodox denominations like the Baptist, the Methodist, and the Anglican. Although the CC does make use of well-known Protestant hymnals, many of their hymns are believed to have been created through divine inspiration, as I have earlier explained. As shown in table 6.1, such hymns include "Jerimoyamo," the opening hymn of the service mentioned earlier, "Káwa Ẹ́lẹ̀ṣẹ̀" (We sinners), and "Padà Ẹ́lẹ̀ṣẹ̀" (Repent, oh sinner). These songs are often accompanied by the organ, just like Protestant hymns.

The repertoire also consists of anthems composed mainly for concerts within and outside the church. Contrasting with these are American gospel and popular music songs, and highlife songs. Originally an exclusively secular popular form, highlife music, which I discuss in chapter 7, now features prominently in Nigerian Christian churches. Because of its popular appeal, highlife represents a means of attracting more people into the church. Indeed many of the musicians who lead CCC choirs and perform music in the church today were once active in the secular world of highlife music.

In spite of the diversity of its repertoire, the music of the CCC is dominated by indigenous and neotraditional Yorùbá song and dance performances. As in the other Aládǔrà churches, the adaptation of traditional Yorùbá performances and musical instruments, notably the dùndún ensemble, represents a most distinguishing feature of the music of the CCC.[23] The incorporation of traditional cultural forms of expression helps members of the CCC to connect Christian worship with traditional Yorùbá life and its associated sense of purity, peace, freedom, contentment—elements generally considered to be in short supply in a city like Lagos, home of the Central Choir. In addition to the respite that marks the recall of traditional life through traditional music, traditional folklore provides a means of exploring didactic themes, which, as I explain below, are particularly enabling in the "truth-claiming" process.

The instruments featured during the CCC worship services and in the performances of the model choir include the organ or keyboard, guitars, and a variety of percussion instruments, including the Western drum set; Yorùbá àkúbà (conga-like) drums; and batteries of Yorùbá talking drums, both the dùndún (bigger)

Table 6.1. Sample of the repertoire of the CCC

Music	Meaning/theme	Genre/type	Instrumental accompaniment
Ìjọ Mímó	Celestial Church (a God-ordained church)	Yorùbá anthem	Organ
Padà Ẹlẹ́sẹ̀	Repent, O Ye Sinner (repentance)	Hymn	Organ, drum set, ìyáàlù dùndún
Ìgbà Mo Gbójú Sókè	When I Lift Up Mine Eyes (prayer/assurance)	Gospel/ Adaptation of Psalm 121	Organ, drum set, ìyáàlù dùndún / àkúbà (shaped like conga drum)
Á ṣeẹ́ṣe Ni Ká Má a Wí	It Shall Be Possible (encouragement)	Yorùbá folksong	Organ, drum set, gángan (small hourglass drum)/ ìyáàlù dùndún / àkúbà
Come Unto Me	Forgiveness	Soul/funk	Guitars
Dáwó Ìdáméwǎ Rẹ	Tithing (Christian living)	Highlife music	Guitars, drum set, gángan
Títóbi L'Olúwa	Mightiness of God (praise)	Yorùbá anthem	Organ only
Tí Kìnìún Bá Bú Ramúramù	The Outburst of a Lion (enemy/devil suppressed)	Yorùbá folksong	Organ, gángan
Títí Lọpẹ́	Thanksgiving	Highlife/funk	Organ, guitar, gángan
Máṣe Dá Ni Léjọ́	Judge Thou Not (homily)	Highlife/àṣìkò/ gospel	Organ, guitar, gángan / ìyáàlù dùndún / àkúbà
Kàwa Ẹlẹ́sẹ̀	Repentance	Hymn	Organ
Jésù Yíó Jọba	The Lord Reigns (praise)	Hymn	Organ
Ònà Kan	One Way (salvation message)	Yorùbá anthem	Organ
Jerimoyamo	A Spiritual Song	Hymn	Organ

and the *gángan* (smaller) hourglass varieties. The organ serves as the instrument through which the religious and sacred ambiance of the music is articulated, a role which derives from the religious identity of the instrument in Nigeria, as in many Christian communities around the world. The sounds of the organ help to lend a reverent quality to songs that originate from urban secular spaces.

In addition to reflecting wide cultural latitude, the use of a variety of musical traditions and instruments in the liturgy of the CCC is reflective of how the Yorùbá Aládǔrà church has been shaped by the social dynamics of life in twentieth century Nigeria. Indeed there is a sense in which musical instruments like the dùndún, àkúbà, organ, guitar, and the modern keyboard each index different historical periods and social cohorts or movements in Nigeria. While the organ symbolizes the continuing impact of colonial Christian denominational practices, the use of traditional instruments in modern cultural or religious spaces is often viewed as symbolizing a form of cultural nationalism that began during the colonial era and continues today. On the other hand, the incorporation of guitars, keyboards, amplifiers, and speakers highlights the growing incursion of popular culture into the church and the increasing attempt of church leaders to respond to the tastes of a rapidly expanding demography of worshippers.

In the remaining section of this chapter, I analyze a specific rehearsal-cum-worship session of the CC to demonstrate the ways in which a religious musical performance is directed to engage and relate to the social needs and experience of members. Although my discussion focuses on one particular all-night music session that took place in June 2007, it draws on my long experience of studying and interacting with members of the CC, as well as on many years of participating in, and observing, the worship services of the CCC.

An All-Night Session with the Central Choir

Performing the Self: Individual Expression in Group Performance

In June 2007, I visited the Ìbàfò home of the Central Choir to observe their activities. As a regular participant in their all-night sessions, I am no longer regarded as a visitor to the CC parish. This fact is particularly advantageous to my work with the group, because members and leaders of the choir are able to conduct the all-night sessions without feeling distracted by my presence. The night vigil, which features prayers, a homily, counseling and thanksgiving, is jointly led by the shepherd in charge of the Central Choir parish, Most Senior Evangelist Tunde Awojoodu, and the director of the CC, Venerable Most Senior Evangelist Oluwole Adetiran.

In their historical connection with colonial musical practices, professional and amateur Christian choirs in Nigeria are often groomed toward achieving what I would like to refer to as the aesthetics of homogeny, marked by the blending

Figure 6.2. CCC choir, with Wole Adetiran. Lagos, 2011, photo by author.

of choral voices, uniform movements, and synchronized gestures. Christian choral competitions in the country are often judged in terms of how voices blend together, that is, how each group is able to perform with "one voice." The musical renditions of the CC are striking, however, for the ways in which these features are undermined, signifying a greater emphasis on the articulation of individual experiences within the group. This deliberate interpretive freedom occurs on different levels and manifests as a unique performance mode that privileges individual agency while also consolidating a sense of group bonding. This performance practice manifests in how the choir sings and in their embodied gestures, including dances. During my visit, I observed that vocal articulation and embodied expressions tend to project and accentuate individual idiosyncrasies. In the course of singing, choristers might close their eyes, rest their hands on their heads, or gaze upward in a manner that suggests that they are in a moment of trance, carried away from their immediate physical surroundings. Such expressions are often sporadic rather than consistent, and personalized rather than synchronized. Many of the choristers with whom I interacted explained that songs do "carry them away." The prevalence of such individualized acts of performance is in tune with the overall goal of the church to facilitate an outlet for individual

Figure 6.3. Omele-dùndún drummers of the CCC. Lagos, 2011, photo by author.

expression and a religious devotion that is suited to individual experience. The music director explained to me that many of his choristers come to the overnight rehearsals to garner a sense of inner strength in the face of the many struggles and challenges that they face in real life. He often conducts the rehearsals in a manner that meets the expectations of his choristers, as I explain below.

Embodied Expressions

Group choreography, often employed by choir groups in Nigeria, is virtually absent in the performances of the CC. Each member tends to engage in individual dances in personally expressive ways. Individual expression takes the forms of dance, facial expressions, and hand movements. While some choristers engage in mild forms of dancing, gently swaying their bodies, others can be seen moving more elaborately. What comes out in the array of movements is a strong sense of individuality. While the raising of hands suggests a sense of expectation and hope, the resting of hands on the head is, in Yorùbá culture, suggestive of a state of apprehension, total surrender, or even hopelessness. None of the singers who engaged in the latter form of expression would confirm this interpretation of their expression. But this is not surprising; Yorùbá people would not publicly confess to be in a state of apprehension and hopelessness. Such expressions in the course of a performance are often spontaneous, reflecting a connection with deep inner feelings.

Facial expressions are as varied as hand movements. Head, facial, and eye movements are forms of expression that provide insights into the ways CC singers mediate their performance, underlining the dual role of the singers as performers and mediators of their music. Many singers who mediate their performance through bodily expressions rely more on the leading of their own emotions than on the directions of the conductor standing in front of them.

Minimal and Surrogate Conducting

It is not surprising that Adetiran's conducting techniques have been framed in response to the diverse needs and idiosyncrasies of his choristers. His musical directing typically ranges from minimal movement and motionless reflection to almost total acquiescence to the whims of his choristers. But this does not imply loss of control. Adetiran is highly respected by his choristers and known generally as a "no-nonsense" man. He would, for example, sometimes stop the choir in the course of a public performance to briefly rebuke an undisciplined member. He is regarded with awe, and his instructions are taken very seriously. Indeed, in their occasional renditions of European-type anthems, his conducting skills are well asserted. But renditions of such anthems are very few in comparison to those in which performances give vent to individual experience. The seeming lack of control that one witnesses in the course of the all-night session emanates from a personal acknowledgment of the vision of the CCC as a place of sanctuary and refuge, designed to facilitate healing and deliverance as well as an outlet for individual emotion. CC performances are thus often enacted to facilitate catharsis and a form of spiritual regeneration that come through uninhibited musical self-expression. In conducting some of the songs, Adetiran barely moves his hands and sometimes pauses as if he, too, is carried away momentarily, just like the members of his choir. At such points no one seems to be in control, or indeed no one can be in control. This performance strategy seems to match the theme of many of their songs about the powerlessness of humans and the need to ascribe all struggles to the care of the Almighty God.

I paid special attention to one of the lead singers for the choir whose sporadic outbursts were hard to miss. His roles were quite varied: singing the part of a soloist within call responsorial sections, providing embellishing and anticipatory phrases, mobilizing fellow choristers, and even sometimes taking over the role of the conductor. Although his loud vocal utterances were musically significant in terms of providing embellishing phrases between the various responses of the chorus, his outbursts often seemed to draw attention to himself while undermining the presence of the conductor. Sometimes he seemed overwhelmed more than any other member of the choir by his own personal experience, as well as by the impact of the music. On occasions, he turned away from the conductor and faced backward or sideward to interact with other members of the choir. Occasionally, he was supported in his expression by other choir members. In the course of performing one particular song, for example, a woman who stood right in front of him in the choir turned away from the conductor and engaged him in a sustained singing and dancing duet. This woman, I later found out, was at that point recovering from emotional stress and had indeed just returned from the hospital. After the vigil, I talked with the lead singer and learned that he too had been facing some challenges, and as a result, had not been attending the all-night meetings regularly. But in spite of his disappearing acts, he was a cherished member of the community, and the conductor was ever ready to admit him back "home" whenever he showed up. It is important to note that dramatic interpretive gestures and emotional vocalizing are not typical of public concert performances outside the church. Music and worship sessions within the church, on the other hand, provide a forum for corporate and individual catharsis, physical therapy, and spiritual regeneration.

Songs of Hope and Restitution

The texts of many of the songs rendered by the CC proclaim and offer alternative conditions of life away from the turmoil and suffering of daily life. Recurring themes include those of assurance, hope, and a new world. The song entitled "Aṣáko Padà Wálé" (Sinners come back home), for example, exhorts sinners to do away with their old life and come back "home"; no matter how grave their sins are, forgiveness awaits all those who repent. This fundamental Christian theme assumes a unique significance in the lives of the CCC choristers. "Home" is both eternal and temporal, symbolic and real; the physical space of the church, which they inhabit as members of the CCC, is home for many of them. It is a sanctuary that is immediate and practical. And those who have wandered away from this space are urged to "run fast back" into the midst of God's people. In another song, "Ìgbà Mo Gbójú Mi Sókè" (When I lift up my eyes), a special arrangement of Psalm 121, the choristers sing, "When I lift up mine eyes, my soul informs me that a door has been opened." The choir sings about a joy that had seemed far away coming to dwell in their bodies, a theme that is also present in another song, "Títí Lọpẹ́" (Our joys are forever). As they sing, the choristers appear to be transformed—lifted away from "here" into a place of comfort where they feel engulfed and surrounded by joy.

In another song entitled "Ijọ Mímọ́," the choristers affirm that their church, the CCC, is divinely ordained and not of this world—an oasis within the social chaos of the larger society. The song, which now functions as the official anthem of the church, is rendered regularly to reinforce this major theme. The opening part of the song establishes the idea that the Celestial Church of Christ is a divine gift from heaven. The last three lines assert that the "world" and all the evil forces therein "cannot prevail over us." The reference to *ayé* (world) here is deeply rooted in Yorùbá religious philosophy. *Ayé* is a multifocal word, which, in one sense refers to a vast humanity that is often evil, negative, and potentially destructive. *Ayé* also refers to the anonymous enemy that lives within the physical and social environment of the victim. This *ayé* could be a relation or a neighbor with evil intentions. But the CCC, as a place of refuge, is fortified against the incursion of any form of *ayé*.

Aṣáko Padà Wálé

Aṣáko padà wálé
Olùgbàlà ń pè ọ́
Ọmọ ìgbàlà gbàdáríjì rẹ
Ẹ̀ṣẹ̀ rẹ́ ti pọ̀ tó
Ó pọ́n bí òdòdó
Ẹlẹ́ṣẹ̀ tètè má a bọ̀
Ìdáríjì ń bẹ fún ẹlẹ́ṣẹ̀ tó ronúpìwàdà
Ọmọ ọ̀ mi sáré má a bọ̀
Lónì kí o fọkàn rẹ fun
Ọ̀la tó ń bọ́ lè lọ ṣòro
Ó dúro lẹ́nu ọ̀nà o
Fẹ́lẹ́ṣẹ̀ tó bá fẹ́ wọlé
Páláyọ̀ ti máyọ̀ de
Ó ń pẹlẹ́ṣẹ̀ kó wá gba ìgbàlà
A yọ̀ ìdùnnú ń bẹ
Fẹ́lẹ́ṣẹ̀ tó ronúpìwàdà
Fétí si, fiyèsi, fayọ̀ sìn
O yára bẹ̀rẹ̀ láti gbe
Ìrẹ́jẹ kò mà sí ní fọ́tò
Iṣẹ́ to bá ṣe láyé ni wà á rí
Fetí sóhùn tó ń kàn pé
Tantan pé má a bọ̀
Ó dé bí olè lóru
Elẹ́ṣẹ̀ kan ò lè lọ

Come back home, O ye sinner
Receive your salvation
The Savior calls you
Come back home
In spite of your sins
The Savior beckons you home

Give him your heart today
Tomorrow may be too late
He stands at the door
Waiting for repentant sinners
He has brought joy to us
He beckons all sinners
With joyful promises
For repentant sinners
Hear Him, worship joyfully
Accept Him now
There is no room for cheating
What you sow is what you will reap
Hearken to His voice
Saying: "Come back!"
He will come back like a thief in the night
No sinner will escape

Ìgbà Mo Gbójú Mi Sókè [First verse only]

Ìgbà tí mo gbé ojú mi sókè
Àkàsò mo rí láti òrun wá
Ọkàn mí wípé Ó ti ṣílèkùn
Ayò morírí, ayò tó ti jìnnà lóòrè
Dé sí ara à mi

When I lift up mine eyes
My soul tells me a door has opened for me
I see nothing but joy
The joy that seemed far away
Has come to me

Títí Lọpé

Títí lọpé, títí lọpé, títí layò o
Káráyé wá bá wa yò
Ayò ayérayé
Títí lọpé, títí lọpé, títí lọpé
Títí lọpé o, ayò bá mi gbé
Ayò ayé rere
Ìbànújé má a lọ
Ìgbà rere jòwó wọlé
Aráyé wá bá mi yò
Ayò ayérayé

Our thanks are for ever
Our joy is for ever
Come and rejoice with us
Everlasting joy
Sadness shall not be our portion
Good times are here

Come and rejoice with us
Everlasting joy

Ìjọ Mímọ́

Ìjọ mímọ́ ti Krístì, látọ̀run wá ni
Kì í ṣe tẹnì kọkan ṣẹ́
Kì mà i í ṣe tẹnì kọkan ṣẹ́
Ìjọ mímọ́ ti Krístì, látọ̀run wá ni
Kì í ṣe tẹnì kọkan láyé
Kì mà i í ṣe tẹnì kọkan ṣẹ́

Ìjọ mímọ́ ti Krístì, látọ̀run wá ni
Ẹ tú yáyá o, ẹ tú yáyá
Ẹ kálelúyà o sí Baba
Oṣó àtàjé, ẹlẹ́bọ lóògún
Ojú ti ti kèfèrí ayé
Ayé ko lè rí wa gbéṣe
À é à rárá rárá!

The Celestial Church
Ordained from above
It is not of this world
Celestial church
Ordained from above
Rejoice, rejoice
Shout Hallelujah, Hallelujah
The unbeliever is put to shame
The world (and its evil) cannot do us any harm
No, no, no, no!

Empowerment through Folklore

Yorùbá folklore in the form of proverbs and folksongs provides enabling resources for constructing a sense of optimism, bliss, and moments of respite from the cruel conditions of life. As I discussed in the last chapter, the appropriation of traditional folksongs as a basis for creating a new music liturgy is almost as old as Christianity in Yorùbáland. In some of the earlier Africanist churches like the Eternal Sacred Order of Cherubim and Seraphim and The Church of the Lord (Aládǔrà), such songs are often completely reworked into new Christian texts. The CC, however, tends to adopt traditional folklore and songs as they are, a creative approach that underlines the strong impact of indigenous Yorùbá thought system on their liturgy. The song "Á Ṣeéṣe Ni Ká Má a Wí" (Let's proclaim always that all is well; CD track 10), based on the melody of a traditional Yorùbá song for twins, titled "Epo Ńbẹ Èwà Ńbẹ" (There's plenty of food for twins), is a good example in this regard. The choristers sing that the future is good, that they have conquered fear, and that each member should continue to proclaim that "there is no fear" ahead of them. All these themes fit easily within the Christian religious philosophy about how God has conquered fear for all his disciples. In the latter part of the song, however, words and proverbs that highlight the Yorùbá perspectives about these thoughts are sung. The choristers admonish one another to believe and be hopeful that they will overcome whatever challenges they may be experiencing, and to be forward-looking because the unripe and "sealed cotton seeds of their farm shall break open and mature to produce plentiful fruits of joy and success." The comparison between the often hard life of worshippers and the anxiety that awaits the ripening of the cotton seed is instructive here. As Adetiran explained to me, Yorùbá farmers typically heave a sigh of relief whenever the (generally hard-to-cultivate) cotton seeds planted on their farm finally break open, signaling that the harvest is near. Although, the moment before the seed breaks open is filled with anxiety, the breaking of the cotton brings relief and joy. The imagery of the cotton seed is evoked here to assure members of the CCC who may be facing tough times that God's solution is imminent. The "cotton seed" of their lives will break open, and joy will come at the end of the day.

Á Ṣeéṣe Ni Ká Má a Wí

i.   Á ṣeéṣe ni ká má a wí o
      Ẹrù kan ò sí níwájú u wa
      Ẹrù kan ò sí táwa ó má a bà
      Á ṣeéṣe ni ká má a wí
      Ta bá fì sósì gbẹ̀dẹ̀
      Ire ló má a a jẹ́ o
      Ọ̀rọ̀ mi ọ̀tún ló n wúkọ́ ẹnu
      Ọ̀rọ̀ mi ọ̀tún ló yẹ kémi o mọ̀
      Ta bá fì sósì gbẹ̀dẹ̀ o
      Ire ló má a a jẹ́ o
      Ṣá ma nìṣó o
      Má wẹ̀hìn mọ́ o
      Òwú tó dinu kunkun
      Yó má a là lọ́nà oko wa

i.   Let us always proclaim that all is well
      Let us always proclaim that all is well
      Let us forge ahead
      We have nothing to fear
      Let us always proclaim that all is well
      Let us sway to the left
      It will be well
      Life may be tough on the right
      That may be true
      Let us sway to the left
      We must forge ahead

We must not look backward
The unripe, sealed cotton seeds of our farm
Shall break open and mature to produce plentiful fruits of joy and success

In another song, the singers liken the power that resides in them to the potent force that is activated in the outburst of a lion. The roaring of the lion and the stillness of the forest that follows are ascribed important symbolic meanings. Members of the choir explained to me that the often powerful and sporadic shouts and yells that characterize their performances are conceived to terrorize and intimidate evil forces that may be lurking in the corner. By musically shouting unto their God, the singers activate the forces of heaven to silence the voices of the "anonymous enemy," just as the lion silences the forest.

Bí Kìnìún Bá Bú Ramúramù

Bí kìnìún bá bú ramúramù
Tigbó tijù á dákẹ́
Omi rọ́ gòkè ó gǔn,
Ó wá ku baba ẹni tí ó gun afárá já
Ẹ̀rù kọ̀bìtì ré, àràbà rìtìbì
Kábíyèsí ti gòkè ńlá ni
B ó ò tiẹ̀ mọ̀sà, o ó jìyọ̀ lọ́bẹ̀
Aṣiwèrè ayé tó sọ pé Ọlọ́run kò sí
Taló wá dá ọ?
Níbo lènìyán tiwá sáyé
Olúwa ńbẹ, yíó sì máa wà síbẹ́ si

When a lion roars
The forest is still and quiet
The flowing river meanders up and down
Who is ready to swim across the bridge?
A big fear, a big riddle
Mighty king
If you do not know the big sea,
You must have tasted its salt
The unwise says there is no God
Who created you, foolish man/woman?
God is alive, and will be forever.

Although the last few lines lead back into a major theme of the Bible, this song emanates from traditional Yorùbá religion and folklore. The phrase "Ó wá ku baba ẹni tí" is used traditionally to rally people into a fight.[24] It is boastful language, meant to anger an enemy and encourage him or her into a duel. The challenger is self-assured that he or she will prevail in the fight. This forceful and boastful theme from Yorùbá culture is meaningful to CC members as they rally to face and even challenge a world that is oppressive and dangerous—a world full of anonymous enemies. As usual, this performance was introduced by the organ. The male lead singer was particularly active in this song, embellishing freely. He seemed lost in a world of his own, closing his eyes and putting his hands on his head.

Prolonging the Song Is Prolonging the Joy

CC performances often reflect a deliberate attempt to prolong the duration of a song. The song itself is a domain of experience within which there is joy and protection. Prolonging a song thus amounts to elongating a temporal experience within which the performer feels safe and invulnerable. This performance device often draws on traditional Yorùbá performance techniques of improvisation, extended dance, and jocular interludes. At such points, all pretences to a conventional European-type choral presentation collapse completely. The song, rather than being controlled by the performers, seems to take over, navigating a life of its own. The performance of "Máṣe Dá Ni Léjọ́" (Do not judge others; CD track 11), which states that "the log in your eyes demands greater attention than the speck in the eye of the other person," vividly illustrates this particular performance device.

This song meanders through a host of musical styles, including highlife, American-derived funk, as well as a folk tradition made popular in the neo-Yorùbá musical genre of fújì.[25] Its eclectic character mirrors the diversity of the CCC musical liturgy. Although relatively short, the song is extended in performance through the introduction of dance interludes as well as the interpolation of song material derived from fújì music. The song begins with an organ introduction, which cues in the choir. Not long after this, the singing stops while a drum interlude ensues. The next few lines of the song are rendered in English after the drum and dance interlude. At this point, the lead singer initiates a new song that is totally unrelated to the piece. The choristers, now directly addressing the conductor, remind him about the blessings he has received from God. They urge him to demonstrate his gratitude by rejoicing. The conductor, now being conducted, responds with a brief dance. It is not until after these interpolated sequences that the conductor regains control of the performance.

In the course of this performance the drummers engage in an extended interlude during which members dance actively. The addition of extended dance and drum interludes and the spontaneous addition of new thematic material are both indicative of the choristers' desire to prolong the span of a song that they deeply enjoy.[26]

Máṣe Da Ni Léjọ́

Máṣe dá ni Léjọ́
Ká má ba à dá ọ Léjọ́

Òṣunwòn tíwọ́ bá wọn fún ni
La ó fi a wọn fún ọ
Otigi tíń bẹ lójúù rẹ
Yọ́ ná ìwọ alágbòròdùn
Òṣunwòn tíwọ́ bá wọn fún ni
La ó fi a wọn fún ọ
Judge nobody, that's the message
'Cause the measure that you meet out
Shall be measured into you; tra la la la
Off the mole away from your eyes
[*Spontaneous diversion to fújì music set to a folk song.*]
Mo ti wípé kẹ́ wálé
Àìfẹ́ yín ló dùn mí jù
Omodé ń yáná
Mo hùwà alàgbà
Mo lọ yá kókó
Òtútù kò lè méja
[*Another digression to an adpated Islamic prayer song, also set to fújì music:*]
Èmí kan sárá sỌ́lọ́run Ọba
Èmí kan sárá sỌ́lọ́run Ọba
Èmí kan sárá sỌ́lọ́run Ọba
Oba tí ò dòjú àdúrà tìmí
Wolé [Adetiran], dakun kan sara sỌ́lọ́run Ọba
[*Conductor stops conducting*]
Èmí kan sárá sỌ́lọ́run Ọba
Ọba tí ò dójú àdúrà tìmí
[*Back to main song*]
Máṣe dá ni léjọ́
Ká má ba à dá ọ léjọ́
Òṣunwòn tíwọ́ bá wọn fún ni
La ó fi a wọn fún ọ
Otigi tíń bẹ lójúù rẹ
Yọ́ ná ìwọ alágbòròdùn
Òṣunwòn tíwọ́ bá wọn fún ni
La ó fi a wọn fún ọ

Judge not
For you will be judged by the same standard [that you apply to others]
Remove the log in your eye first
You will be judged by the same standard
[*Spontaneous diversion to fújì music set to a folk song.*]
I have asked you to come home
Your unfriendliness makes me angry
A little child by the fireside [trying to keep warm]
I responded with wisdom
I gave [the child] kókó [hot corn meal]
A fish never feels cold inside a river
[*Another digression to an adpated Islamic prayer song, also set to fújì music:*]

I salute the Almighty God
I salute the Almighty God
Wole [conductor's name], please, salute the Almighty God
[*Conductor stops conducting*]
He always answers my prayers
I salute the Almighty God
[*Back to main song*]
Judge not
For you will be judged by the same standard [that you apply to others]
Remove the log in your eye first
You will be judged by the same standard

Religious Music as Sanctuary

My discussion of the music of the CCC demonstrates how Christian musical practices in a Yorùbá Aládùrà church have been employed to demarcate a space of sanctuary and a place of refuge for congregational members for whom Christian music worship is more than a religious event. With its inclusions of elements of traditional Yorùbá practice, CCC religious music reflects indigenous cultural perspectives and mediates social experience in a creative performance technique that corroborates the observation that Yorùbá performances do not constitute "mere reflections of a pre-existing sensibility analogically represented; they are positive agents in the creation and maintenance of such sensibility."[27]

The use of music in this manner also illustrates how the Nigerian church has evolved from colonial times to the present. In its early years in Nigeria, Christianity was embraced mainly by a Western-educated elite whose needs were clearly different from those of the vast majority of today's Christians, many of whom are poor and needy, and whose embrace of the religion is anchored in a desperate need to survive economically. Further, by moving away from the metropolitan convention of European missions through the use of musical styles that are relevant to the social and cultural experience of modern-day worshippers, the CCC music liturgy, in conception and practice, exemplifies "more than the flourishing of Christianity" in Yorùbáland. It represents the ways in which Christianity has been decentered in Africa.[28] The physical space of religious activities, the musical repertoire, and the manner and mode of performance are channeled to demarcate a zone of empowerment for the vastly underprivileged members of the CCC.

Furthermore, the performative devices displayed in the music of the CCC speak to an embodied mode of musicality that distinguishes the African experience on the continent as well as in the Black Diaspora. These devices collectively demonstrate what Samuel Floyd has described as the performance of "musical individuality within collectivity," and speak to how Christianity has been given a new form of identity, away from the European cultural and ideological framework that characterized its early form in Yorùbáland.[29] The musical construction of social empowerment is grounded in the creation of a new form of aesthetics that speaks to the existential reality of life in modern Yorùbá society.

Chapter Seven

Yorùbá Popular Music

Hybridity, Identity, and Power

Popular music genres are often studied as part of a "world music" phenomenon whose significance has been interpreted in different ways. The works of Mark Slobin and Veit Erlmann, which date back to the 1990s, are particularly significant in setting the main analytical positions on the study and impact of globalization. Slobin's position stresses a cross-cultural dialectic involving the "subculture, interculture and superculture," and characterized by "code-switching and cultural counterpoint,"[1] while Erlmann's analysis proceeds from the perspective of a "global ecumene," a musical order, which, in its encompassing manner, generates a dichotomized, unequal, and hierarchical relationship between the global and the local.[2] Reflecting on these two positions, Ingrid Monson has noted that although Slobin's position is less apathetic than that of Erlmann's, both arguments tend to marginalize the significance of individual agency, and the diverse nature of the ethnographic contexts within which musical behavior and social practices are shaped.[3] Perhaps too much analytical emphasis has been placed on the dialectic between the local and the global, to the detriment of the internal social factors that help define social and musical practices of individuals and groups within the local space. My discussion of Yorùbá popular music in this chapter is driven by the need to accord greater attention to exploring how the performances of individual African musicians reflect on the issues of power and identity as shaped within their respective local communities. To engage such issues is to accord greater significance to "practical actions and agency" than to globally framed "ontologies of identity,"[4] and thus pave the way for a more robust exploration of alternative spaces of social activity. In navigating the depth and breadth of such alternative spaces, I take cognizance of Slobin's concept of "cultural counterpoint," and Monson's observation that "hybridities are not random."[5]

Without denying or ignoring the apparent imbrications of Yorùbá popular music with the Western/global music order, I focus mainly on the local sphere, and argue, first, that for most Yorùbá popular musicians, the "cultural counterpoint" that pervades their music-making decisions is defined ultimately by the social dynamics of their immediate locality, in spite of the constant forging of hybridized musical forms that incorporate Western and globalized elements and speak to global issues of power. Second, I explain that although Yorùbá popular music displays a natural process of interculturalism, a mode of "organic hybridity"[6] that often typifies works emanating from colonial encounters, I am particularly interested in the process of "intentional hybridity"[7] through which the syncretic language of Yorùbá music is deployed to construct, preach, or support specific ideological positions as well as the interests of specific cohorts as locally configured within Nigeria and among the Yorùbá people. I explain that musical hybridities or syncretic forms, though they might have been formed initially to subvert, resist, engage, or undermine colonial cultural and political domination, are dynamic in their indexical connotations and structural configurations because Yorùbá musicians continue to reshape such hybrid forms to engage new and emerging social realities and identity politics as constituted within Nigeria. I confer full agency on each musician studied in this chapter by arguing that Western or global elements which often saturate their music must be assessed mainly in terms of how they are used as accessories in the process of reflecting on local issues and experiences. As a prelude to my analysis of these issues, I begin with a short reflection on hybridity and syncretism, two terms that recur in my discussion.

The term "hybridity" has been used at different points in history for different purposes. In the nineteenth century, for example, it was used with reference to plant biology, and to characterize racial categories. The term gained a new significance in the late twentieth century, however, when it began to feature in postcolonial studies to characterize literary expressions resulting from colonial encounters. More recently, it has been used by social scientists to describe cultural expressions linked to globalization and transnational encounters, migrant movements, and diaspora populations. With specific reference to music studies, "hybridity" and a related term, "syncretism," have been used in world music discourses that "mediate Northern metropolitan hegemony."[8] And as I explain later, both terms, in various degrees, confer agency, inventiveness, and intentionality either as a "strategic reversal of domination"[9] or as a "conscious process" of appropriation, rather than a dormant or passive form of multi- or interculturalism.[10]

Implicit in the multivocal power and gestures of syncreticsm and hybridity are the "politics of the multiple"[11] and a pervasive alterity, qualities which carry notions of power, struggle, and resistance. These qualities are particularly resonant in musical narratives linked directly or indirectly to the dynamics of colonial power. In Yorùbá popular music, for example, the interaction of Western and African elements, almost always a constant, is replete with symbols of power and resistance. The wave of cultural nationalism that attended the construction and conception of new Yorùbá music forms aimed at attenuating the impact of Western culture and domination during and after the colonial era was, as I explained earlier in chapter 5, characterized by strong notions of power and resistance.

But while the terms syncretism and hybridity are often used interchangeably, each actually references a different mode of relations. For while syncretic expressions often represent a relatively stable resultant that emanates from the interaction or the mixing of different cultural elements, hybridity references a less stable, more dynamic process of interaction between multiple cultural elements, characterized by flux and variable subject positions.[12]

Reflecting on how the disparity between these two terms may be useful as a prism for analyzing the social and political significance of Yorùbá popular music, I propose that, while it is true that stylistic categories like *jùjú*, *highlife* and *Afro-beat* may be described as syncretic in the sense that the forms are well formed and easily identifiable, they, and indeed Yorùbá popular music as a collective, continue to exist as hybrid forms in the sense that they are subject to a continuing process of reshaping—both as individual works and as exemplars of specific stylistic categories. It is not surprising, for example, that a musician like Lagbaja has struggled with the issue of how to describe his music, and thus has over the years used terms like "higherlife" and "africano" to describe his music, an issue which highlights the constant process of reconfiguration that goes on in his work.

There is a sense, therefore, in which Yorùbá music is syncretic and hybrid. But hybridity, as I use it here, suggests neither an inferior category nor an aberration from a norm. I use the term to highlight the dynamic nature of Yorùbá popular music and the agency of individual musicians in the constant process of shaping diverse cultural material to generate meanings that traverse class, ethnic, and social boundaries. The power of Yorùbá popular music thus lies in its syncretic-hybridity, a quality that speaks to the capability of Yorùbá musicians to constantly alter and reorder the intercultural language of their music to generate multiple meanings. In the process, global or Western elements are manipulated, undermined, demystified, minimized, and mirrored—in short, subjected to multiple facets and levels of signification. The musical discourse so generated is thus defined by an inclusive language in which global elements are teased out to reflect on the divisions and contradictions that typify Yorùbá (and Nigerian) society in and beyond the twentieth century.

The history of modern popular music across Africa interweaves intimately with social and political developments associated with the European colonization of the continent. It is not surprising that the number of research projects analyzing the sociopolitical significance of popular music within and beyond the colonial era in Africa has grown significantly, especially since the last decade of the twentieth century. Prominent studies include those by Afolabi Alaja-Browne and Christopher Waterman on jùjú music and those by Michael Veal and Tejumola Olaniyan on Fela Anikulapo-Kuti's Afro-beat music.[13] This chapter focuses on three performers of popular music whose lives and work highlight the continuing dialectical engagement between Yorùbá popular music and the social, cultural and political cross-currents that have shaped Nigerian society since the colonial era. The musicians are Victor Olaiya, Fela Anikulapo-Kuti, and Bisade Ologunde, popularly known as Lagbaja. The works and careers of these three musicians illuminate important issues and mark important phases within the social and political history of Nigeria of the twentieth century. Understood within the specific context of the Yorùbá society, their works, like those of many other Yorùbá practitioners of modern popular music, highlight the gradual emergence of a pan-Yorùbá idiom of music, one whose popularity cuts across subethnic boundaries.

But although they are generally considered to be representative of a pan-Yorùbá musical culture, many of these musical forms, in their predominant use of the Ọ̀yọ́ language and in their incorporation of musical instruments like the dùndún and bàtá, maintain a stronger cultural relationship with Ọ̀yọ́-Yorùbá than with any other Yorùbá subethnic group. And although notable Yorùbá popular musicians like I. K. Dairo, Jide Ojo, Ebenezer Fabiyi (a.k.a. Ebenezer Obey) and Sunday Aladeniyi (a.k.a. Sunny Ade) do occasionally incorporate non-Ọ̀yọ́ elements in their music, prominent Yorùbá popular music forms like jùjú and fújì are, in their strong connectedness to the Ọ̀yọ́-Yorùbá culture, reflective of the cultural hegemony of Ọ̀yọ́.

Their assumed pan-Yorùbá identities notwithstanding, many of these forms, especially prominent ones like rap-music, fújì, jùjú, àpàlà, Afro-beat and highlife, tend to reflect ideological, class, and religious differences that define modern Yorùbá society. Waterman partially explained the relationship between the sonic world of Yorùbá popular music and the divisions and hierarchies of Yorùbá society when he observed that "the role of neo-traditional music in enacting and disseminating a hegemonic Yorùbá identity is grounded in the iconic representation of social relationships as sonic relationships"[14] and the fact that the "hierarchical values [of Yorùbá culture] are embodied in the aural structure of Yorùbá popular music.[15]

The dissemination of popular music through modern technology—mp3 files, CDs, audio cassettes, DVDs, the electronic media, cable TV, the Internet, and smart phones—is, as we know, not restricted or curtailed by ethnic or national boundaries. Thus, although I discuss works by Yorùbá musicians, my analysis of the significance of their music probes well beyond its Yorùbá and Nigerian boundaries. Furthermore, the development of Yorùbá popular music since the beginning of the twentieth century has been characterized by shifting degrees of integration between Yorùbá and Western musical elements to generate forms that demonstrate hybridity, or "cultural fusion in performance."[16]

Victor Olaiya, who remains active to this day, was one of the major pioneers of highlife music in Nigeria, and the most celebrated Yorùbá musician during the colonial era. Fela Anikulapo-Kuti, the sole inventor of Afro-beat, a radical anti-establishment music, could be described as one of the most influential musicians of the twentieth century, a fact partly attested to by the success of the Broadway musical *Fela!*, which provides a free-flowing exploration of the ideological and cultural significance of his music. Lagbaja's musical ensemble, which came into force in the last two decades of the twentieth century, illustrates the transformation of modern Yorùbá popular music into an increasingly pluralistic syntax that draws on multiple forms and style elements to create a variegated musical landscape—a hybrid and syncretic form in which resides a complex interplay of meanings. In this chapter, I focus on how these musicians have reconfigured materials from the same pool of musical resources to create unique forms of popular music expressions and to articulate specific identities while exploring issues of social and political significance. My discussion derives substantially from ethnographic material obtained through interviews, observations, and participation in live performances, as well as from recorded material. I rely in particular on interviews that I conducted with Victor Olaiya and Lagbaja, and on live performances that I witnessed at Olaiya's Stadium Hotel nightclub, venue of his weekly performances in Lagos. My discussion also derives from interviews that I conducted over several years of fieldwork with Yorùbá and non-Yorùbá listeners in Western Nigeria. In order to fully understand the enlarged cultural space within which Yorùbá music has been shaped, I begin with a brief discussion of its historical context.

Yorùbá Popular Music in Nigerian Society

Highlife music, one of the earlier examples of Yorùbá popular music, drew on African, European, and Caribbean elements to meet the social and aesthetic demands of the emerging Nigerian elite of the colonial era and the period shortly after independence. As reflected in its name, it was performed in social spaces well beyond the means of the average Nigerian.[17] Its displacement by jùjú music in the 1970s and 1980s represented a major step in the evolution of a more culturally relevant form of popular music. Although jùjú also serves the interests of the elite and draws on European elements, it is significantly marked by indigenous Yorùbá performance elements and thus more suited to the taste of the average Yorùbá listener. In the colonial era, the two most notable practitioners of jùjú music were Tunde Nightingale and Tunde King. Tunde Nightingale pioneered a form of jùjú called ṣó wàńbẹ̀. Ṣó wàńbẹ̀ was preceded by another genre, àṣìkò, which Tunde King and a few others had performed many years earlier as informal evening entertainment music. Àṣìkò was performed in Lagos bars patronized largely by the working-class community. These two early types anticipated the music of Isaac Kehinde Dairo in the 1950s. Dairo, whose music is unique in using the accordion, reconfigured jùjú by incorporating the talking drum and provincial Yorùbá dialects and folklore from Èkìtì and Ìjẹ̀ṣà.

Metamorphosing from I. K. Dairo and the Morning Star Band to I. K. Dairo and his Blue Spots in 1957, Dairo's band helped to weaken, albeit marginally, jùjú's strong link to the Òyó-Yorùbá culture.[18]

Dairo's pioneering efforts later received a strong boost in the music of jùjú musicians like Sunny Ade, Ebenezer Obey, Shina Peters, and Dele Abiodun. Representing jùjú in its full maturity, notably in the 1970s and 1980s, the works of these musicians are noted for an even greater use of traditional instruments, mainly dùndún and àkúbà drums as well as the Yorùbá rattle (ṣèkèrè) and bell (agogo), and a concomitant cultural adaptation of, or reduction in the use of, Western instruments. For example, brass and woodwind instruments, the staples of highlife instrumentation, are completely eliminated in jùjú. Although the guitars continue to feature prominently, they are made to imitate the cyclic and layered rhythmic structures of indigenous Yorùbá drumming. Furthermore, European harmonic procedures, which typify highlife music and Dairo's accordion-propelled jùjú, are less prominent in jùjú since the 1970s. Other prominent elements of the more recent form of jùjú include the abundant use of traditional folklore and the simulation of the Yorùbá festival celebration spectacle, known in jùjú parlance as àríyá (merrymaking). Jùjú music also emphasizes a greater degree of interaction between musicians and their dancing audiences than is found in highlife music.

Contrasting with highlife and jùjú, both of which are historically, culturally and stylistically linked to Christianity, are other Yorùbá popular music genres like àpàlà, sákárà, wákà and fújì, all of which are strongly attached to Islam.[19] Anikulapo-Kuti's Afro-beat, which was widely embraced by Nigerian youth and radical intellectuals, especially in the last two decades of the twentieth century, reworks highlife music, indigenous Yorùbá elements, and jazz to create a highly political genre, noted for its antiestablishment ideology. There is an accretive dimension to the practice of Yorùbá popular music; old styles are never completely abandoned as new styles emerge. Thus, although highlife music is no longer as popular as it used to be, its impact is continuously felt in the works of contemporary musicians who have used the original form of the music as a foundation for developing new ones.

The Yorùbá popular music scene has, since the late 1980s, been particularly invigorated by a new generation of musicians, playing global and American forms like reggae, R&B, soul, pop, disco, rap, and the new post-Anikulapo Afro-beat. The emergence of this new class of musicians speaks to the increasing visibility of a much younger demography of musicians. Prominent names in this group include Majek Fashek (reggae) and Dizzy K. Fashola (funk/disco), both of whom were active in the 1980s; Afro-beat-influenced artists like Lagbaja (Bisade Ologunde) and Tunji Sotimirin; and Paul "Play" Dairo (R&B). More recent names include D'Banj (Dayo Oyebanjo), who collaborated with Snoop Dogg (Calvin Cordozar Broadus, Jr.) on a remix of "Mr. Endowed"; Ṣọla Allison, who has in recent times composed and performed some of the best folk-derived songs; 9ice (Abolore

Adegbola Akande), a hip hop artist of note; and the phenomenal singer Aṣa (Bukola Elemide), who plays a mixture of R&B, reggae, and Yorùbá folk music, as illustrated in albums like "Asha" (2007) and "Beautiful Imperfection" (2010). For many of these musicians, Yorùbá performance idioms, notably oríkì and dùndún drumming, represent indigenous cultural tropes that provide the basis for the appropriation of global and African American traditions in Nigeria.

Lagbaja's music, one of the examples to be extensively discussed in this chapter, is particularly illustrative of how older musical styles are juxtaposed with new ones, and reworked to convey contemporaneous social and political messages. In the remaining part of this chapter, I focus on selected works by Victor Olaiya, Fela Anikulapo-Kuti, and Lagbaja to analyze in specific ways how multiple social identities have been configured, and how the development of Yorùbá popular music has been shaped by the changing dynamics of the Yorùbá social and political environment.

Olaiya's Highlife

It is important to note that Olaiya's music is part of a pan-regional style that extends to other West African countries, including Ghana, Liberia, and Sierra Leone. As Collins (1992) has observed, the Ghanaian musician Emmanuel Tetteh Mensah (1919–96) was one of the major pioneers of highlife music in West Africa. He toured Nigeria and other West African countries in the 1950s and played a significant role in consolidating the growth of highlife as a regional musical genre. Akin Euba underscores the regional status of the idiom when he observes that "highlife exists in other parts of West Africa," and that "Ghanaians contributed a great deal toward its development."[20] In the same vein, Waterman explains that "Western-derived marching bands, ballroom dances and Accra-based highlife bands contributed towards the development of *highlife* in Nigeria,"[21] while the "growth of pan-West African urban musical traditions was grounded in the demographic flow linking colonial entrepots."[22]

Born in 1929, Olaiya is probably the oldest active highlife musician in Nigeria. His music developed as part of a new cosmopolitan tradition that was enjoyed and patronized by the emerging Nigerian political elite in the colonial era. Olaiya's highlife was first forged in the 1950s and was performed in elite social contexts of nightclubs, dinner parties, and banquets—social spaces that highlighted the social gap between the emerging elite of the time and the rest of the local populations who resided in villages and small towns. The Nigerian elite of the time consisted mainly of Western-educated citizens (many of whom had lived in Europe or the United States) as well as the descendants of ex-slaves who had settled in places like Lagos and Badagry and whose cultural tastes and lifestyles followed European practices. To this day, Olaiya plays regularly at his Stadium Hotel, Surulere, Lagos.[23] My discussion of his song "Ìlú Le" demonstrates how

Figure 7.1. Victor Olaiya. Lagos, 2011, courtesy of Victor Olaiya.

highlife music, in its original form, was structured to appeal to elite patrons during and immediately after the colonial era.

Olaiya's "Ìlú Le"

This song, first released as a recording in 1983, had been part of Olaiya's repertoire for many years before then.[24] "Ìlú Le" (Times are hard; from the album *Leading Gentlemen*) illustrates important features of highlife music—notably its Western-style harmonic language that revolves primarily around the primary chords. Chordal ostinatos however tend to function in a manner similar to the cyclic rhythmic patterns which pervade the music, the most notable of which is the Yorùbá konkolo and the clave rhythm.[25] Also typical of highlife, and illustrated in "Ìlú Le," is an instrumental layout that consists of guitars, woodwind and brass instruments (mainly the saxophone and the trumpet); and a percussion section comprising of conga drums, drum set, Yorùbá rattles (ṣẹ̀kẹ̀rẹ̀) and the clave. As in the American big band tradition, the instrumentation of highlife is marked by a rather light use of the percussion—serving mainly to provide background support to the more dominant retinue of wind instruments and guitars. To understand the ways in which these basic stylistic elements cohere, a short description of "Ilu Le" is instructive.

"Ilu Le" begins with an instrumental introduction that features guitars and percussion, with the trumpet joining in at 0:11 (see table 7.1) to play hints of the main theme.[26] This section introduces two main musical materials, which recur continuously in the piece. One is the Yorùbá standard rhythmic pattern, the konkolo (ex. 7.1), while the second is a derivative of the main melodic material, example 7.2. Example 7.1 is played by the claves as a recurring cyclical pattern throughout the piece, while example 7.2 is played in turn by each of the melodic instruments and the voice. At 0:37, example 7.2 is introduced in its full form by a vocal chorus that is dominated by Olaiya's voice. The song comments about the harsh economic conditions of life in Nigeria, a problem which has refused to go away since 1960, when Nigeria gained its independence. In the first stanza, Olaiya sings that everyone feels the economic meltdown, while, in the second stanza, he informs us that women bear the effect of the problem mostly, and many of them are forced to turn to men for a bail-out. Separated by a guitar interjection, the two stanzas are provided below.

	Ìlú le O
i.	Ìlú le o kò sówó lóde
	Obìrin ń kígbe ọkùnrin ń kígbe
	Kálukú lóń kígbe owó

ii.	Bọ́mọge bá múra gẹ̀gẹ̀ wọ́n á ká ẹ mọ́lé
	Bọ́mọge bá múra gẹ̀gẹ̀ wọ́n á ká ẹ mọ́lé
	"Wọ́n á ní mo bèrè ẹ títí wọn ò jíṣẹ́ fún ẹ ni?"
	Irọ́ lóń pa owó lóń wá yẹn.

i.	Times are hard, money is scarce
	Times are hard, money is scarce
	Women and men are complaining
	Everyone is complaining

ii.	Gaily dressed women would come looking for you
	Gaily dressed women would come looking for you
	They would say: "I have been looking for you. Were you not told?"
	All they want from you is money

The two stanzas are followed by improvised solos based on the main melody, featuring the guitar and the saxophone. The chorus returns with the main melody at 3:48, echoing the same two-stanza strophic form and the guitar interjection. The guitars return once again at 4:52 for a much shorter instrumental version of the main song. The trumpets are featured in 4:57 with a variant of the main song. These instrumental parts reflect the strophic structure of the main song. The music ends emphatically at 5:17.

Example 7.1. Konkolo pattern in Victor Olaiya's "Ìlú Le O," transcribed by author. Reproduced with permission from Victor Olaiya.

Example 7.2. "Ìlú Le O" by Victor Olaiya, transcribed by author. Reproduced with permission from Victor Olaiya.

The piece is monothematic; a single musical material dominates the narrative. As table 7.1 shows, all the component sections of "Ìlú Le" revolve around the theme of example 7.2, which, though it first appears fully at 0:37, has been anticipated in the opening introduction. This same theme forms the basis of the guitar improvisation that begins at 1:42; and of the saxophone improvisation from 2:42. The trumpet part of 4:57 explores the same material. Furthermore, the recurring punctuating guitar material of 0:31, 1:07; 3:43; 4:17 and 4:52 (see table 7.1), which in each case leads to the main song and separates its two stanzas, is also derived from example 7.2. The monothematic structure of this piece is typical of Olaiya's music, and conforms to the relatively simple and highly predictable structure of most highlife songs. In "Ìlú Le," this form is framed by a continuous variation of one single theme. The vocal sections bring back the main theme in its invariant form while instrumental sections subject it to different variations. Other features of the song include its striking diatonic melodies and a tonal quality that point to its strong cultural links to British church music.

It is also important to note that "Ìlú Le," like most highlife songs, is music particularly suited to listening. Compared with the more recent jùjú music of Ebenezer Obey, Sunny Ade, and Shina Peters, highlife music is less connected to Yorùbá music associated with social occasions like naming ceremonies, weddings, and moonlight games. As one of the earlier genres of modern Yorùbá popular music, highlife is more like Western popular music of the early twentieth century—associated with banquets, dinner parties and the ballroom. Cocktail parties and banquets held by the emerging Nigerian elite of the fifties, as well as nightclubs located in the big cities like Lagos and Ìbàdàn, constituted the new social spaces within which highlife flourished for the pleasure of the emerging Nigerian elite.

Although the song focuses on economic hardship, its treatment is casual, noncommittal, and nonanalytic; it provides neither a reflection on the remote and immediate factors responsible for economic problems nor a mention of possible solutions. The statement that women constitute the category of the population mostly hit by economic austerity, though well informed, is patronizing, rather than reflecting a genuine empathy. Both the form of the music and the lyrics must be understood as light entertainment dance-music conceived for the pleasure of the emerging Nigerian elite of around the mid-twentieth century, rather than as social critique. Olaiya's music, like many examples of the Nigerian highlife of the colonial and postcolonial era, should be read in terms of its attachment to the process of defining and consolidating the identity of the Nigerian political elite, rather than as representing the voice of the ordinary folk. Its syncretic language is shaped in conformity to this fundamental role: Yorùbá traditional elements like the "standard pattern" (the konkolo pattern), the Yorùbá language, and vocal style exist mainly as nostalgic reminiscences within a predominantly European instrumentation, form, and style.

By the early seventies, the status of highlife as the foremost popular music genre in Nigeria had begun to decline, giving way to the rise of jùjú music. The Nigerian oil boom of the seventies and eighties helped to produce a new class of wealthy businessmen and women and politicians who amassed their wealth through fraudulent means, and celebrated their wealth with elaborate weddings, funerals, house-warmings, and birthdays. At these occasions, jùjú musicians sang the praise of their wealthy patrons, employing the traditional Yorùbá praise-epithet (oríkì). Dance, in its most invigorating and flamboyant form, was a vital aspect of such ceremonies. The demands of such occasions were clearly beyond the social and aesthetic reach of highlife. Jùjú music, with its emphasis on the use of praise-song and a powerful percussion ensemble featuring dùndún

Table 7.1. Victor Olaiya's "Ìlú Le": Form and structural process

Time	Description	Main thematic material	Subsectional divisions	Formal design
0:01	Guitar, percussion set groove	Examples 7.1 and 7.2	Intro	Introduction
0:11	Trumpet/guitar/ percussion; guitar interjection at 0:31	Echoes of example 7.2		
0:37	Harmonized vocals on main theme; brief guitar interjection separates the two verses at 1:07	Based on example 7.2	Vocal section	Main body
1:42	Guitar improvisation	Example 7.2	Instrumental interlude	
2:42	Saxophone improvisation			
3:43	Guitar interjection			
3:48	Harmonized vocals on main theme; brief guitar interjection separates the two verses at 4:17	Example 7.2	Vocal section	
4:52	Guitar interjection; last take on the main theme by trumpet [04:57]	Example 7.2	Instrumental postlude	Postlude
5:17	Music ends			

drums, became more fashionable, and replaced highlife as the dominant form of Yorùbá popular music. In its new status, highlife music became restricted to a few nightclubs in cities like Ìbàdàn and Lagos.

Olaiya's Stadium Hotel in Surulere, Lagos, is one of the few remaining places featuring regular highlife performances in Nigeria. The sprawling complex is now a haven for lovers of Olaiya's music, many of whom come to watch him perform on a regular basis, although the dingy atmosphere of the nightclub contrasts sharply with the glamour and the visibility that the music enjoyed in the 1950s and 1960s. In order to provide an insight into the context in which Olaiya's highlife is performed in present-day Nigeria, I now present a brief ethnographic

description of my experience during one of my numerous visits to the Hotel in
July 2006.[27]

Performing Nostalgia: An Evening of Music at the Stadium Hotel

At exactly 10:00 p.m., the band began with tunes like "Iye Jẹ́mílá" (Jẹmila's mother),
"Ìlú Le" (Times are hard), and "Ọmọ Pupa" (Lady with a fair skin), all of which I
had heard on the radio as a child growing up in Western Nigeria. Each piece was
greeted with occasional applause by the gathering party of the faithful, who spent
most of the time chatting over alcoholic beverages. The performance, at this point,
was relatively relaxed and laid-back. Although the band was made up of male musicians, some women joined intermittently as dancers and lead singers. Meanwhile,
the size of the audience began to increase, and by a little after midnight, it had
become much larger, though still not large enough to fill the considerable space
of the unroofed quadrangle. At 12:30 a.m., Olaiya came into the nightclub from
his office in the hotel complex. In spite of his unassuming personality, the atmosphere became charged as he walked in, accompanied by his manager and a few
staff members. Members of the audience sitting close to his passage rose to greet
him. It was at that point that I realized that the seats that we (I, a colleague, and
my research assistant) occupied were in an area usually reserved for dignitaries. I
definitely did not look like a dignitary in my casual t-shirt. But we must have drawn
attention to ourselves because of our video and audio cameras. Olaiya paused by
us to exchange greetings. He knew we were coming, and had granted us permission to do limited and unobtrusive recording of the show. Rather than proceeding
to the bandstand, Olaiya sat in a centrally-placed seat, while the band continued
to play for the club visitors, who by now had started to pay greater attention, and
were applauding more enthusiastically.

I checked with Olaiya's manager to ask whether he was going to perform,
reminding him that my main purpose of visiting that night was to record Olaiya
in performance. He responded that Olaiya would perform only if he was spon-
sored to do so. Just at that point, a member of the audience announced loudly
that he wanted to sponsor Olaiya. Olaiya proceeded to the band stand, made the
players retune their instruments, brought out his trumpet and his trademark
white handkerchief, and led the band in a series of old-time favorites. The club
atmosphere became electrified as many members of the audience made for the
center arena to dance. I too joined. I and other sponsors came up with more
money to ensure that Olaiya did not leave the bandstand. The night then moved
on more quickly; the band performed till about 5:00 a.m., when the show ended
with Olaiya's signature close tune, "Olaiya's Incantation."

Many of the people at the show that night later explained to me that Olaiya's
music reminded them of "the good old days," when Nigeria was "enjoyable."
Younger people who were not yet born during the "good old days" of the 1950s

and 1960s said they loved the music because "it is cool and relaxing to the ear." Based on such comments and my observations at the show, it is clear that Olaiya's music is nowadays imbued with a strong element of nostalgia and a cool, reflective character, both of which have continued to endear the music to his committed admirers. Furthermore, the nightclub context of the performance cannot but bring memories of the colonial era as well as the 1960s and 1970s, when highlife was the music of expensive nightclubs like the Caban Bamboo, the Kakadu, and the Yábǎ Rex Club, all in Lagos.

Olaiya's performances are now largely restricted to the confines of his night-club, a relatively detached social space that tends to ascribe a "classic" quality to the music. He has refused to join the àríyá (open-air merry-making) spectacles of jùjú and fújì bands.[28] Olaiya's performances generally retain the "good-old-days" standard highlife instrumentation—brass instruments, guitars, a Western drum set and one single Yorùbá talking drum. By performing old songs, Olaiya's live shows maintain a relative degree of aloofness to current cultural, social, and political developments. His music rarely makes any direct comment on topical political issues in Nigeria. A musical oasis of some sort, the performance ambience of Olaiya's Stadium Hotel constitutes a powerful medium for recalling the social landscape of the colonial era and the decades immediately following it.

Fela Anikulapo-Kuti's Afro-Beat

A comprehensive discussion of Anikulapo-Kuti's music is not possible within a single chapter such as this. Indeed, as I mentioned earlier, extensive discussions of his career, his biography, and music have been provided by writers like Olaniyan and Veal,[29] and I do not intend to duplicate those efforts here. What has yet to be done is an analysis that demonstrates the basis for the coherence of Anikulapo-Kuti's musical style, and a detailed discussion of the relationship between musical structure and political narrative. My intention is to show that the effectiveness of Anikulapo-Kuti's political discourse derives from, and is grounded in, the coherence of his musical language. I begin, however, with a biographical summary.

Fela Anikulapo-Kuti, the sole inventor of Afro-beat, was born in 1938 to a middle-class family. His father was an Anglican priest, while his mother was one of the pioneer political leaders in Nigeria. Following an initial collaboration with Victor Olaiya, he proceeded to England in 1958 to study music at the Trinity College of Music, London, against the wishes of his parents, who had wanted him to study medicine.[30] On his return to Nigeria in 1963, he worked briefly at the Nigerian Broadcasting Corporation, and later, at the University of Lagos as a music lecturer. None of these jobs could satisfy his first interest, which was to lead a band. While in London, he had spent his spare time leading a band known as the Koola Lobitos, a jazz ensemble, which he later revived in Lagos in

Figure 7.2. Fela Anikulapo-Kuti. Reproduced with permission from Tunde Afolayan.

the mid-1960s. Throughout this time, he remained relatively unknown and did not produce any chart-breaking music.

In 1969, Fela and his band embarked on a tour of the United States during which he met leading African American artists and political activists and was introduced to the work and philosophy of prominent black leaders, including Malcolm X. He also developed a greater level of interest in African American music, notably that of John Coltrane.[31] On his return to Nigeria, his musical activities began to reflect a strong political consciousness, drawing connections between racial discrimination in the United States and colonial oppression in

Africa. These connections also resonate strongly with the pan-African philosophy of his mother, an ardent follower of Kwame Nkrumah, Ghana's first president and a prominent figure in the pan-African movement of the early twentieth century. Anikulapo-Kuti's pan-Africanist orientation is well demonstrated in the changing of the name of his band to Fela Ransome-Kuti and the African 70 before leaving the United States. In the 1980s, he changed the name of the band once again, to Egypt 80. Years later, he changed his own name from Ransome-Kuti to Anikulapo-Kuti. *Aníkúlápó* means "the man who has death in his pouch."

A series of events and activities underlined Anikulapo-Kuti's increasing political and antiestablishment activism. In 1974, he erected a fence around his Lagos home and called it Kàlàkútà Republic, a space constructed as a site of defiance to the Nigerian state. He also performed regularly at his nightclub, the Afrika Shrine, using virtually every occasion to draw attention to official corruption and political dictatorship in Nigeria, issues which featured prominently in his recorded music. In 1979, he formed a political party named Movement of the People (MOP), and tried to run in the presidential election. He was arrested and jailed many times because of his constant criticism of the Nigerian political leadership, the longest of such incarcerations being a twenty-month imprisonment in 1984 on a trumped-up charge of illegal possession of foreign exchange.

Although his music focuses on a wide range of issues, political criticism dominates. More importantly, his embracement of a pan-African philosophy guided by a strong yearning for the liberation of the "black man" is complemented by an equally pan-Africanist musical style that incorporates a variety of musical resources and styles, notably from jazz, the West African highlife and his native Yorùbá musical tradition. In discussing the political theme and musical style of Anikulapo-Kuti's music, I focus on *Zombie*, a work which I consider to be marked by an organic synthesis of musical and political discourse, and which perhaps represents his most successful politically directed musical composition.

The Music of the Zombie

Released in 1977, the album *Zombie* paints the Nigerian military class as a thoughtless and mindless group, incapable of critical thinking and ever-ready to kill and destroy. Nigeria was ruled by a series of military regimes between 1966 and 1979 and from 1983 to 1999, periods marked by dictatorship, arbitrariness, electoral malpractice, and religious conflicts resulting from economic deprivation and an uneven access to opportunities.[32] *Zombie* is one of many works by Anikulapo-Kuti that explore one or more of these themes. In 1977, when *Zombie* was released, the country was ruled by Major General Olusegun Obasanjo, the man who would later rule again from 1999 to 2007 as a civilian president. Anikulapo-Kuti's *Zombie* also serves as a critique of the Nigerian political class as whole, a group considered by him to posses neither the will nor the capability to provide effective and positive leadership.

Two striking features of *Zombie* are the use of style elements from diverse cultural sources and the manipulation of the density of sound as an important form-building technique. Throughout the music, Anikulapo-Kuti varies the density of sound by reducing or increasing the number of participating instruments to generate, increase, and resolve dramatic tension. This technique begins right from the opening moments of the piece. As shown in table 7.2, the music commences with guitar-based layers of ostinato patterns which combine to generate a groove in which there are at least four important layers of melo-rhythmic phrases, as shown in example 7.3.[33] This groove is boosted 10 seconds later when additional instruments, notably the bass guitar and percussion, enter. Each of the melo-rhythmic strands of the groove is unique. The most active of the lot is motif *r*, which is played by a rhythm guitar. Based on my transcription, motif *r* consists of four notes (F, G, D, and B♭, in order of appearance). The note G, which is often approached from a major second below, features most prominently. Another fairly prominent material within the groove is a middle-range pattern, which I have designated as motif *s*. This pattern moves in quarters, eighths, and sixteenths, with punctuating silences in between. Next is motif *t*, a bass pattern, which helps to deepen the groove and energize the music. Throughout the song, motif *t*, the rhythmic patterns of the drums, and the punctuating sounds of brass instruments are periodically withdrawn from or put back into the music to generate undulating sequences of calm and storm, which, as I explain later, help to enhance the political message of the song. The last strand within the opening groove is motif *u*, a monotone figure that moves in quarter notes (as shown in my transcription) and marks every other beat of the groove. The entire groove, through the tonal, melodic, and rhythmic features of its separate strands, helps to clarify important structural features of the song: a persistent periodicity, a consistently polyrhythmic texture, a tightly-knit motivic process, a sense of drama achieved through a regular tinkering with the density of sound and texture, and a fast tempo. A general description of the remaining sections of the piece provided below reveals how these features are employed to convey the political message of the song.

Example 7.3. Layered instrumentation in *Zombie* by Fela Anikulapo-Kuti, transcribed by author.

The main body of the piece begins with Anikulapo-Kuti's first solo passage at 0:29, playing to the accompaniment of the opening groove. The entry of the saxophone here further strengthens the accretive orientation of the music as a new layer adds to the already dense texture. Anikulapo-Kuti's improvisation brings in new thematic material, the opening of which is shown in example 7.4. A powerful chorus of brass and wind instruments, a regular feature of his music, interjects at 1:12 corroborating, as it were, Anikulapo-Kuti's solo narrative and bringing the density of the musical texture to an orchestral proportion. The melodic profile of the piece thus continues to grow when the brass-wind section of the ensemble introduces example 7.5. Examples 7.4 and 7.5 are related to the opening groove, example 7.3. For example, the first measure of motif *t* of example 7.3 is echoed in the opening and closing parts of example 7.4, which is the beginning part of Anikulapo-Kuti's improvisation at 0:29. The motivic connections between example 7.4 and the opening groove can also be observed by comparing phrase r of example 7.3 with motive w of example 7.4. At 1:34, his saxophone solo resumes with a short thematic material (ex. 7.6) followed again by corroborative answers from the brasses and woodwinds. The alternation of Anikulapo-Kuti's solos with responses from the brass-woodwind group as illustrated here is a major dialogical narrative pattern of his music.

As shown in table 7.2, the main body of the instrumental section, which begins from 0:29 and continues until 5:20, is realized in three broad parts. The first two sections here, 0:29–1:53 and 1:54–3:41, mirror one another through the use of the same set of thematic ideas, shown in examples 7.3, 7.4, 7.5 and 7.6. The third part of the instrumental section, 3:42–5:20 functions as a transition to the vocal section, which begins at 5:21. At this point, new material based on example 7.7 appears, culminating in example 7.8. In addition to introducing a new thematic idea, this transition is marked by a less agitated mood, thus generating an air of relative calm that contrasts with the drama of the previous sections, while anticipating the beginning of the vocal section.

Example 7.4. Improvisation phrase I in *Zombie* by Fela Anikulapo-Kuti, transcribed by author

Example 7.5. Brass-woodwind response in *Zombie* by Fela Anikulapo-Kuti, transcribed by author.

Table 7.2. Fela Anikulapo-Kuti's *Zombie*. Form and structural process

Time	Striking events/features	Thematic material	Density of texture	Sub-sectional delineation	Overall form
0:01	Instrumental introduction	Example 7.3 without motif t	Layered melo-rhyhmic groove	Introduction	Instrumental section
0:10	Instrumental introduction	Example 7.3 with t	Joined by bass guitar and drums		
0:29	Saxophone improvisation [first strophe, example 7.4]	Examples 7.4 and 7.3	Saxophone with full band	Saxophone-solo dominated	
1:12	Brass/wind response: three-fold reiterations of example 7.5	Examples 7.5 and 7.3			
1:34	Saxophone improvisation [second strophe, example 7.6]	Example 7.6, example 7.3 initially without t; example 7.5	Instrumental solo-group exchange; phrase t, drums and brass/woodwind initially withdrawn		
1:54	Sax improvisation [first strophe, based on example 7.4]	Example 7.4, and example 7.3 with motif t	Saxophone with full band		
2:28	Brass/wind response: three-fold reiterations of example 7.5	Examples 7.5 and 7.3			

2:50	Sax improvisation [second strophe, based on example 7.6]	Example 7.6, example 7.3 initially without *t*, example 7.5	Instrumental solo-group exchange ; phrase *t*, drums and brass/woodwind withdrawn		Vocal continuation
3:09	Saxophone improvisation [first strophe, based on example 7.4]	Example 7.4 and example 7.3 with *t*	Saxophone solo with full band		
3:42	Saxophone improvisation; less agitated	Example 7.7; example 7.8; example 7.3 with *t*		Transition to vocal section	
5:21	Lead voice and chorus sing "Zombie"	Example 7.9; example 7.3 with *t*	Vocals with full band	Vocal section	
6:12	Lead voice and chorus with band: Tell am to go straight	Example 7.9; example 7.3 without *t*	Bass guitar's phrase *t*, drums and brass/woodwind withdrawn		
6:33	Solo voice and chorus with band	Example 7.3 with *t* [joro jáárá joro]			
6:54	Fermata on "joro" [7:08–7:13]	Example 7.3 with phrase *t*		Transition	
7:14	Solo and chorus; parade drill; drum stroke at 07:13; chorus back with "zombie;" Fela sings "attention; quick march"—leading to "Halt!"	Example 7.3 with *t*; example 7.9	Full band with chorus	Military parade section	
7:37	Solo and chorus with band; "Halt!"	Example 7.3 without *t*, parade calls	Bass guitar's phrase *t*, brass/woodwind and drums withdrawn		

Table 7.2. *Continued.*

Time	Striking events/features	Thematic material	Density of texture	Sub-sectional delineation	Overall form
7:50	Solo and chorus with band	Example 7.3 with *t*; parade calls	Vocals with full band		
8:14	Solo and chorus with band; "Halt!" at 8:15; drum stroke at 8:16 and at 8:31	Example 7.3 without *t*; parade calls	Bass guitar's phrase *t*, brass/woodwind and drums withdrawn		
8:33	Solo and chorus on "Zombie" with band; drum stroke on 8:33;	Example 7.3 with *t*; parade calls	Chorus on "Zombie" back		
8:58	Voice/band; "Halt!" At 8:59 desperate/sarcastic parade calls; "zombie" chorus stops	Example 7.3 without *t*	Bass guitar's phrase *t*, brass/woodwind and drums withdrawn		
9:18	Keyboard	Example 7.3 without *t*	Keyboard/ synthesizer/ Skeletal percussion	Chorus resumes	
9:52	Chorus and band	Example 7.9; example 7.3 with *t*	Keyboard, chorus and band		
10:25	Chorus ends sharply at 10:25	Example 7.9; example 7.3 with *t*			
10:31	Keyboard resumes	Example 7.3 with. *t*	Keyboard and band	Reprise	Instrumental reprise

10:39	Full ensemble, keyboard with brass chorus; spaced drum strokes	Example 7.5; example 7.3 with *t*	Brass punctuations with band	
11:01	Band with brass punctuations; section ends abruptly	Example 7.6; example 7.3 without *t*; example 7.5	Phrase *t*, brass/woodwind and drums initially withdrawn	
11:18	Postlude/cessation of regular beat; section evokes solemn military ritual; dissonant chords	New improvisatory passage	Saxophone solo with sporadic drum rolls and bell.	Coda
12:23	Music ends			

Example 7.6. Improvisation phrase 2 in *Zombie* by Fela Anikulapo-Kuti, transcribed by author.

Singing the Zombie

The vocal section lasts from 5:21 to 10:25. As in the purely instrumental section, it is realized in different subsections, each of which propels the piece in a specific way. The first part consists of exchanges between solo and chorus (ex. 7.9) about a zombie who must take instruction for every single activity. This is ultimately a narrative on neocolonialism, a theme that recurs relentlessly in Anikulapo-Kuti's music. It is about how African postcolonial economic and political institutions are shaped by Western concerns rather than by the interests of Africans, and how African leaders behave as zombies and are manipulated by their former European colonial masters rather than relying on their own initiative to work for the betterment of their people. After the initial exposition of the zombie theme, Anikulapo-Kuti (6:12) sings, "Tell am to go straight, na joro jáàrá joro," which refers to a zombie person who moves ahead thoughtlessly. This section is marked by the cessation of the bass guitar part (that is, motif *t*) and drumming. These instruments return, however, at 6:33 when Anikulapo-Kuti sings, "Come and kill, come and dance, come and quench," while the chorus responds with "joro jáàrá joro."

Example 7.7. Instrumental transition phrase 1 in *Zombie* by Fela Anikulapo-Kuti, transcribed by author.

Example 7.8. Instrumental transition phrase 2 in *Zombie* by Fela Anikulapo-Kuti, transcribed by author.

Example 7.9. Vocal Section in *Zombie* by Fela Anikulapo-Kuti, transcribed by author.

At 6:54, the "joro jáàrá joro" phrase ends with a vocal fermata on the word "joro" (7:08–7:13) after which the chorus resumes with the zombie chorus. As shown in table 7.2, each of these minisections is delineated through the constant return and withdrawal of the bass guitar/drum component of the instrumentation, a technique which helps to periodically lessen the role of instrumental accompaniment, privileging the lyrics and consequently enhancing the rhetorical impact of the message. This procedure draws attention to how instrumental and vocal parts work together to project the political message of the song.

The Parade Section

In the remaining part of the vocal section (7:14–10:25), the music evokes the activities of a military parade to further explore the zombie theme. Many of the listeners that I interviewed in Nigeria confirmed that this section reminds them of military parades at which instructions are never disobeyed or questioned because the line of command originates from officers who give orders to noncommissioned members who, in turn, must obey. The notion of a command carries a force of obligation that may not be questioned. The allusion to a neoimperialist power structure is thus quite evident. There is, however a change of technique in the ways in which the zombie theme is projected here. For while the previous sections of the lyrics merely explain the qualities of a zombie, the military parade section demonstrates these attributes by musically evoking the activities of a parade ground. At the lower level of Anikulapo-Kuti's attack here are the junior military and police officers who have on many occasions carried out instructions "from above" to harass, punish, or even kill citizens, usually on very flimsy grounds. For example, Anikulapo-Kuti's home was invaded on many occasions by junior police and soldiers acting under instruction "from above." During one such invasion, his mother, Funmilayo, was thrown through the window.

In the parade section (7:14–10:25), vocal and instrumental parts are judiciously integrated to articulate the zombie theme. The section begins with Anikulapo-Kuti singing parade instructions like "Attention! Right march! Quick march!" These instructions are answered by the chorus singing "Zombie." At 7:37, Anikulapo-Kuti gives the order "Halt!" at which point singing stops and the bass component of the groove is withdrawn. As can be observed in table 7.2, this procedure (the alternation between sung "command instructions" and a "guitar ostinato" section devoid of singing and initiated with a shouted "Halt!") is done three times. Also distinctive of the parade section are sporadic drumbeats at 7:13, 8:16, 8:31 and 8:33; and the shouting of the word "Halt!" at 7:37, 8:15, and 8:59.

The temperament of the music changes considerably after the parade instructions. The entry of the keyboard at 9:18 and the chorusing for the last time of the word "zombie" from 9:52 to 10:25 anticipate the beginning of what could be described as the reprise. Here Anikulapo-Kuti brings back two of the main thematic ideas of the piece (exx. 7.5 and 7.6 at 10:39 and 11:01, respectively). The end of the reprise is marked emphatically by the cessation of a regular beat. But we still have a few more minutes before we are finally done. There is what could be described as a coda, which, though it helps to cool off the piece, is not politically neutral. The wailing saxophone solo, punctuated only by drum rolls and a bell, sounds like a lamentation for Nigeria. The music approaches its final moments through two dissonant jazzlike chords and a final drum stroke at 12:23.

Zombie is full of drama, with its varied instrumental texture, constantly shifting and fast-paced musical events, a powerful use of the voice, dramatic drum-strokes, and the interweaving of speech and song. The fast tempo of the music makes possible the incorporation of many musical events within a short time.

A look at the overall form of *Zombie* reveals the importance of the stylistic elements that I earlier mentioned. One of these is the use of texture; the constant addition and cessation of the *t* motif, the drums and the brass-woodwind punctuations from the "rhythmic bed,"[34] represents a principal means of articulating subsectional divisions. The gradual buildup of texture, in spite of the fluctuations within the various sections of the piece, reaches a climax from 9:52 to 10:25, where the main body of the piece ends emphatically. The reprise takes the music back to a less dense texture, leading to a coda where a virtual cessation of all instruments provides an important form of resolution.

The vocal section of the piece (5:21–10:25) is sung to lyrics which describe the attributes of a zombie. The motivic relationship between the vocal section and the instrumental section, the ways in which the vocal section contributes to and sustains the increasing density of the piece, the consistency of the melo-rhythmic bed of the piece across instrumental and vocal sections all underline the complementary relationship between the opening instrumental section and the ensuing vocal section. Rather than existing as a long introduction, the main instrumental section is realized as an integral part of the piece, working in concert with the vocal section. What the vocal section does is to provide a vivid articulation of the theme of the zombie through the use of lyrics, while continuing the structural buildup that was initiated in the instrumental section. We know however that musical instruments lack the "voice" to articulate extramusical ideas in a clear and distinct manner. The instrumental section of *Zombie* cannot therefore on its own, convey the theme of zombie. In the parade section, melodic and rhythmic materials, which dominate the earlier instrumental section, combine with vocal parts to vividly describe the activities of a zombie. The parade section thus retroactively helps to clarify the orientation of the instrumental section as a narrative on the zombie theme.

Zombie by Fela Anikulapo-Kuti

Zombie o zombie
Zombie no go go unless you tell am to go
Zombie no go stop unless you tell am to stop
Zombie no go turn unless you tell am to turn
Zombie no go think unless you tell am to think

That this piece has been carefully knit and structured almost in a mirrorlike manner is revealed in the temporal span of the corresponding sections. As can be observed in table 7.2, identical thematic areas are given almost equal durations. For example, the music shown in example 7.6 lasts about equally long in its two appearances (1:34–1:53; and 2:50–3:08). Similarly, the music in example 7.5 lasts for almost the same duration (about 22 seconds) in its two appearances (1:12–1:33 and 2:28–2:50). In the same vein, the two appearances of the saxophone solo last for almost the same number of seconds (1:54–2:28 and 3:09–3:41 in table 7.2). The only exception to this procedure is at 0:29, where, in exposing an important thematic material (ex. 7.4), Anikulapo-Kuti improvises for about 42 seconds. This detailed attention to temporal design also shows in the fact that the instrumental and vocal sections are almost of equal duration, with each lasting for about five minutes.

The structural use of the element of periodicity to accomplish unity and diversity, stability and progress, and thus a high degree of coherence in this piece is also noteworthy. The pervading melo-rhythmic bed of the piece provides a regular element of stability, which sets into sharp relief the shifting vagrancies of musical material and texture. The constantly evolving saxophone improvisations are particularly important here. In addition to the inherent movement that takes place within each strophe of the improvisation is the fact that each strophe represents a continuation of the previous one. Also important is the constant shift in instrumentation as occasioned by the alternation of improvised saxo-phone passages and brass-wind punctuations.

Anikulapo-Kuti's *Zombie* represents the apotheosis of his musical craftsman-ship and the most pungent of his musico-political narratives. The success of this work derives from his ability to weave musical structure from diverse sources with political narrative, balancing the two sides of the work in a most organic manner. Tejumade Olaniyan has observed that Anikulapo-Kuti's music often suggests a programmatic conception within which musical elements are deployed sugges-tively to reflect nonmusical, often political meanings.[35] It is important to note, however, that the articulation of political narrative is grounded in a coherent musical language within which thematic elements are meticulously crafted such that there is a continuous correspondence between local structural moments and macro-level form. As I have shown, this work is propelled through an accre-tive profile in which texture plays a prominent role. The exploitation of timbral and sonic resources through the use of dynamics, sectional delineations around key thematic material, and thematic linkages across various sections are critical to the piece's coherent musical structure.

Stylistic elements that define the work's syncretic language include the use of a layered melo-rhythmic groove that evokes the cyclic character of Yorùbá drumming that I discussed in chapter 2; the employment of a singing style that imitates the call-and-response organization of indigenous Yorùbá singing; a relatively large instrumental texture reminiscent of the American big-band tradition; the use of jazzlike chords; and saxophone improvisations that some-how recall John Coltrane. Furthermore, European instruments are superim-posed over a rhythmic language that is decidedly African. Indeed instruments like the guitars are used almost pervasively to imitate the cyclic patterns of the Yorùbá drum language, while brass and woodwind instruments are used in a manner that recalls the Yorùbá (and African) call-and-response procedures. Some of these elements—for example, jazz-like chords and Coltrane-type improvisation procedures—although specifically associated with American and even global musical practice, notably point to the historical and cultural connections between Africa and Black America. But Anikulapo-Kuti's *Zombie*, in spite of hinting at diasporic and global historical, cultural, and power rela-tions, focuses mainly on the local dynamics of power within Nigeria. Insisting on the social aesthetics of the local, Anikulapo-Kuti confers on these "world music" elements a local topicality within Nigeria by juxtaposing and blending them with Yorùbá stylistic and structural elements and, more importantly, by using them to articulate and convey his message about dictatorial politics and neoimperialism in Nigeria. Unlike the music of Olaiya in which global and cul-turally diverse musical material is made to serve the interests of an elite politi-cal leadership within Nigeria, the syncretic music of Anikulapo-Kuti's Afro-beat music is designed as a critique of the ruling military and political elite within the country.

Lagbaja's "Skentele Skontolo"

Lagbaja (real name Bisade Ologunde), a graduate of the Obafemi Awolowo University, Ilé-Ifẹ̀, and the son of a Baptist church organist in Ìlọrin, Kwara state, is one of Nigeria's most successful popular musicians in recent years. His rise to stardom is part of the emergence of a new generation of college-educated professional musicians in Nigeria. Gone are the days when parents discouraged their children from pursuing a career in popular music after graduating from college. The success of some older college graduates in the music business has changed the attitude of many parents who would otherwise have discouraged their children from taking up a career in music. Following his graduation from college, Lagbaja moved to Lagos to become fully engaged as a professional musician. In addition to performing at concerts within and outside Nigeria, he runs a concert center known as Motherlan', where he has performed fairly regularly. Lagbaja has released a good number of albums, including *Africano: The Mother of Groove*, and *We and Me*.[36] He has carved a unique image for himself by wearing a mask modeled on the traditional Yorùbá masquerade.[37] Symbolic representations of departed spirits, Yorùbá masquerades (egúngún) act as intermediaries between humans and deities (Òrìṣa), especially in moments of trouble or to help prevent trouble. He explains that the use of a mask speaks to his role as an advocate for the faceless masses of Nigeria who experience economic hardships and political oppression and who lack the wherewithal to protect themselves. Not all his songs focus on political issues, though.

As a vital tool for reinforcing his role as a social mediator, Lagbaja's music often draws on antecedent Yorùbá styles that range from indigenous traditions to modern neotraditional forms. Non-Yorùbá style elements, including European and African American features also recur, although Lagbaja is sometimes eager to draw attention to the Yorùbá source of certain features of his music, when such features bear apparent links with well-known foreign styles. For example, he traces the use of rap-like utterances in his songs to traditional Yorùbá practices rather than to the American hip hop tradition, explaining that "we don't use rap in our music, that's really more of traditional Yorùbá chant, done in a style that has been around forever. Here they call that rap, but in Africa it's just always been a part of the music."[38] Commenting on the influence of antecedent Nigerian forms on his music, Lagbaja explained to me in an interview: "I would say both of them [highlife and Afro-beat] are major modern influences, and what I mean by that is that both of them come from Yorùbá music in contemporary times to become urban style music forms, musicians like Roy Chicago, Adeolu Adesanya, Victor Olaiya. All these musical styles are contemporary forms which are heavily influenced by Yorùbá music, just like I employ traditional Yorùbá style in my music."

By retaining important style-defining elements of Yorùbá music, Lagbaja maintains close affinities with Yorùbá tradition and audiences in spite of global influences. In assessing the stylistic and the cultural significance of his music, I

Figure 7.3. Lagbaja. Reproduced with permission from Tunde Afolayan.

shall now examine one of his most popular songs, "Skentele Skontolo" from the album *Africano: The Mother of Groove*, which was released in 2007.

"Skentele Skontolo"

My discussion here relies on the video edition of the music, the version in which the social and ceremonial qualities of the music are vividly articulated through dance, costume, movement, and dramatic action. Released in 2007, the album *Africano: The Mother of Groove* is considered by Lagbaja to be representative of his musical style in its mature form. Writing about the album, Lagbaja explains as follows:

> For many years the controversy brewed. People categorized my music as afrobeat, higherlife, afrojazz, crossover etc. I always insisted that none of these was appropriate as I was digging for something more fundamental. But no one could deny the impact our music had with its use of traditional African drums and percussions. Now, I christen that drum driven sound Africano, and wish to invite lovers of music to come on board for an exciting journey.[39]

"Skentele Skontolo," which begins with phrases announcing the sophistication of the Yorùbá culture (exx. 7.10 and 7.11), is a witty, "gender-play" piece, which refers to two items of Yorùbá ceremonial dress—*gèlè* (traditional female headgear), and *fìlà* (traditional male cap)—as tokens of gender.

Example 7.10. "Kò Sí Fashion Kan" by Lagbaja, transcribed by author. Reproduced with permission from Lagbaja.

In constructing a quasi-oppositional relationship between the male and female genders, Lagbaja also employs two nonlexical words, *skentele* and *skontolo*, to represent woman and man respectively. The men sing, "If you tie your gèlè in a skentele manner, we will respond by putting on our fìlà in a skontolo manner." Musically, these words perform contrasting functions within the melody as can be observed in examples 7.12 and 7.14. The statement-counterstatement relationship between the two words mirrors the overall theme of the song, which, as depicted in the series of dramatic actions within the performance, portrays women's dressing habits as a gendered performance that demands a response from their male counterparts. Throughout the video, two groups of men and women engage in a game of wit, as each group tries to affirm its superiority over the other. The pervading question is: Who looks better—women in their headgear or men in their caps? Another theme of the music is the promotion of a pan-Yorùbá culture as represented in the Yorùbá ceremonial dress, and as prominently announced in the very opening phrase of the performance, example

Example 7.11. "Skentele Skontolo" by Lagbaja, transcribed by author. Reproduced with permission from Lagbaja.

7.10: "Kò sí fashion kan tó ju tia lọ" (There is no fashion better than ours). This theme is projected right at the very opening moments (see transcription of text below). Following this confident and positive representation of the Yorùbá formal costume, Lagbaja sings about the beauty of the headgear of a particular woman. Thereafter, he asks if the woman's flamboyant headdress was meant to intimidate him, and, without waiting for an answer, he promises to "retaliate" by wearing his own cap.

Example 7.12. "Onígèlè Yí Ẹrọra" by Lagbaja, transcribed by author. Reproduced with permission from Lagbaja.

Example 7.13. "Ẹ Wo Gèlè Gẹngẹ" by Lagbaja, transcribed by author. Reproduced with permission from Lagbaja.

Example 7.14. "Tẹ Bá Gẹ Gèlè Gẹngẹ" by Lagbaja, transcribed by author. Reproduced with permission from Lagbaja.

1. Opening:

Kò sí fashion kan tó ju tia lọ
Ìró àti bùbá yẹn pẹ̀lú u gèlè
Skontolo

There is no cultural style better than ours
The Yorùbá wrapper, the dress, and the headgear all look great
Skontolo

2. Gèlè ó dùn

Gèlè ò dùn bíi ká mọọ wé
Ká mọọ wé kò dàbí kò yẹ ni

Èyí yẹ ẹ́ o
Bàbá ta ló sọ pé kò yẹ ẹ́?
Kí kẹ́kẹ́ pa kó pa mọ́ wọn lẹ́nu
Kẹ́kẹ́ ti kẹ́ pa mọ́ baba wọn lẹ́nu
Kí kẹ́kẹ́ pa sẹ́ kó pa mọ́ wọn lẹ́nu sẹ́
Kẹ́kẹ́ ti kẹ́ pa mọ́ baba wọn lẹ́nu
Ọ̀rọ̀ hùrù hùrù inú ẹlẹ́dẹ̀ ló mí gbé
Tó bá sọjú ló ń dùn wọ́n ka gba jígí fún wọn
Ṣé torí mi lẹ lọ gẹ gèlè skentele

The beauty of a headgear lies in its shape
This one is good for you
Whoever thinks otherwise should shut up
An offensive statement chokes the pig (should not be spoken)
Perhaps they are blind (not smart enough)
If so, we should get them a pair of glasses
Are you trying to impress me with your eye-catching headgear?
Skentele

3. Kí ló dé

Kí ló dé
O ti lọ wà jù baby
Ẹ ṣáa má fi gbá wa lójú
Èyí wà ńlẹ̀ ẹ dẹ̀ ní ò sí ńkankan
Àà kí ló dé?
Why o màmá
Mì ò màmà réyìn mà, à ẹ jọ́ọ́
Ẹ bá mi sún síbí

What is the matter?
Do not let [the headgear] fall off
Should I help you hold it in place?
Otherwise it will fall
Is this load [the headgear] not too heavy?
If you move backwards, it [the headgear] will fall
Please move to one side [so as not to block my view]

In the opening moments of the performance, as a woman prepares to put on her headgear, we hear an unaccompanied introductory vocal solo performance by Lagbaja, singing verse 1. The main body of the piece thereafter follows, outlined in three broad sections. As can be observed in table 7.3, the first section (of the main body) runs through 3:42; the second section from 3:43 through 5:45; while the third section lasts from 5:46 through 7:10. These sectional divisions are delineated by specific musical materials and dramatic actions.

The piece features two main categories of melodies. The first category includes melodies of considerable length, mainly Yorùbá folk tunes and Lagbaja's own melodies. Three such melodies (exx. 7.11, 7.13 and 7.15) are introduced at strategic points within the piece. The reenactment of traditional Yorùbá social habits in the song relies significantly on the use of folk tunes (exx. 7.13 and 7.15) in the section that I have labeled the Yorùbá ceremonial section in table 7.3. Example 7.11 appears in the first and last sections, thus helping to lend to the song a quasi-ternary form. The second category of themes consists of what I would like to refer to as "tail thematic material" (exx. 7.12 and 7.14). These are much shorter, usually appearing as appendages following a longer melody, and are rendered as call-and-response phrases. Example 7.12 appears prominently in the opening and closing sections, while example 7.14 appears prominently in the ceremonial section.

Sectional delineation in the piece also relies considerably on the use of a syncretic instrumentation. The opening vocal introduction (0:28–0:38) is unaccompanied. The first section begins with the entry of the entire band, consisting of drums and guitars. The transition from the first to the second section (see 3:33) is conveyed through a prominent use of the guitars and a corresponding softening of the percussion section. The ceremonial section is distinguished by the cessation of guitars and the overwhelming presence of Yorùbá drums, which are comprised of a battery of smaller talking drums (gángan) and indigenous Yorùbá conga-like drums. In the last section of the piece, the guitars return. The beginning of this last section is also marked by the return of example 7.11. By restoring the syncretic instrumentation and the thematic material of the first section, the last section constitutes a close variant of the first, lending to the piece an overall tripartite form.

The overall form of the piece is also defined by a sequence of dramatic actions. The first section of the piece (0:28–3:42) is (from the point of view of dramatic action) outlined in two main parts. In the first part (0:28–2:11), beautifully clad women walk or dance across the stage. In the second part of this section, we see gaily dressed women in ceremonial attire and tall headgear sitting in a crowded bus, called a *molue*. The glamor of their costumes contrasts sharply with the rough, dusty, and rickety conditions of the bus in which they are precariously seated. Lagbaja, acting as a typical *molue* driver, drives dangerously and pokes fun at the ladies. The music responds to this dramatic action by digressing into witty, short melodic, at times speechlike phrases. Here, Lagbaja sings, in Yorùbá:

Table 7.3. Lagbaja's *Skentele Skontolo*: Form and structural process

Time	Description of musical/dramatic events	Main dramatic scenes	Theme	Sectional divisions	Overall form
0:25	Sounds of *gèlè* (Yoruba female headgear)	Women tying headgear		Introduction	A
0:28	Unaccompanied vocal introduction		Example 7.10 [Kò sí fashion kan]		
0:39	Instrumental entries: guitars and percussion	Gaily dressed women walk across the stage as in a fashion parade	Example 7.11 [Gèlè ò dùn]		
1:10	Entry of chorus	Gaily dressed women inside *molue* (commercial bus)	Example 7.12 [Oní gèlè yí]	Chorus/solo/instruments combine	

Time	Description	Scene	Example	Notes	Section
3:33	Guitar transition to next major section				
3:43	Cessation of guitars; Yoruba drumming intensified; prominence of *ṣẹ̀kẹ̀rẹ̀* and *gángan*; singing/spoken descriptions of *gèlè*			Yoruba ceremonial section begins	B
3:46	Parade of *gèlè* styles; women (and young girls) pitched against men.	Female fashion parade scene resumes; women display an aura of self-confidence	Example 7.13 [Ẹ wo gèlè gẹngẹ]		
4:41	Lagbaja sings		Example 7.14 [Bobá gẹ gèlè skentele]		
5:04	Drum; call-and-response vocals				
5:18	Definitive response by women/Lagbaja enraged		Example 7.15 [Ẹ má torí mi]		
5:46	Tutti: guitar/voice/ percussion		Example 7.11 [Gèlè ò dùn]	Resumption of opening songs	A
6:27			Example 7.12 [Oní gèlè yí]		
7:10	Music ends				

What is the matter?
You look beautiful
This dress is overwhelmingly beautiful
You are blocking my rear view [with your rather tall headgear]
Do not let it [the headgear] fall off; it is about to fall off
Is this headgear not too heavy?
It will fall off if you move backward
Please move to one side.

Example 7.12, one of the tail melodies, features quite prominently here. It is rendered at intervals, appearing in between the fun-poking phrases quoted above. The gender-play theme of the piece is given its strongest articulation in the second section (3:43–5:45) where the intersection of music, drama and dance—elements which define Yorùbá ceremonial performance—is most vividly illustrated. Musically, the section is dominated by the percussion sounds of the *gángan* and conga-like drums and those of the ṣẹ̀kẹ̀rẹ̀, which continue unabated, and without the support of guitars. In the section, the same set of gaily dressed women that we had seen earlier flaunting their gorgeous dresses, especially the headgear, in front of a group of men (the musicians) who stood by, watching, teasing but also admiring, reappear in a fashion parade. Women and men are pitched against each other, standing on different parts of the stage, but sometimes crossing each other's spaces. The women sometimes move to display their elaborate costumes right in front of the men, while the leader of the male group, Lagbaja, occasionally moves nearer to take a better look and poke fun at the women.

The women wear different types of headgear, each of which is identified by the male group with humorous labels like "kọjú sọ́hŭn" (look away), "umbrella," "labalábá" (butterfly), "ice-cream," "ceiling fan," "national theatre," and "boys follow me."[40] The parade features both the young and the not-so-young, including a pregnant woman. Although much of the commentary is made in plain speech, songs mocking the female gender feature prominently in this section. One of the songs talks about the headgear of *ajígbọ́tọkọ,* women who are passionate about their men:

4. Ewo Gèlè Gẹngẹ

Ẹ wo gèlè gẹngẹ lórí ajígbọ́tọkọ
Ayé ni nó jẹ n ò ní jìyà
Ẹ wo gèlè gẹngẹ lórí ajígbọ́tọkọ

Ajígbọ́tọkọ's flamboyant headgear begs for attention
Life is good, and I will enjoy it
Ajígbọ́tọkọ's flamboyant headgear begs for attention

This song suggests that women dress beautifully to please men, a chauvinistic conclusion that rationalizes a woman's choices in terms of her husband's desires.

It is important to note that up to this point, representations of Yorùbá women in the music are marginal. They have only been dancing and showing off in response to the singing, teasing, and drumming of the male folk. We are not really sure whether or not they agree with the statements of the male group, who control and dominate the discourse as drummers, guitarists, singers, bus drivers, jesters, and teasers. It is not until after five minutes into the music that we finally have a definitive response from the women. At 5:19, the band's lead female singer, whom we have not seen up until now and who takes the role of the spokesperson for other women, renders a definitive response thus:

5. Ẹ Má Torí Mi

Ẹ má torí mi, ẹ má torí mi rèé jàjàkú o. . . [ìwọ. . . lẹ́nu ẹ]
Ẹ má torí wa, ẹ má torí wa rèé jàjàkú o
Ẹni gèlè mí bá wọrí ẹ̀ ló mí a we
Ẹ má torí mi, e má torí wa rèé jàjàkú o

You (men) should stop bickering because of me/us
Only the best (amongst you) is worthy of my love
You should stop bickering
You should stop bickering because of me/us

The leader speaks not just for herself but for the entire female group. This response, example 7.15, is an adaptation of a traditional Yorùbá wedding song. In the original song, the bride seeks the prayers of her parents as she prepares to go away with the bridegroom. In Lagbaja's "Skentele Skontolo," the women's spokesperson affirms that all the taunting by the men is really an expression of admiration for the women. This assertive response is supported by dances by the women, who have suddenly become more confident and assertive. Lagbaja, as the leader of the male group, seems enraged by this boldness, and threatens to confront the women by attempting to move closer to them. He is held back by his fellow musicians. The definitive response of the women (the phrase: "You (men) should stop bickering because of me/us") marks the end of the second section.

The third section, basically a slightly varied repeat of the first, returns immediately in 5:46, with the reappearance of examples 7.11 and 7.12. Also marking the return of the A section is the restoration of the ensemble in its full syncretic force, notably through the return of the guitars. Example 7.12 is repeated continuously as the music runs into its final moments.

The middle section is further demarcated through a change of key from the preceding G-flat major to an A-major scale (as represented in my notation of the music examples).[41] The return of the opening section is marked by the return of the guitars, which, together with example 7.15, restore the G-flat major of the piece. It is interesting to note how key and scale changes

Example 7.15. "Ẹmá Torí Mi" by Lagbaja, transcribed by author. Reproduced with permission from Lagbaja.

help to articulate the differences in the cultural orientation of each of the sections. The location of the Yorùbá ceremonial section of the music in the middle section, framed by the opening and closing sections in which Western instruments and tonal language feature strongly, underlines Lagbaja's objective, as musically announced in the opening moments of the performance, to showcase a united, homogeneous, and glamorous Yorùbá culture within a larger multiethnic Nigerian society. While it is true that Western and Yorùbá elements run through all the sections of the performance, the strong emphasis on certain prominent Yorùbá elements—folk-singing, traditional drumming, dance and the pentatonic scale—in the middle section lends a strong Yorùbá identity to that section.

Although the performance of gender in this piece is enacted humorously, interesting perspectives on the nature of the social relations between males and females in Yorùbá society emerge. First, the male domination of Lagbaja's ensemble is striking, and it is typical of many modern-day popular Yorùbá bands. Second, the attitude of the male group to the women is distinctly patronizing. They seem to be challenging the women into a competition by boasting of the elegance of their own attire. But the women are not in any way fooled—they know that the men just want them to display their beauty. Hence their assertive response. All actions are enacted in a playful, good-natured, and witty manner, and spiced with a hint of romance. Throughout the performance, humor is expressed musically in a manner that is reminiscent of indigenous Yorùbá ceremonial performance. In traditional situations, it is within such playful moments that important issues of social significance are debated and analyzed, though, quite often, without a concrete resolution. The exchanges between the men and the women in Lagbaja's song mirror such traditional models of play.

Globalized Language, Local Concerns

It should be clear by now that political themes, although they pervade the music of Anikulapo-Kuti, represent only one facet of Yorùbá popular music. As I mentioned earlier, the music of Victor Olaiya, grounded in the dynamics of the preindependence social and political environment, rarely focuses on controversial political issues. The fact that Olaiya's music does not derive from or convey any substantial oppositional philosophy does not, however, divest of his music of political significance. The pragmatic dispensation of the Nigerian nationalist politics of the period shortly before and after independence influenced the direction of Olaiya's musical career and resonates vibrantly in his music. Although lacking the militancy of Anikulapo-Kuti's oppositional music, his music, both in its social orientation and style, reflects the neoliberal identity of the emerging political elite of the time.

One of the main political challenges faced by the first generation of the Nigerian political elite of the twentieth century was how to forge a shared sense of national unity among the various ethnic groups in the country. That challenge remained even after independence, and continues today. Toeing the line set by the nationalist leaders of the time, highlife musicians of the period before and after independence avoided controversial political issues, while projecting the values of the country's political elite. Lagbaja's "Skentele Skontolo," which, like Fela-Anikulapo's *Zombie*, is framed by a chain of musical events, contrasts remarkably with the relatively simple and monothematic form of Olaiya's "Ìlú Le." The narrative form of "Skentele Skontolo" and *Zombie* underlines the structural grounding of the two works in the Yorùbá chain-song format, the type of which is featured in the music of Emure chiefs that I discussed in chapter 4. Lagbaja's music explores both political and nonpolitical themes, reflecting a deliberate philosophy to entertain as well as to express a viewpoint. His syncretic music also draws on key musical developments in Yorùbá culture, including the highlife era of the 1950s and 1960s, the jùjú music of Ebenezer Obey and King Sunny Ade of the 1970s and 1980s, and the Afro-beat of Fela Anikulapo-Kuti of the same period. Like Anikulapo-Kuti's music, and quite distinct from genres like àpàlà, fújì and jùjú, which I discuss in the next chapter, Lagbaja's music uses pidgin language, Western instruments, and idioms emanating from African American traditions to reach out to an audience within and outside Nigeria about issues of local significance. All three examples illustrate important features of modern Yorùbá popular music. These include: the interpenetration of culturally diverse styles in a single work; the evocation of traditional Yorùbá ceremonial music and indigenous social habits; the recontextualization of global musical styles in Yorùbá socio-aesthetic terms; and the cultivation of a multimedia network of elements (song, drumming, dance, costume, speech narratives, and dramatic sequences) to generate a holistic cultural expression.

My study of the works of Victor Olaiya, Fela Anikulapo-Kuti, and Bisade Ologunde has demonstrated how the issues of power, class, and identity in Nigeria are expressed in selected examples of their music. In each case, stylistic preferences are representative of the musicians' "indices of identity,"[42] locally constituted, rather than reflecting an exclusive response to the dynamics of global power relations. Olaiya's music articulates and celebrates the ideology of the Nigerian elite of the colonial and postcolonial era, a group to which he belongs, drawing largely on Western and Afro-Caribbean forms while nostalgically recalling indigenous Yorùbá elements in his music. His use of global elements serves mainly a local purpose. Anikulapo-Kuti's music, although it reflects the global impact of a Black Diaspora, focuses on economic and political exploitation and asymmetric power relations in Nigeria. His predilection for hybrid "simultaneous periodicities"[43] recalls the use of similar materials by musicians from other parts of Africa and the Black Diaspora, including West Africa, the United States, Haiti, Cuba, and Brazil.[44] While these materials are replete with global dimensions of power, their use by Anikulapo-Kuti in *Zombie* addresses specific issues of power and the crisis of leadership within Nigeria. Globalized musical elements, like Western-derived chords, jazzlike improvisation, and European instrumentation, are mediated by a local musical dialect that carries specific meanings of local significance. Lagbaja's "Skentele Skontolo" promotes and preaches pan-Yorùbá cultural values within a musical language that is defined essentially by the juxtaposition of Western, Yorùbá, and African American elements. The syncretic language of this song, in spite of its apparent incorporation of world music/global music elements, is best understood from the perspective of power relations within Yorùbá society and Nigeria, rather than in terms of the dynamics of global power. The juxtaposition of multicultural musical sections in his song is conceived to paint a glamorous and homogeneous picture of the Yorùbá culture. In addition to promoting a pan-Yorùbá identity—a musical action that resonates with political undertones when viewed within the competitive multiethnic structure of the Nigerian federation—Lagbaja also engages in a gender and power discourse that is apparently sympathetic to the male gender. The emphasis on local rather than global issues of power by these three musicians should also be understood against the background of the local economy. As an oil-rich nation, Nigeria provides a relatively favorable commercial environment for local musicians. Many Nigerian musicians need not seek international or global patronage to survive as musicians. The is particularly true for Yorùbá jùjú and fújì musicians who are legendary for exchanging praise (oríkì) for cash and smiling all the way to the bank. Anikulapo-Kuti, Lagbaja, and Olaiya have also achieved considerable commercial success because of impressive record sales made possible by the huge purchasing power of Nigeria's large population and the country's oil economy.

Chapter Eight

Yorùbá Islamic Popular Music

My discussion of Yorùbá popular music would be glaringly incomplete without an examination of the impact of Islam, a religion which, like Christianity, has played a major role in the generation of new Yorùbá musical idioms, especially since the beginning of the twentieth century. As I have explained in another study,[1] Islam was introduced into parts of present-day northern Nigeria as far back as the eleventh century through the activities of Berber and Arab traders, and the Moroccan invasion of the area. The acceptance of Islam by the ruling dynasty of the Kanem-Borno would later facilitate a rapid growth of the religion in northern Nigeria, from the fourteenth century onward. The spread of Islam to Yorùbáland further south was pioneered by Islamic jihadists who, upon conquering areas formerly under the control of the Old Ọ̀yọ́ kingdom in the nineteenth century, helped to consolidate the growth of the religion in towns like Ìlọrin, Ògbómọ̀ṣọ́, Ọ̀yọ́, and Ọ̀ffà. Although the onslaught of the jihadists was contained successfully in the more southerly parts, especially in Òṣogbo, where they were fiercely repelled, Islam is today a major religion in Yorùbáland, notably in states like Ọ̀yọ́, Ọ̀ṣun, and Lagos.[2]

By Yorùbá Islamic musical popular music, I refer to musical practices and styles that are associated with Islamic religious events outside the mosque, and which often, but not necessarily always, project Islamic themes. It should be remembered that musical renditions other than call-to-worship chants are forbidden inside the mosque, a practice which contrasts vividly with the prominent use of music—instrumental and vocal—within Christian liturgy. Islam-influenced Yorùbá music has therefore had to develop outside the context of religious worship, mainly as a form of social entertainment in which Islamic themes are projected within quasi-religious events outside the mosque. Such musical activities, although dominated by Muslim performers, have been transformed into specific popular idioms enjoyed and patronized by the generality of Yorùbá people, irrespective of their religious affiliation.

The most prominent genres of Yorùbá Islamic popular music are sákárà, àpàlà, fújì, and wákà. The first three are male-dominated, while wákà is performed mainly by women. All of these genres present a singing style that reflects Arabic influences in the use of "prosaic monodic cantillations and chants, which are characterized by microtonal glides and slurs";[3] the use of the Ọ̀yọ́ dialect;

and the use of musical instruments strongly associated with the Ọ̀yọ́ culture. In spite of their strong association with the Islamic culture of northern Nigeria, these genres are marked by a distinct performance style, defined by the incorporation of traditional Yorùbá cultural elements, especially those from the Ọ̀yọ́ tradition. For example, while instruments like the *gòjé* (one-stringed fiddle) and the *ahá* (calabash drum) index the culture of the Hausa-Fulani people of northern Nigeria, and therefore the Islamic religion, they are, in the music of Yusuf Olatunji (Yorùbá master of sákárà music), often appropriated within a rhythmic language that recalls indigenous Yorùbá drumming. They are combined with Yorùbá instruments like the sákárà (frame drum) and gángan hourglass talking drums. Likewise, although Olatunji's singing style reflects the impact of the microtonal gliding of Islamic chants, it retains the inflectional and linguistic contours of Yorùbá words as often found in traditional music.

Yorùbá Islamic genres are also conceptually different from European and Christian-affiliated genres like highlife and jùjú music, mainly because they rarely feature European musical instruments and tonal harmony, which typify Christian-affiliated forms. Yorùbá Islamic popular music, as shown in these four genres, thus reflects an independent identity that is carved differently from the musical traditions of northern Nigeria (the area from which Islam penetrated to Yorùbáland and noted for the use of Hausa, Fulani, and Arabic languages in Islamic musical performances),[4] and distinct from Christian-affiliated popular music genres. In their use of the Ọ̀yọ́ dialect and musical instruments like the dùndún and gángan, these genres affirm, once again, the cultural dominance of Ọ̀yọ́ in modern Yorùbá expressive forms, an issue which I have discussed before. The practice of Islam in Yorùbáland is strongest in Ọ̀yọ́-dominated areas, and it should therefore not be surprising that Ọ̀yọ́ musical and cultural elements are strongly projected in the main Yorùbá Islamic music genres, almost to the total exclusion of musical influences from non-Ọ̀yọ́ areas. I expand on these issues in the discussion below, which focuses on representative performers and musical examples. My discussion is divided into two parts. First, I examine the work of a major pioneer of these idioms, Haruna Ishola, to illustrate how Islam has provided the forum for Yorùbá musicians to respond to social change in Africa,[5] and to show how indigenous Yorùbá musical and cultural elements are reinterpreted within the framework of Islamic religion. In the second part, I discuss the music of Monsurat Gbajumo, a female performer of wákà based in Ìkìrun. My main objective in this part is to provide an ethnographic demonstration of how Islamic popular music connects with the social and cultural life of local communities. My discussion of Gbajumo's music derives from interviews with her and members of the Ìkìrun local community, as well as from watching and analyzing a live performance by her group. Although I have provided brief descriptions of sákárà, àpàlà, wákà, and fújì in a previous study,[6] an overview of these genres is necessary here, as a background to my discussion of specific examples.

Haruna Ishola's Àpàlà Music

Àpàlà, like fújì and sákárà, grew out of *wéré*, an informal musical perform-ance associated with the Islamic fasting season in Nigeria. Its emergence in the 1930s was linked to the rivalry between sákárà musicians and traditional Yorùbá dùndún drummers who felt uncomfortable with the growing popularity of sákárà. Àpàlà was consequently evolved by traditional dùndún drummers in their bid to match, or even beat, the rising profile of sákárà. Akin Euba explains this succinctly: "*Sákárà* quickly assumed wide popularity among the Yorùbá and threatened the position of the *dùndún* hour glass tension drum players, who had hitherto been regarded as the superstars of Yorùbá music. Concerned that they would be relegated to the background, the *dùndún* players created their own brand of pop music, and this they called *àpàlà*."[7]

The dùndún players who created this new type of music were mostly Muslims. Also significant from this origin history is the fact that àpàlà started basically as an adaptation of Yorùbá dùndún drumming to create a social dance music that, though it remains dominated by Muslims, is not thematically restricted to Islamic messages. By the 1950s, àpàlà had become popular all over Yorùbáland, notably through the music of Haruna Ishola (popularly known as Baban Gani), its main exponent. Other important performers of the genre have included Sefiu Ayan, Kasumu Adio, Ayinla Omowura, and Musiliu Haruna Ishola, Haruna Ishola's son, who has sought to revive àpàlà in the last few years.[8]

Haruna Ishola's àpàlà features a percussion-dominated ensemble, with Ishola himself playing the role of lead singer, backed by a male chorus. Instruments typically featured include the *àgídìgbo*, a Yorùbá lamellophone;[9] several hour-glass-shaped talking drums (the small àdàmò type), àkúbà (conga-like upright drum); ṣèkèrè (rattle); and agogo (gong). Àpàlà thus features a dense instru-mentation and carries a strong element of dance.

Haruna Ishola (1913–83) was born in Ìjẹbú-Igbó in Ògùn state, the town where he formed a band named Haruna Ishola and his Àpàlà Group in 1947.[10] His first major recording, entitled *Orimolusi Adeboye*, a tribute to Oba Orimolusi, the late king of Ìjẹbú-Igbó, was produced in 1948.[11] His next major album was another tribute, an obituary for the same king when he died seven years later. Released in 1955, and produced by Decca West Africa, this second tribute was the one that popularized Ishola all over Yorùbáland. But it was another album, entitled *Oroki Social Club*, released in the late 1960s, that would sell millions and bring him considerable wealth. A successful musician and businessman, he collaborated with I. K. Dairo[12] to set up one of Nigeria's first indigenous record companies, the STAR Records, in 1969. And in the 1980s, he established Phonodisc, a thirty-two-track recording studio.[13]

Haruna Ishola's song "Ìbà Akọdá" (Homage) from the album *Late Oba Adeboye—The Orimolusi of Ijebu Igbo*, recorded in 1955, illustrates important com-positional and performance features of àpàlà music.[14] Particularly striking is the very interactive relationship between the lead solo and the chorus. The song features a continuous process of exchange between Ishola's solo singing and the responses of the chorus. Although there is no apparent attempt to structure the piece beyond its framing as a continuous solo-chorus dialogue, two types of solo-chorus interchange are discernible. The first features a process in which a solo and its chorus are based on two different phrases. In this example, the solo phrase and the chorus response are relatively independent. This procedure is illustrated in the opening part of the song, where the soloist pays homage to the creator when he sings, "Ìbà akọ́dá aṣẹ̀dá ayé ìbà o" (I salute the First, the Creator). The second phrase, sung by the chorus, extends the homage: "Àgbà kí mo sí fìlà, orẹ́rẹ́ mo júbà kí n tó kọrin" (I doff my cap, I pay homage before performing my music). Thus, although the chorus part continues with the theme of homage that is initiated in the opening solo line, it is a complete and independent phrase. This procedure is visually observable in the transcription of the lyrics below, where the solo and chorus phrases (of lines 1 and 2) each start at the beginning of the line. Other examples of this procedure can be observed in lines 3–4, 7–8, and 11–12.

In the second type of arrangement, a single sentence is broken into two and shared between the solo and the chorus parts. In this procedure, the solo part merely starts the phrase, which is completed by the chorus. In line 5, for example, the soloist begins with the phrase "ẹ̀bẹ̀ la bẹ̀ yín" (we plead), a hanging phrase whose meaning is completed only when the chorus part enters in line 6 with the phrase "olọ́yan ń lògbà ẹ jẹ́ kó yẹwá làwa ń tọrọ" (that we may live and prosper). A similar procedure is illustrated in line 9, where the solo initiates the phrase, singing, "Òrọ̀ yí le koko" (It is serious). We are only made to know what is "serious" when the chorus enters in line 10 with the phrase "tó mọ́ba kùrò lÓyọ́" (the forced abdication of the king of Ọ̀yọ́). To indicate this form of relationship, I have transcribed the chorus part of the second type of procedure to start not at the beginning of the line, but indented, as can be observed in lines 6, 10, 15, 19, 21, 23, and 25. As can also be observed, the two procedures seem randomly arranged, thus underlining the loose narrative sequence of the song. This interactive relationship between solo and chorus represents a vocal technique that typifies *àpàlà* and other Islamic popular genres.

Haruna Ishola: "Ìbà Akọ́dá"

1. Solo: Ìbà akọ́dá aṣẹ̀dá ayé ìbà o
2. Chorus: Àgbà kí mo sí fìlà,
   Orẹ́rẹ́ mo júbà kí n tó kọrin
3. Solo: Ọmọ eyẹ wọ́n ṣomi ṣálá ṣolo
   Abẹ̀lẹ̀ tọ́mọdé ò gbọdọ̀ wọ̀
4. Chorus: kọ́mọdé torí ẹ̀ kó kú gangan
   Ìyá ńlá abẹ̀lẹ̀ fún mọ lọ́run bí ẹ̀gbẹ̀ṣu

5.   Solo: Ẹ̀bẹ̀ la bẹ̀ yín
6.   Chorus: ọlọyan ń lògbà ẹ jẹ́ kó yẹwá làwa ń tọrọ
7.   Solo: Ọ̀pẹ àtÀkùkọ ẹ má gbàgbé
         Ọgbẹ́ni wa Ejòngboro
8.   Chorus: Bàbá le sẹ̀mù
         Ìbà fún Macaulay tó kó wa jọ[15]
9.   Solo: Ọ̀rọ̀ yí le koko
10.   Chorus: Tó mọ́ba jáde kúrò lỌ̀yọ́ o
11.   Chorus: Bọ̀dé Thomas, ayé pa kádàrá ẹ̀, ikú mu lọ[16]
12.   Solo: Àkùkọ ń ṣagbára kÁláàfín lè padà wálé[17]
13.   Chorus: Àwọn Ọ̀pẹ kọ̀, wọn ò gbà pe kÁláàfín bọ́ sórí ọba
14.   Solo: Ká tó rérin ó digbó
         Awólọ́wọ̀ ló sọ̀rọ̀ kan, ẹ wá gbọ́[18]
15.   Chorus: Ó lọ́nà ó mà jìn kátó rírú ẹni Bọ̀dé tó lọ
16.   Chorus: Àwọn ò gbà yen àfi bá a bá rí Bọ̀dé lọbá le darí wálé
17.   Chorus: Tọ̀tún tòsín ẹ dákun ẹ má ṣe fòyà
18.   Solo: Baba Démọ́lá
19.   Chorus: Bánkọ́lé ọkọ Àdùkẹ̀ Àńkúrí, London ni dúníà
         Ẹní ní sùúrù ni ó jogún ayé
20.   Solo: Tí ò gbọdọ̀ kanni lójú
         Ẹni tí ò dáni lókòwò tí ò yáni lówó ṣiṣẹ́
21.   Chorus: Ẹgbọ́ bó bú mi mà á bu
         Bó sọ̀rọ̀ tí ò tẹ́ mi lọ́run mà á sọfun
22.   Solo: Àkéte lowó
23.   Chorus: ẹni tó bá wojúu wa ni ó fi délé, èní la rí
         Baba lókè lómọ̀la
24.   Solo: Bánkọ́lé mo fẹ́
25.   Chorus: Àtowó àtọmọ mo fẹ́
         Kó o darí owó tùtù sílé e wa

1.   Solo: I salute the First, the Creator
2.   Chorus: I doff my cap, I pay homage
         before performing my music
3.   Solo: The offspring of the bird that muddies
         the water
         A child cannot behold its face
4.   Chorus: The child dies for doing so
         The big mother that squeezes
         the neck of a child
5.   Solo: We plead
6.   Chorus: that we may live and prosper
7.   Solo: The palm-tree and the cockerel[19]
         Our friend Ejòngboro [honorary title for Herbert Macaulay in Lagos]
8.   Chorus: The father
         Salute to Macaulay, our leader
9.   Solo: It is a serious matter
10.   Chorus: that forces the king
         of Ọ̀yọ́ to abdicate
11.   Chorus: Bode Thomas was killed by the enemy

12. Solo: The cockerel is working hard to bring the king back home
13. Chorus: But there is great resistance to this
   effort by the palm-tree
14. Solo: An elephant could only be found in the
   big forest
   It was Awolowo who once remarked
15. Chorus: that it will be difficult to find
   another person like Bode
16. Chorus: The palm-tree [a political party] say it is only when we
   find Bode that the king could come back
17. Chorus: Be calm everyone
18. Solo: Demola's father [reference to the Aláké—king—of Abẹ́òkúta]
19. Chorus: Bánkọ́lé the husband
   of Àdùkẹ̀ Àńkúrí whose [second] home is London
   Only those who are patient will
   inherit the earth
20. Solo: He/she has no reason whatsoever to make troubles with us:
   Who has not done us any favor
21. Chorus: If he/she abuses me, I will
   abuse him back
   If she says any unpleasant thing
22. Solo: Àkéte lowó
23. Chorus: Only those who love us will find money
   Only God knows tomorrow
24. Solo: Bánkọ́lé—I want
25. Chorus: money and good children
   May we have both of these

This song begins with a Yorùbá traditional homage in which a singer or a drummer appeases and salutes the elders and deities before proceeding to the performance proper. In invoking this traditional practice, Ishola prays to the Creator, "the one who existed before anyone else," to protect and to guide. This is followed by homage to some powerful elders, including Herbert Macaulay, one of Nigeria's pioneer eminent nationalists. The mention of Macaulay highlights the song's focus on political events of the 1950s when there was a bitter rivalry between leading political parties, especially the Action Group (AG) and the National Convention of Nigeria and Cameroon (NCNC). As the song recounts, the king of Ọ̀yọ́, the Aláàfín, was forced to abdicate his throne in the midst of the political crisis of the time, while an important politician, Chief Bode Thomas, died in tragic circumstances. The song briefly extols the wisdom of the late Chief Awolowo, leader of the Action Group political party, the man generally hailed by most Yorùbá people as their greatest leader in recent history and one of the leading architects of Nigerian nationalism. Ishola continues his song with the statement that everyone has the right to protect himself/herself against their enemies. He ends the song with a prayer for God's blessings, wealth, and good children.

There are a number of interesting aspects to this song. Its emphasis on politics underlines the depth of knowledge of topical social and political issues often displayed even by indigenous Yorùbá musicians. Ishola's take on the turbulent political events of the 1950s in Western Nigeria (a geopolitical area often referred to, especially in the early sixties, as the "wild, wild West") is descriptive and narrative rather than critical or evaluative. In taking a neutral position, Isola describes the chain of events: the disagreement between the defunct AG, which had the palm-tree image as its symbol, and the defunct NCNC, which had the cockerel image as its symbol; the forced abdication of the Alaafin (king) of Ọ̀yọ́, and the death of Bode Thomas, a prominent Yorùbá politician, during that time. Ishola states the position of each of the two political parties without apparently taking a stand, although he somehow betrays some sympathy for the leader of the AG, Chief Obafemi Awolowo, by drawing on the politician's "words of wisdom," and his praise for Bode Thomas.

The strong impact of Yorùbá music in Ishola's song is immediately recognizable in the employment of the traditional Yorùbá homage right at the beginning of the song, and the prominence of the Yorùbá drum language. The slow, meditative, and sparse instrumentation of sákárà, which, in its use of instruments like the fiddle and calabash drum reflects Northern Nigeria's Islamic influences, is, in this àpàlà song, replaced with a dùndún-dominated dance music. Of course, there are similarities: they include the use of an exclusively male chorus; a vocal style that reflects the influence of Arabic/ Islamic chanting (notably the use of microtonal glides); Yorùbá call and response procedures; and vocal melodies whose contours correlate with the tonal inflections of their Yorùbá words. The disparity in the use of instruments and the organization of ensembles, however, speaks to the lingering impact of the identity politics that motivated the emergence of àpàlà in the first place. Thus, although sákárà and àpàlà are representative of a Yorùbá Islamic musical tradition that is conceived and constructed away from the character of the Christian-type genres that I discussed in chapter 7, and while it is true that both genres provide syncretic mixtures of indigenous Yorùbá elements and Arabic/Islamic influences, each articulates a different shade of identity, a fact which underlines the strategic and competitive nature of identity construction in Yorùbá musical culture. Practitioners of the Yorùbá Islamic popular music, although they incorporate musical elements and strategies through which they resist, reinterpret, or even reject Christian/Western elements that typify musical genres like juju, highlife and Afro-beat and are representative of a different social demography of listeners, do not constitute a monolithic or homogeneous group. The politics of identity, which highlight the interest of specific cohorts of Muslim musicians and their audiences, are made manifest through the organization and structure of music. One such marker of identity construction is gender, which resonates prominently in my discussion of wákà music below.

Wáká Music

Wáká is performed exclusively by women, contrasting with sákárà, àpàlà and fújì, all of which are performed mainly by men. Wáká was initially performed within Islamic events like naming and marriage ceremonies, and to welcome returning pilgrims from Mecca.[20] The allocation of musical roles according to gender, as shown in these examples, brings into focus the critical role of gender in the practice of Islam in Africa.[21] Developed as an amateur genre in the late 1950s, wáká had by the 1980s become the music of professional female Muslim musicians like Batili Alake and Salawa Abeni, two figures who popularized the genre well beyond the confines of Islamic devotional and ceremonial music. In its professional form, it began to incorporate traditional instruments like the dùndún, agogo, and ṣèkèrè, and later, the Western drum set and synthesizer. The texts of the music changed too, featuring nonsacred, even sometimes vulgar subjects, as illustrated especially in the music of Salawa Abeni.[22] In spite of its new status as a form of commercial music, wáká has stayed connected to its erstwhile Islamic roots and remained a mode of religious expression and a medium for social interaction amongst Muslim female groups and their communities. My discussion of wáká below focuses on this particular model of wáká, as illustrated in the music of Monsurat Ibrahim, a wáká singer based in Ìkìrun.

Ìkìrun, an ancient Yorùbá town just about ten miles north of Òṣogbo (the capital of Òṣun state), illustrates the typical social and religious set up within which Islamic Yorùbá popular music has grown and thrived as a type of music owned and enjoyed by a local community of Muslims. This town was on many occasions a point of transit during my numerous journeys from Ìlọrin, where I once lived, to Iléṣà to visit my father-in-law. In order to avoid the usually very busy traffic in Oshgbo, I often branched off the main road (from Ìlọrin to Òṣogbo) to drive through Ìkìrun and a host of towns like Ìrágbìjí, Adà, Ìdómìnàsi, and finally Iléṣà. It was not until I was conducting the research for this book that I really took time to savor the sights and sounds of the rusty ancient city. And there are many things to absorb: its narrow, winding, partly tarred and dusty streets where cars struggle against a regular horde of commercial motor cyclists (popularly known as òkadà), roadside traders who have managed to seize a significant portion of the motor road to sell food items that range from roasted plantain and corn, peppers and tomatoes and yam tubers to domestic utility items like candles, kerosene lanterns, and detergents wrapped in small white nylon bags. There are also roadside artisans like the ubiquitous "vulcanizers" who fix tires, and tailors—both men and women—who sew a variety of traditional Yorùbá garments. The presence of these various traders and artisans is articulated sonically: the ear-jarring sounds of the vulcanizers' air-vending machines; those of the roadside mills grinding corn and pepper; the relentless honking of commercial buses and motorcycles; and the voices of women who periodically advertize their goods to passers- and drivers-by. All these sounds are overlaid by Muslim clerics' periodic call-to-worship chants, urging devout worshippers to fulfill their prayer obligations at the appropriate hour. Blaring over mounted speakers, these chants can be heard from everywhere in the town.

The big Kajola downtown central mosque is just a few yards from the tailor's shop where my research assistants waited for me each time we had an appointment. I recall vividly the hot July afternoon in 2008, when I first met Monsurat Gbajumo, the rising wákà queen whose Islamic Youth band typifies small groups that are integrally connected with local community and germane to the strengthening of ties amongst adherents of Islam in the town. Performances by such community groups take place within formal religious events outside the mosque and as informal events for the entertainment of community members. I conclude my discussion of Islamic Yorùbá popular music with a brief discussion of the music of Monsurat Gbajumo.

Monsurat Gbajumo was born in 1984 in Ìkìrun, and has lived there all her life. Although she started her own group in 2005, Ibrahim had earlier been involved in a host of musical activities connected with Islamic religious events. She explained to me that she started as a member of the Samsudeen Society, a Muslim youth musical organization, members of which met regularly at the Central Mosque in Ìkìrun. As the song leader, Gbajumo led the group on many occasions to perform during Malidinabin (a ceremony celebrating the birth of Prophet Mohammed) and wedding ceremonies—all outside the mosque. The group depended on monetary gifts received during performances to buy items of equipment like amplifiers and loudspeakers. The activity of the group was not limited to musical performance. Members also took Koran lessons and learned about Islamic laws.

Gbajumo later joined another Muslim society, known as the Ìkìrun Youth Muslim Organization, an umbrella organization for all Muslim societies in Ìkìrun. It was while she was a member of Samsudeen that she was approached by one Alhaja Jelilah who at that time was leading another Islamic organization known as Mobin. Jelilah wanted Gbajumo as a background singer in her group, an invitation which Gbajumo accepted. In 2005 Gbajumo left Jelilah's group to form her own group, the Islamic Voice of Solieena—Al Rishad. The group consists of a core ensemble of four female singers (including Gbajumo, the lead vocalist). Other members are a male backup singer and a manager who sees to the business aspect of things. Her ensemble often features two small drums known as the kànàngó, and a slightly larger one known as the àdàmọ̀. As illustrated in "Orin Ìgbéyàwó" (CD track 12), the two kànàngó drums play their usual repetitive patterns, while the àdàmọ̀ engages in occasional improvisations as appropriate to a vocal-based performance rather than following the more dynamic tradition of Yorùbá dùndún master drummers. For performances involving a large audience, she may engage a larger group of drummers, cosisting of one àpàlà drummer (playing the àdàmọ̀); two omele

Figure 8.1. Monsurat Gbajumo and her male instrumentalists. *Back row, from left,* Taye Ayinla, Saheed Oladejo, and Kayode Olagunju; *front row,* Monsurat Gbajumo, Ibrahim Asimiyu. Ìkìrun, 2011, photo by author.

drummers (each playing a small hour-glass tension drum); an ìyáàlù player (playing a bigger hourglass drum, the dùndún); two players of ọ̀rúnṣà (frame drums—consisting of a smaller one known as kod, and the larger sákárà). The smaller drum ensemble, consisting of three drums, is more typical, however. Gbajumo also explained to me that her group had in the past experimented with the use of keyboards and electronic guitars in an attempt to make her music gain wider acceptance among the youth.[23] In addition to performing during Islamic ceremonies, Gbajumo's group performs recreational music for her predominantly Muslim community. My discussion of Gbajumo's music below is based on a public performance specially arranged for me in Ìkìrun in July 2008, and a recording session in a small sitting room following the public performance. Ibrahim's musical activities exemplify how Muslim women have used "their agency in the public and private spheres" in the process of appropriating and recrafting "characteristics of identity traditionally associated with the male other and their mobilization toward particular women-centered ends."[24]

Figure 8.2. Monsurat Gbajumo and her backup singers. *From left,* Rukayat Tijani, Ganiyat Abdulasis, Monsurat Gbajumo, and Rasida Jomoh. Ìkìrun, 2011, photo by author.

Monsurat Gbajumo's Wákà

The song entitled "Mi Ó Ní Sìn Wọ́n Wá Sáye" (CD track 13) is a prayer for Allah's blessings in the form of riches and the gift of a child. The singer explains that such blessings await all true believers in Allah. This song does not feature a slow free-rhythm introduction, but begins with a solo part that subsequently becomes the response of the chorus. In the song, the chorus alternates with the verses of the soloist, each of which is reworked to accommodate the inflectional patterns of new words. The phrase "Fàlùbáríkà sọ́rọ̀ mi má jẹn sìn wọ́n wá sáyé" (I pray not to be an idle person) alternates with the names of prominent Islamic leaders in Ìkìrun, each of whom the lead singer praises. The combination of religious prayer with human praise is not uncommon in Yorùbá songs, especially those that are performed as entertainment.

Mi Ó Ní Sìn Wọn Wá Sáyé

Verse 1: Solo
Mi ò ní sìn wọn wá sáyé
Mi ò ní bá wọn wá wòran
Fàlùbáríkà sọ̀rọ̀ mi
Má jẹn sìn wọn wá sáyé

Chorus:
Mi ò ní sìn wọn wá sáyé
Mi ò ní bá wọn wá wòran
Fàlùbáríkà sọ̀rọ̀ mi
Má jẹn sìn wọn wá sáyé

Verse 2: Solo
Ṣe bẹni tó sìn wọn wáyé
Lẹni tó wáye tí ò lówó
Ó wáye kò bímọ
Kò lálàfíà kọkan
Títí tó fi kú kò mà tún ṣe sí Islam
Má jẹn sìn wọn wá sáyé
Má jẹn bá wọn wá wòran
Ọlá bàbá mi pẹ̀lú màmá mi

Chorus
Mi ò ní sìn wọn wá sáyé
Mi ò ní bá wọn wá wòran
Fàlùbáríkà sọ̀rọ̀ mi
Má jẹn sìn wọn wá sáyé

Extended Coda
Solo: Fàlùbáríkà sọ̀rọ̀ mi
Chorus: Má jẹn sìn wọn wá sáyé
Solo: Ọlọ́run fàlùbáríkà sọ̀rọ̀ mi
Chorus: Má jẹn sìn wọn wá sáyé
Solo: Lọ́lá bàbá wa Shehu Yunusun
Chorus: Má jẹn sìn wọn wá sáyé
Solo: Shehu Yunusun bàbá wa nÌkìrun
Chorus: Má jẹn sìn wọn wá sáyé
Solo: Shehu Yunusun Yunusun Sunusi
Chorus: Má jẹn sìn wọn wá sáyé
Solo: Ọlá bàbá mi Shehu Adamo
Chorus: Má jẹn sìn wọn wá sáyé
Solo: Shehu Adamo Aliliori o
Chorus: Má jẹn sìn wọn wá sáyé
Solo: Ọlá bàbá mi Shehu Rawelu o
Chorus: Má jẹn sìn wọn wá sáyé
Solo: Shehu Rawelu baba mi lÓmùpo
Chorus: Má jẹn sìn wọn wá sáyé

Solo: Má jẹn sìn wọ́n wá sáyé
Chorus: Má jẹn sìn wọ́n wá sáyé
Solo: Ọlọ́run má jẹn sìn wọ́n wá sáyé
Chorus: Má jẹn sìn wọ́n wá sáyé

Verse 1: Solo
I pray that I will not be a failure
Not be a spectator (an idle person)
Bless me (oh God)
I pray that I will not be a failure

Chorus
I pray that I will not be a failure
Not be a spectator (an idle person)
Bless me (oh God)
I pray that I will not be a failure

Verse 2: Solo
A spectator is one who is poor
Has no child
Has no peace
Not a practicing Muslim
I pray that I will not be a failure
May I not be a spectator (an idle person)
Bless me (oh God)
I pray that I will not be a failure

Chorus
I pray that I will not be a failure
Not be a spectator (an idle person)
Bless me (oh God)
I pray that I will not be a failure

Extended Coda
Solo: Bless me (Oh! God)
Chorus: I pray that I will not be a failure
Solo: Oh God bless me
Chorus: I pray that I will not be a failure
Solo: Our king Shehu Yunusun
Chorus: I pray that I will not be a failure
Solo: Shehu Yunusun our father in Ìkìrun
Chorus: I pray that I will not be a failure
Solo: Shehu Yunusun Yunusun Sunusun
Chorus: I pray that I will not be a failure
Solo: Ọlá bàbá mi Shehu Adamo
Chorus: I pray that I will not be a failure
Solo: Shehu Adamo Alilori
Chorus: I pray that I will not be a failure
Solo: The honor of Shehu Rawelu my father

Chorus: I pray that I will not be a failure
Solo: Shehu Rawelu my father in Ómùpo (a town in Kwara State)
Chorus: I pray that I will not be a failure
Solo: I pray that I will not be a failure
Chorus: I pray that I will not be a failure
Solo: I pray that I will not be a failure
Chorus: I pray that I will not be a failure

In its relatively simple form and thematic choice, Monsurat Gbajumo's song reflects a community-based performance, contrasting with the tendency for Ishola's àpàlà to discuss issues that are more philosophical or even political within the context of a wider Yorùbá, even Nigerian, social space. Gbajumo's community-directed performance is also underlined by her extensive praise of community leaders who are identified by name and town and, at times, her own relationship to them. Phrases like "our king Shehu Yunusun, Shehu Yunusun, our father in Ìkìrun" emphasize her commitment to local community networks. Gbajumo's emphasis on the sanctity of marriage in her live performances is particularly instructive in this regard. While funeral performances are often the provenance of male musicians in Yorùbá traditional societies, those of weddings tend to attract the participation of women more than men. Her repeated emphasis on the need for all to embrace the institution of marriage as commanded in the Koran in "Orin Ìgbéyàwó" (CD track 12) could be seen as linked to this Yorùbá practice and represents an important means of strengthening community bonds.

Gbajumo's performances boost the visibility of women and project women-friendly themes; she challenges male domination of popular music ensembles like those of àpàlà, sákárà and jùjú, where women are not featured at all, and those of afro-beat and fújì where women function only as dancers and backup singers. Gbajumo's leadership of her wákà band challenges the gender equation in a most significant manner. But she also acknowledges the leadership of men, particularly in her praise of male Islamic leaders. It is also pertinent that all the drummers featured in her ensemble are male. The allocation of drumming to the male gender is common to many traditional Yorùbá ensembles, especially those of the Òyó-Yorùbá, and also finds support within Yorùbá Islamic practices. Her concession of this gender role to the male group within her band is very strategic. Indeed, the various musical choices displayed by Gbajumo speak to a delicate process of strategic conciliation, a give-and-take approach that assures the inviolability of Islamic values and respect for traditional Yorùbá gender practices while securing her own visibility as the leader of a modern community-based ensemble. It is a strategic process that helps to boost the effectiveness of her role as an accepted public-square performer who molds opinions and helps to build social and community networks. It is important to note, however, that Gbajumo's performances are constructed in a manner that limits the performance latitude of her male drummers, while enhancing her own visibility as the undisputable leader of her group. Contrasting with the restricted role of the drummers is the more exuberant and relatively uninhibited expressions of Gbajumo's female singers/dancers. Although they wear veils, as expected of women in many Yorùbá communities, Gbajumo's female dancers often display the relatively uninhibited, even suggestive, movements found in secular Yorùbá dances.

The performance strategies displayed in Gbajumo's wákà performances recall those of earlier musical groups in other parts of Africa, who sought an alternative aesthetic platform for identity construction—one that avoided or was subversive of the oppressive force of European colonial power. In an article on music in the Belgian Congo, Bob White has observed that such a platform was found in Afro-Cuban music. White explains that for Congolese musicians, Afro-Cuban music offered a new mode of musical and cultural association that provided a respite from the oppressive and suffocating power of the Belgian rule; and for Congolese audiences, Afro-Cuban musical traditions provided a form of cosmopolitanism that promoted individual freedom and an authentic form of group identity.[25] Gbajumo's wákà music reflects an intricate process of appropriation and selectivity that seeks different layers of affiliation in a cosmpolitan spirit, recalling the Congolese example. It is a multilayered process of musical and cultural negotiation that traverses the domains of gender, class, religion, ethnicity, and social space in a number of ways. Firstly, her wákà music navigates musical, religious, and social-cultural terrains that are defined in contrast to those of Christian-affiliated Yorùbá popular music, thus providing interesting perspectives on the ways in which religion and musical practices intersect to aid identity constructions.

Her music presents a cultural interpretation that departs from Islamic practices in northern Nigeria, the region from which Islam spread to Yorùbáland, and which is often associated with political domination in Nigeria. Gbajumo's music, while reflecting religious connections with the Islamic northern Nigeria, rejects a northern cultural imposition by affirming a strong Yorùbá culture. Parallels could be drawn between such a musical practice and the well-known Yorùbá people's political resistance to the northern Nigerian oligarchy.

Gbajumo's community-based, rural oriented music is configured in opposition to the urban character of many Nigerian popular forms, notably by focusing on themes of local significance and using musical instruments more connected to local tastes and rejecting the technology-driven instrumentation of the male-dominated urban forms. And finally, the three drums often featured in her ensemble, in their sizes and the ways in which they are used, constitute a minimalist variant of the more powerful configuration of the traditional all-male dùndún drum ensemble. The musical functions of the dùndún are curtailed, as it were, by the vocal force of Gbajumo's singing.

Islamic Music and the Performance of Identity

As this discussion shows, Yorùbá Islamic musicians are masters of the word, crafting traditional proverbs and idiomatic expressions to reflect on Islamic ideas as well as social and political issues of their times. Their performances demonstrate once again how African musicians have interpreted Islamic values in African terms and how oral performances have taken on Islamic influences.[26] As illustrated in the various examples, Yorùbá Islamic popular music is a predominantly word-based style in which musical instruments merely provide accompaniment or interlude between verses. The crafting of verbal exchanges, the corroborating relationship between solo and chorus, the use of indigenous Yorùbá idiomatic expressions, the narration of stories, the employment of traditional Yorùbá panegyrics—all these constitute the techniques through which Islamic themes are reinterpreted in Yorùbá cultural terms.

Also shown in the discussion is the fact that Islamic themes are more dominant in some of the genres than in others. For example, wákà, as performed by Monsurat Gbajumo, remains more connected to Islamic teachings and communities than Haruna Ishola's àpàlà. This difference draws attention to how Yorùbá Islamic genres have, over the years, developed from their Islamic roots into secular popular forms. Indeed, as shown in my discussion of the music of Ishola, Islamic themes are often marginalized, a feature which underlines the capability of the musicians to reach out to a larger, non-Muslim audience. And apart from the use of Arabic/Islamic singing styles, Yorùbá cultural elements are more prominent than specifically Islamic elements in the music. As mentioned earlier, Gbajumo's wákà does not represent the only form of wákà. Indeed, the more popular brand of wákà is that which, as typified in the music of musicians like Salawa Abeni and Batili Alake, is commercialized and does not restrict itself to projecting Islamic themes. The existence of these two forms, the commercialized and the community-based, also shows how Yorùbá Islamic forms have continued to relate to a variety of social identities, in spite of an overarching Islamic connection.

In their sole dependence on traditional Yorùbá musical instruments, sákàrà, àpàlà and wákà contrast sharply with jùjú and, especially, highlife, both of which bear strong Christian influences, and rely strongly on the use of Western instruments. Yorùbá Islamic genres are also distinct from the music of the Islamic northern Nigeria, not only because of their predominant use of Yorùbá elements, but also through their creative reworking of musical elements associated with Arabic-Islamic as well as Hausa-Fulani musical traditions. Although an exception has to be made for fújì (a genre which features heavy electronic amplifiers and keyboard synthesizers), instrumentation in these Islamic genres consists mainly of Yorùbá talking and frame drums, rattles, gongs and the one-string fiddle, gòjé. Western melodic instruments like guitars and synthesizers are rarely used, except, of course, in fújì, where they tend to function rhythmically rather than melodically, and serve mainly to increase the density of the music. The heavy reliance of these Islam-affiliated genres on traditional Yorùbá music underlines their strong conception as neotraditional forms that identify a distinct Yorùbá Islamic culture, and accounts for their appeal in Yorùbá society. Western and Christian-affiliated forms, notably highlife and the jùjú music (of musicians like Victor Olaiya and Sunday Aladeniyi) are sustained largely through the patronage of the elite. Conversely, Islamic genres, although they do benefit from the support of rich Muslims, are sustained largely through the patronage of millions of artisans, drivers, car mechanics, carpenters, and tailors. These are the people whose lives and experiences are often captured in the music.

Conclusion

My discussion of Yorùbá music in this book has demonstrated how a unique and socially responsive musical culture has been shaped and sustained in a variety of forms since the late colonial period. In painting a multiple and an accretive profile of Yorùbá music, I have discussed how modern musical genres have evolved out of ancient Yorùbá traditions in response to new existential realities, and how such realities have been interpreted, appropriated, and filtered according to the vision, understanding, challenges, and experiences of musicians and audiences. I have also explained that although various Yorùbá musicians and musical practices draw on what may be described as pan-Yorùbá elements, each musical genre or style is strategically grounded to respond to specific needs and interests. Yorùbá musical traditions are thus conceived, performed, and experienced as narratives of identity through which drummers, dancers, singers, and chanters express self-mediated visions of their social and cultural environment. Dating from the antiquated era of Àyànàgalú (the Yorùbá pioneer drummer-turned-deity) and extending into the colonial and postcolonial world of modern musicians, Yorùbá musical traditions have been shaped as a form of social and cultural expression in which communality, spirituality, negotiation, resistance, critique and, of course, social entertainment are inscribed.

The process of reworking Yorùbá and non-Yorùbá elements is shaped by a need to challenge, resist or reconfigure existing or imposed conventions, and identify a group or an individual through music. The process is strategic and competitive, even when a sense of unity or solidarity is thematized in a musical performance, or when traditional institutions are valorized, as in the case of Aírégbé and Olorì musical performances. For example, although Aírégbé and Olorì songs project the values of their larger (Emùré-Èkìtì) community and extol the qualities of the king, they are anchored in unique musical styles that have come to define the identities of the two categories of women who perform them. In the case of Olorì, we see two parallel uses of their music. The first one is occasional, occurring when there is a public event such as the annual new yam festival. At such a forum, the women sing in honor of their king and articulate shared values. The second, more regular use of the music, however, takes place at weekly meetings where the music is performed exclusively to reinforce the identity of the performers as a distinct group and facilitate interactive sessions dealing with group-specific problems. Within such an exclusive space, the interests of participants as members of a distinct social group are paramount. By performing Olorì songs to themselves at such meetings, the women consciously connect musical expression with group identity, and demonstrate the power of their music as a form of social action and as a facilitator of group bonding.

A similar conclusion can be drawn regarding the musical activity of the more powerful female group in the town, the female chiefs who perform Aírégbé music. The process of composing and recomposing pieces, the context of performances, and the unique structural and stylistic features of their songs all provide the medium and the tools for configuring a group identity that sets female chiefs apart from other groups within the town. Promoting and extolling traditional institutions is to the political advantage of these chiefs, because they constitute an integral part of the political leadership of Emùré-Èkìtì. These female chiefs are very conscious of their status as a distinct social entity. They often sing about themselves in the course of a performance. And although the activities of the female chiefs are intended to serve the interests of the entire community, they also enhance the status of the women themselves. The musical performances of these two female groups are thus strategically deployed to articulate their status to differentiate them from other social groups within the Emùré-Èkìtì community.

The conception of musical activities to articulate the interests of distinct social groups assumes a sharper focus in a fast-changing, economically challenging environment. The narratives of bàtá drummers and the ways in which they have repositioned themselves to challenge the rising profile of dùndún drummers are particularly instructive in this regard. Also instructive is how dùndún drummers have moved from the periphery of Yorùbá musical culture to dominate sacred and secular performances and to integrate themselves into modern social spaces. By organizing themselves into a formidable group of musicians who meet regularly, analyzing the social factors responsible for their declining status, and taking a resolute stance to resist marginalization and reshape their music to meet the social demands of life in modern Nigeria, bàtá drummers articulate the interests of their group over those of a collective Yorùbá identity.

The statements of bàtá drummers that I discussed in chapter 1 should be seen from the perspective of how musical activities are connected to social action and ideas. Ingrid Monson, following Michel Foucault, explains that such statements constitute "constellations of discourses" that advance "the process of framing arguments and justifying positions, and possess the authority and prestige to order how we think about the world."[1] The statements of the drummers constitute discourses, deployed not accidentally or innocently, but rather as strategic utterances, which articulate specific positions and arguments. It is also possible to interpret the activities of the Bàtá Drummers Association—their discontent with their dùndún counterparts, and the decision to stand for themselves—as a form of performance framed along the trajectory of Victor Turner's social drama.[2] The story and the decisions of the drummers bear all the marks of Turner's paradigm, namely, a dislocation in social relations, a marked state of crisis and the mapping out of specific actions to resolve the crisis. Their resolution to stand for themselves represents a form of redressive action, which finds its manifestation in the process of generating new forms of bàtá ensembles to compete with dùndún drummers.

Although their music is a powerful symbol of Yorùbá identity, recent musical decisions by members of the Bàtá Drummers Association speak directly to the need to redefine themselves as a distinct group with specific interests. Westernization and the growing profile of Islam and Christianity have combined to significantly undermine the status of traditional religious institutions, thus narrowing the social and cultural space within which traditional drummers could perform. These factors, coupled with the increasingly desperate economic climate in Nigeria, have put pressure on each group of traditional drummers to seek new ways of surviving. Thus, although bàtá drumming shares many important musical and cultural features with dùndún music, the activities of bàtá drummers are shaped differently from those of their dùndún counterparts, and propelled by the specific interests of the musicians.

My discussions in chapters 7 and 8 situate Yorùbá popular music, in its various manifestations, within the historical development of popular music in Nigeria, and analyze the syncretic language and the local power dynamics revealed within it. Responding to the growing impact of a dominant foreign culture on their environment, Yorùbá musicians display creative choices that reflect different degrees of adaptation. Reflecting on this phenomenon, Jocelyne Guilbault has observed that subdominant countries, "in the face of a world-wide homogenization" caused by globalization, may either adopt a protectionist approach distinguished by a purist renewal of indigenous practices, or reassess their creative choices in terms of the social and cultural challenge of their environment.[3] For many Yorùbá popular musicians, the choice to resist or adapt Western elements is determined by the need to evolve musical styles that address and reflect the unique challenges of their immediate environment rather than engaging in a globalized power struggle. As in the music of Olorì, Aírégbé, bàtá, and dùndún, the process of configuring modern popular forms is typified by hierarchies, strategic interests, and resistance as locally defined within Yorùbá and Nigerian society. Thus, although popular music forms like Victor Olaiya's highlife, Fela Anikulapo-Kuti's afro-beat, Lagbaja's "higher-life," Ishola Haruna's àpàlà, Yusufu Olatunji's sákárà, Ishola Kollingon's fújì, and Monsurat Gbajumo's wákà all derive from or incorporate core Yorùbá conventions of musical practice and European, Arabic-Islamic, or Caribbean music elements; they articulate the interests and identities of distinct groups and individuals, and are homological of the hierarchies and the relations that define the larger Yorùbá and Nigerian society. Olaiya's highlife music, coming after the music of an earlier generation of musicians that imitated Western ballroom styles like the foxtrot and waltz, infuses imported musical styles, notably Western instrumentation and tonal harmony, and Caribbean elements with Yorùbá elements like dùndún drumming, Yorùbá folktales, and traditional poetry. Western harmonic progressions are simplified, appropriated, and attuned to support an ostinato-driven music, and made to reflect the nuances of the Yorùbá tonal language. Although Olaiya's use of these elements to dilute imposed British and Western musical styles could be interpreted as constituting a subtle act of resistance, it must be seen mainly as a musical act deployed in support of an emerging local elite to which he belongs. The symbolic and nostalgic recall of traditional Yorùbá life within an urban-centered musical genre in his music is elitist, serving mainly the interests of the ruling class of the 1950s and the 1960s, and reflecting the newly emerging hierarchies of a modern Yorùbá society shaped by colonial rule. Olaiya's highlife speaks to this hierarchy more than it does to any notion of a collective Yorùbá identity. His music appeals to neither the tastes nor the aspirations of the average Yorùbá person, and contributes very little to the sustenance of indigenous Yorùbá institutions.

Anikulapo-Kuti's Afro-beat, on the other hand, speaks strongly to the impact of colonial domination of Nigeria, and the antinomies inherent in the process of making sense of the complex nature of that domination. Afro-beat music thematizes the negative impact of colonialism in Nigeria—the unmanageable social and political structures, inept and corrupt leadership, an internal oligarchy, and an exploitative political class. In configuring his music to engage these issues, Anikulapo-Kuti reworks Yorùbá elements differently from other popular musicians. Yorùbá-derived call-and-response phrases, traditional folklore, and multilayered and cyclically conceived rhythmic structures are synthesized with jazz elements and a modal melodic structure that simultaneously recalls John Coltrane and Yorùbá musical folklore. The use of these elements serves the purpose of configuring a pan-African musical style that addresses local issues of power in Nigeria. Rather than imitating the praise-dominated language of traditional Yorùbá music, Anikulapo-Kuti opted for the use of Yorùbá songs of abuse, which he considered more suited to engaging the antics of Nigeria's exploitative ruling class. Again, as in highlife music, Anikulapo-Kuti's projection of the Yorùbá voice is nuanced by a cosmopolitan language, albeit a politically charged one, within which Yorùbá elements are deployed to draw attention to social inequalities rather than to articulate a collective identity. But in spite of this apparent altruistic goal, Anikulapo-Kuti's Afro-beat also emanates from personal experiences, and is reflective of his personal interests—it bears a strong imprint of his personality, his ego, his narcissism—and speaks to his personal frustration with the Nigerian military institution, whose force was deployed against him many times.

Powered by the use of traditional drums like dùndún and bàtá, and the infusion of traditional folklore, Lagbaja's music also displays a strikingly unique style in spite of drawing syncretically from the categories of musical cultures that serve the music of Olaiya and Anikulapo-Kuti.

By de-emphasizing the "self" in order to give valence to the voice of the faceless majority, Lagbaja's music and performance and his wearing of a mask evoke Foucault who, in his writing, also aspired to the loss of a "fixed identity" through a symbolic wearing of a "succession of masks."[4] The mask that Lagbaja wears and the Yorùbá masquerade cult of egúngún that is invoked by wearing it are associated with departed ancestors who act as impartial mediators of social conflict among the living, and intercede between humans and the deities. Lagbaja's wearing of a mask represents his desire to project a perfect state of objectivity as a social critic and mediator. The evocation of death in his quest for objectivity also recalls Foucault's belief that death symbolizes the state in which the "abolition of subjectivity" can be completely achieved.[5] "Killing" the self, as Lagbaja attempts to do through the invocation of the egúngún cult is, however, a utopian project. His contribution to the Yorùbá gender discourse in "Skentele Skontolo" shows that he is not an impartial arbiter. The presentation of a positive image of a pan-Yorùbá culture within a competitive multiethnic framework of the Nigerian federation, as boldly announced in the opening of the song, is nuanced by a gendered position that, in spite of the lighthearted nature of the performance, seeks to affirm the superiority of the male gender. This brings us back to the point that I have made several times about the strategic nature of identity construction and how a seemingly altruistic expression can camouflage a hidden agenda.

The syncretic musical language of these three musicians, though relying essentially on the same cultural resources—Yorùbá, Western European, and Black Diaspora—mixes these elements differently to generate what I would like to call a syncretic hybridity that promotes three different political and social identities: an elitist ideology (Olaiya), a populist and radical ideology (Anikulapo-Kuti), and a patriarchal ideology (Lagbaja). Each of the subject positions and ideological viewpoints presented in the music of these three figures relies on specific modes of integrating disparate cultural forms to generate socially and politically expressive forms. And in spite of the impact of global and European musical practices, the works of these three musicians, like those of many other practitioners of Yorùbá popular music, should be understood largely in terms of their local relevance. Although their works do carry implicit messages about global dimensions of power, issues of power relations within Yorùbá and Nigerian society provide the immediate context for what the musicians do.

Yorùbá Islamic popular music navigates musical, religious, and cultural terrains that contrast strongly with those of Christian-affiliated Yorùbá popular genres. Often, it also contrasts with the image of Islam that is projected in northern Nigeria, the region from which Islam spread to Yorùbáland, and which is often associated with political domination in Nigeria. The unique nature of Yorùbá Islamic music, while reflecting religious connections between Yorùbáland and northern Nigeria, rejects a northern cultural imposition by affirming a strong Yorùbá culture, thus generating a musical form that parallels Yorùbá people's uneasiness with and resistance to northern oligarchy, in spite of the popularity of Islam in Yorùbáland. Yorùbá Islamic popular music also departs from the cultural and social orientation of Christian-affiliated genres (like highlife, jùjú, higher-life and Afro-beat), thus providing interesting perspectives on the ways in which religion and musical practices intersect to illuminate crucial demographic contours of modern Yorùbá society. Although Christianity is now widely embraced by Yorùbá of differing social backgrounds, the elitist nature of its early history in Nigeria continues to impact its practice. Most of Nigeria's Western educated professionals and intellectuals are Christians. And they are the people who provide the most economic support for Christian-affiliated genres like highlife and jùjú. Islam tends to be more popular among the less-educated Nigerians who occupy the lower rungs of the social ladder. Islamic law allows marriage to multiple wives, a freedom that is particularly attractive to the less-educated and underprivileged tradesman and artisans, whose social experiences are often reflected in Islamic popular music. Furthermore, performers of Yorùbá Islamic music, notably fújì musicians, often project a big-man image of themselves, and an opulent lifestyle that contrasts sharply with their humble origins while appealing strongly to the tastes and yearnings of their working class audiences who are inspired by the rags-to-riches stories of the musicians, and are hopeful that they, too, will "make it" one day. Taking all these factors into consideration, it is clear that Yorùbá Islamic popular music displays an intricate process of appropriation and selectivity that is framed to resist hegemonic imposition from multiple directions.

It is also clear from my discussion in chapter 8 that Yorùbá Islamic popular music does not articulate a monolithic framing of Yorùbá Islam. For while fújì and wákà tend to be popular with young Islamic audiences, genres like sákárà and àpàlà are enjoyed mainly by the elderly who relate positively with both the Islamic orientation of the music and its grounding in indigenous Yorùbá philosophy and musical aesthetics. There is also the factor of gender. As I discussed in chapter 8, wákà is a musical genre dominated by women, in contrast to the domination of sákárà, àpàlà, and fújì by men. Like the music of Aírégbé women, community-based wákà, as performed by Monsurat Gbajumo, does not challenge the position of religious male leaders, a task that would be almost impossible, given the Islamic context of the music. It does however provide a forum for issues of interest to Islamic women. Thus, although all these Islamic genres are also patronized by non-Muslims, they reflect a general Islamic culture as shaped locally in Yorùbá society, while speaking to class, age, and gender divisions. In spite of their connections to a larger Yorùbá musical and cultural tradition, they articulate the interests and experiences of specific segments within the Yorùbá society.

The spread of Christianity in Nigeria in the nineteenth century constituted the principal medium for the growth of European music in the country and, more significantly, provided a major catalyst for the emergence of new musical practices that have come to define the musical landscape of modern Nigeria. The evolution of these new musical traditions was marked, first, by the introduction of European musical instruments and musical forms; and, later, by the practice of synthesising European and indigenous Yorùbá musical practices to create new musical forms. At every stage within the process, Yorùbá musicians explored how to make Christianity more relevant to Yorùbá life and culture through musical compositions and activities that connected with precolonial traditions. The process began with the attempt to translate English hymn texts into Yorùbá while retaining their original tunes, an attempt that did not work, because the contours of the tunes did not match the inflections of Yorùbá speech. To overcome this problem, Yorùbá organists and choirmasters adapted or composed Yorùbá tunes to newly written Christian texts, using Western staff notation and solfège, thus championing a new mode of composing. Songs that had been used in connection with indigenous Yorùbá religious practices were purged of their "pagan" texts and recomposed to biblical texts. They were set to melodic patterns that merged European tonal systems with indigenous Yorùbá modal scales, and followed the inflectional contours of Yorùbá speech.

Western hymns were not completely abandoned; they continued to exist side by side with new compositions. The elitist way in which pioneer composers of Yorùbá church music responded to Western European music was to later have a long-lasting impact on modern musical practice in Yorùbáland. Ekundayo Phillips and Reverend I. O. Kuti, to mention just two of the pioneers of European-influenced Yorùbá music in the first few decades of the twentieth century, were musically literate in the European tradition, and were more attuned to that tradition than to the indigenous Yorùbá musical tradition. Though they tried to incorporate some Yorùbá folk tunes in their anthems, their approach in resisting European cultural imposition was mild rather than decisive. Ekundayo Phillips's interpretive approach was guided and limited by the dynamics of the colonial environment within which he operated, and by the nature of his own upbringing. His evolutionary approach to musical history, which hailed Western music as a progressive model to be imitated, reflected the general thinking of many colonized Africans of the period. It also shows the ways in which the philosophy of political colonization filtered into to the process of cultural planning. Phillips's influential position among Yorùbá church musicians of the era helped him to popularize his vision about how Yorùbá music should be "developed." His books, which represent the few examples of published material on Yorùbá music from that period, were widely distributed and very influential in shaping the nature of what other Yorùbá composers did and what Yorùbá Christians sang in the church.[6] His activities illustrate very vividly the ways in which the views of an influential individual could shape the musical tastes of a large group of people.

The rise of the Yorùbá Aládŭrà church was guided by a more decisive form of cultural resistance to the imposition of European Christian liturgy. Although the initial founders of the Yorùbá Africanist church were drawn from the same rank of the elite Yorùbá Christian leaders of the early twentieth century, their project has since blossomed into a large movement, now dominated by working- and lower-class Yorùbá Christians. The humble origins of the Yorùbá Aládŭrà church are well illustrated in the life of Reverend Oschoffa, one of the most influential Yorùbá Aládŭrà leaders of the twentieth century. In chapter 6, I discussed how this barely educated but very charismatic leader founded the Celestial Church of Christ, a church that boasts of millions of worshippers around the world today. The missionary orientation of the CCC, like that of other Aládŭrà churches, is conceived differently from the doctrinal policies of orthodox denominations like the Anglican, the Catholic, and the Baptist. For the CCC, the church is more than a place to prepare candidates for everlasting life in heaven; it is a refuge for the poor, and a place that responds to the real-life needs of its members. Musical performances in the CCC are conceived as an integral part of the overall mission of the church to give hope to those of its members who are going through hard times. Imported Western hymns, though not completely abandoned, exist peripherally within a folkloric and populist musical liturgy that challenges Western musical conventions through its African-based performance practices. Caricatures of Western performance modes, which I described in chapter 6, highlight how musical activities of the CCC reject Western forms that were introduced and imposed during the colonial era, and speak once again to the ways in which class divisions nuance religious musical activities. Rather than aspiring to the notion of a pan-Yorùbá identity, these musical activities are conceived to meet the needs of a particular segment of the society, defined essentially by their relatively low social class. The increased popularity of Yorùbá Africanist churches in the late twentieth century was linked to the declining economic fortunes of Nigeria as a whole, a situation which has fuelled the need for people to seek spiritual solutions to economic woes. It is important to note that, in an apparent response to the growing popularity of such churches, orthodox churches have started to incorporate a greater level of populist and traditional music into their liturgy in an attempt to stem the tide of defections from their ranks.

I have also explained that some musical genres and forms like dùndún, bàtá, and neotraditional forms like jùjú and fújì, which are now generally assumed to represent a unified or pan-Yorùbá identity, are indeed grounded in Òyǫ́-Yorùbá culture more than they reflect "universal" Yorùbá traditions. The popularity of such forms in non-Òyǫ́ areas speaks to and derives from a pervading cultural hegemony of Òyǫ́-Yorùbá, a phenomenon which was initiated during the ascendancy of Òyǫ́ kingdom in the seventeenth and eighteenth centuries, and promoted by the British during the colonial era. The continuing domination of such musical forms and genres even now is a reflection of the enduring cultural dominance of Òyǫ́.

The various musical activities discussed in this book draw attention to the performativity of Yorùbá music, that is, its malleability and responsiveness to the specific needs of individuals and groups of people as defined at specific moments and as shaped by specific social and political dynamics. Complicating the idealism of a unified or pan-Yorùbá identity is a complex terrain of multiple identities and interests delineated according to status, gender, age, religious inclination, political ideology, economic interests, and ethnicity. My discussion throughout the book demonstrates how Yorùbá musical practices are shaped by individuals and groups to reflect, construct, and reconstruct these identities and interests. I stress the notion of a Yorùbá musical identity that is nuanced and responsive to individual experiences; one that reflects conflicts, competition, contradictions; and one that is marked by a constant process of adaptation, rejection, and resistance as envisioned by specific individuals and groups.

Appendix A

Fieldwork

Interviews and Performances

Musibau Ayanlere's Bàtá Ensemble (performances and interviews, Ìbàdàn; summers of 2006–11)

Musibau Ayanlere (ìyáàlu bàtá)
Amusa Ayanwole (omele abo)
Kasim Babatunde Ayanyemi (omele akọ)
Wasiu Ayangbemi (omele akọ)
Isiaka Ayanyemi (omele akọ)

Bata Drummers' Association, Ọ̀yọ́ State (performance and interview, Ìbàdàn; summer of 2007)

Chief Laisi Ayanwoola, Ààrẹ Oníbàtá of Ìgànnáland
Chief Ayangbekun Adigun, Ààrẹ Alubàtá of Ògbómọ̀șó
Chief Amusa Ayantayo, Baálẹ̀ Alubàtá of Ìbàdàn
Mr. Tafa Ayansola, alubàtá from Ìsẹ́yìn (deceased)
Chief Shittu Ayanleye, President, Oníbàtá of Ọ̀yọ́ State, and Ààrẹ Alubàtá of Ìsẹ́yìnland
Chief Matiu Ayanyemi, Ààrẹ Alubàtá of Ìsemi-Ilé
Pa Ayanriola Yekini Adigun, alubàtá from Ìbàdàn

Ayantunde's Dùndún Ensemble (performance and interview, Ò̩șogbo; summers of 2006–11)

Sule Ayantunde (iyáàlù)

Ayansola Oladosu (kánran ìsáájú)
Yinusa Ayanbiyii (kánran àtèlé)
Lasisi Ayanwale (gúdúgúdú)

Nigerian National Museum Cultural Troupe (performance and interview, Òşogbo; summer of 2006)

Sule Ayantunde (dùndún-ìyáàlù)
Mufutau Babatunde (a.k.a. Mambo; ìgbin)
Moshood Muritala (dùndún-kánran ìsáájú)
Sakirat Gbadamosu (dancer, lead chanter/singer)
Toyin Ajayi (dancer/singer)
Omotola Ojuade (dancer/singer)
Risikat Adewole (dancer/singer)
Nike Obisesan (dancer/singer)
Suleiman Aderibigbe (a.k.a. Şàngó; dancer/singer)

Monsurat Gbajumo's Wákà Group (performance and interview, Ikirun; summers of 2008 and 2011)

Monsurat Gbajumo
Ganiyat Abdulasis (singer/dancer)
Rasida Jimoh (singer/dancer)
Rukayat Tijani (singer/dancer)
Kayode Olagunju (àpàlà)
Taye Ayinla (omele ìşááju)
Saheed Oladejo (omele ikèhìn)
Ibrahim Asimiyu (manager)

Celestial Church of Christ Central Choir (performances and interviews, Ibafo-Lagos; summers of 2006–11)

Oluwole Adetiran (on the music of the CCC)
Rotimi Olaosebikan (on the music of the CCC)
Tunde Balogun (on the music of the CCC)
Kemi Adeneye (on the music of the CCC)

Olorì and Aírégbé Female Ensembles (performances and interviews, Emure-Ekiti; summers of 2006–10)

Her Royal Highness, Olori Funke Oshin (Queen of Emure-Ekiti)
Chief Morenike Awopetu (Iyalode, leader of Emure women)
Chief Lucia Ajayi (group lead singer)

Other Interviews

Elder Dafidi Ayandola (bàtá master drummer, on bàtá; June 2006, Òṣogbo)
Bisi Adeleke (dùndún master drummer; on dùndún; Atlanta and South
Hadley, MA, USA, 2006–10)
Baba Ramonu-Yekini Adigun (retired drummer at the Oyo State Arts
Council; on bàtá; Ìbàdàn, August 2007)
Dr. Segun Oyewo (on bàtá, Ilorin, 2000–2004, sundry occasions)
Dr. Tunde Adegbola (on bàtá, Ìbàdàn, July, 2011)
Dr. Yemi Olaniyan (on dùndún, Ile-Ife, July 2007)
Dr. Femi Fasheun (on the music of the CCC, Lagos, summers of 2006–11)
Kehinde Alake (on the construction of Yorùbá drums, Ibadan, July 2011)
Ayo Bankole jr. (on the music of Ayo Bankole Sr., Lagos, July 2011)
Christopher Ayodele (on Christian church music, Ìbàdàn, July 2010 and
2011)
Olaolu Omideyi (deceased, on Christian Church music, Ìbàdàn August
1999, 2000, sundry occasions)
Chief A. Ayelaagbe (on Christian church music, Ìbàdàn, September 1990)
Dr. Femi Abiodun (on Christian church music, Ìlọrin, 1999–2004, sundry
occasions)
Taye Adeola (on Christian church music, Ìlọrin, 1999–2004, sundry
occasions)
Dr. Moloye Bateye (on the music of Ayo Bankole, September–December
1984)
Dr. Victor Olaiya (on popular music, Lagos, January 2001, June 2006)
Mr. Bisade Ologunde (a.k.a. Lagbaja) (on popular music, by phone, 2007)

Appendix B

Audio Track List

Track No.	Title
1	"Aroko Bódúnde" (ìyáàlù dùndún part; ex. 2.1; Sule Ayantunde)
2	"Olúkòso Ọbakòso" (ìyáàlù dùndún part; ex. 2.2; Sule Ayantunde)
3	"Afasẹ́gbèjò" (ìyáàlù bàtá with omele; ex. 2.3; Musibau Ayanlere and his bàtá group)
4	"Moṣákẹ́kẹ́" (ìyáàlù bàtá with omele; ex. 2.4; Musibau Ayanlere and his bàtá group)
5	"Ọba Ko Yẹ Á" (ex. 4.1; Airegbe group, Emure-Ekiti)
6	"Olúṣẹgun, Àjàṣẹ́gun" by Dayo Dedeke (ex. 5.6; The Polytechnic Choir, Ibadan, directed by Christopher Ayodele)
7	"Kérésìmesì Odún Dé" by Dayo Dedeke (ex. 5.7; The Polytechnic Choir, Ibadan, directed by Christopher Ayodele)
8	"Èmi Yíó Gbẹ̆ Ojú Mi Sókè Wonnì" by Ekundayo Philips (ex. 5.9; The University of Ibadan Choir, directed by Tolu Owoaje)
9	"Olúwa Lo Lùṣọ́ Àgùntàn Mi" by Christopher Ayodele (ex. 5.10; The Polytechnic Choir, Ibadan, directed by Christopher Ayodele)
10	"A Ṣéẹ̀ṣe Ni Ká Má a Wí" (Central Choir, Celestial Church of Christ, directed by Wole Adetiran)
11	"Maṣe Dá ni Léjọ́" (Central Choir, Celestial Church of Christ, directed by Wole Adetiran)
12	Orin Ìgbéyàwó (Monsurat Gbajumo and the Islamic Voice of Solieena—Al Rishad)
13	Mi Ó Ní Sìn Wọ́n Wá Sáyé (Monsurat Gbajumo and the Islamic Voice of Solieena—Al Rishad)

Notes

Introduction

1. See Merriam, "Characteristics of African Music," 32–35.
2. Waterman, "Our Tradition Is Very Modern," 372.
3. Waterman, "Big Man, Black President," 20.
4. Turino, *Music as Social Life*, 116.
5. Ibid., 102.
6. Reily, "Discipline or Dialogue," 331.
7. Numbering close to 30 million people, the Yorùbá are perhaps the single largest ethnic group in Nigeria, if we consider the Hausa and the Fulani as two separate ethnic groups.
8. Munoz, *A Living Tradition*, 17. Oduduwa, the son of Lamurudu, is believed to have had seven sons, each of whom would become the founder and crowned king of a separate Yorùbá territory.
9. For further discussion on this, see Law, "Heritage of Oduduwa," 208.
10. Munoz, *A Living Tradition*, 17. For more discussions on this, see Johnson, *The History of the Yorùbás*; Idowu, *Olodumare in Yorùbá Belief*; Lloyd, *The Political Development of Yorùbá Kingdoms in the Eighteenth and Nineteenth Centuries*; Smith, *Kingdoms of the Yorùbá*; Falola and Oguntomisin, *Yorùbá Warlords of the Nineteenth Century*.
11. The geographical area known as Nigeria today was declared a British protectorate in 1901. In 1914, the northern and southern territories of that region were unified in a major move that would define the political map of Nigeria.
12. In chapter 1, I discuss the ways in which this notion of a pan-Yorùbá group, one that was defined largely around the more visible culture area of Ọ̀yọ́, has led to a greater level of patronage for the music of Ọ̀yọ́-speaking areas (especially in terms of research work on Yorùbá music) and the relative marginalization of the music of the non-Ọ̀yọ́-speaking areas.
13. The status of the Ọ̀yọ́ dialect as the standard written language received a major boost in 1884, when the Bible was translated into Yorùbá.
14. Ẹgbẹ́ Ọmọ Odùduwà provided the foundation for the Action Group, a Yorùbá-based political party formed by Obafemi Awolowo in 1951 to contest regional and national elections.
15. Munoz, *A Living Tradition*, 22.
16. This scenario applies, albeit in varying dimensions, to other Yorùbá states created from the old Western region. In the state of Ondo, for example, the cultural practices and the dialects of Àkúré, Ọ̀wọ̀, Oǹdó, and Àkókó, four of the main ethnic groups in the state, now enjoy a level of patronage similar to that of the Èkìtì in Èkìtì and the Ìjẹ̀bú in Ògùn.

17. Rattray, "The Drum Language of West Africa," 226.
18. Ward, "Music of the Gold Coast."
19. Jones, "African Rhythm."
20. Ibid., 26.
21. Agawu, *Representing African Rhythm*, 55–58.
22. Chernoff, *African Rhythm*; Anku, "Principles of Rhythmic Organization"; Locke, "The Music of Atsiagbekor"; Agawu, "Structural Analysis"; and Tang, *Masters of the Sabar.*
23. See, for example, Beier, "Yorùbá Vocal Music"; Laoye, "Yorùbá Drums"; and Bankole, Bush, and Samaan, "The Yorùbá Master Drummer."
24. See, for example, Thieme, "Three Yorùbá Members," and "A Descriptive Catalogue."
25. King, "Employment of the 'Standard Pattern'" and King, *Yorùbá Sacred Music from Ekiti.*
26. King, "Employment of the 'Standard Pattern,'" 52.
27. Olaniyan, "Compositional and Performance Technique"; and Euba, *Yorùbá Drumming.*
28. Villepastour, *Ancient Text Messages*, 1.
29. Brandel, "Africa," 17–24.
30. Agawu, "Structural Analysis or Cultural Analysis?" 41.
31. Klein, *Yoruba Bata Goes Global*, xxii.
32. Babalola, *Content and Form*; Olajubu, "Iwi Egungun Chants"; Barber, "Oriki, Women and Proliferation"; and Barber, *I Could Speak.*
33. Barber, *I Could Speak*, 249.
34. Phillips, *Yoruba Music*; Sowande, "The Catholic Church"; Beier, "Yoruba Vocal Music"; Mary Adebonojo, "Text-Setting in Yoruba Vocal Music"; Vidal, "Oriki in Traditional Yoruba Music"; Vidal, "Oriki, Praise Chants of the Yoruba"; Adegbite, "Oriki"; Euba, "Multiple Pitch Lines"; and Welch, "Ritual Intonation."
35. Sowande, "The Catholic Church," 42.
36. Welch, "Ritual Intonation," 156.
37. Hornbostel, "African Negro Music"; Schneider, "Tone and Tune"; Fiagbedzi, "Music of the Anlo"; Ekwueme, "Linguistic Determinants"; and Agawu, "Impact of Language."
38. Euba, *Essays on Music*; "Music Adapts"; "Islamic Musical Culture"; and "Concept of Neo-African Music."
39. Alaja-Brown, "Diachronic Study"; Waterman, *Juju*; Veal, *Fela*; Veal, "Jazz Music Influences"; and Olaniyan, *Arrest the Music!*
40. Euba, "Islamic Musical Culture"; and Omibiyi-Obidike, "Islamic Influence on Yoruba Music." From a religious perspective, Yorùbá popular music falls into two main categories: Christian-influenced and Islamic. Thus, while genres such as highlife, jùjú and Afro-beat reflect strong Euro-Christian influences, and are often performed by Christians, fújì, àpàlà, sákárà, and wákà belong to the category of Yorùbá Islamic popular music. See chapters 7 and 8 of this book for a discussion of these two categories.
41. Barber and Waterman, "Traversing the Global," 240.
42. Harnnerz, "The World in Creolization," 546–59.
43. Barber and Waterman, "Traversing the Global," 240–43. In a related study, based on the music of Ge (mask) performances of the Dan people of Western Côte d'Ivoire, Daniel Reed makes a similar observation about how Dan musicians integrate

the old and the new to generate modern musical performances that combine Western and traditional African elements. This phenomenon is particularly resonant in the title of the third chapter of Reed's book, which is derived from a traditional Dan proverb: "When a rooster goes for a walk he does not forget his house." This saying captures the attitude of Dan musicians toward the use of new and foreign musical material. Reed discusses how a Dan drummer incorporates modern "popular-music references" into his "personal expression of musical and cultural identity" (*Dan Ge Performance*, 63–64). Dan performers who appropriate modern and foreign elements do not represent a "blank slate upon which is inscribed the hegemonic imprint of mass-mediated popular culture" (ibid.). Reed's discussion also accounts for the role of modern African musicians as agents who invest the diverse elements that they engage in their creative and performance work with new meaning and significance (ibid., 65).

44. Chernoff, *African Rhythm and African Sensibility*, 153–54.
45. Bourdieu, *Outline of a Theory*; Certeau, *The Practice of Everyday Life*.
46. Stokes, *Ethnicity, Identity and Music*, 4.
47. Stokes, *Ethnicity, Identity and Music*, 4.
48. Shelemay, "Ethnomusicologist, Ethnographic Method," 201.
49. Turino, *Music as Social Life*, 94.
50. Linton, *The Study of Man*, 113, quoted in: Waterman, "I'm a Leader Not a Boss," 70.
51. Nettl, *Study of Ethnomusicology*, 278.
52. Barz, *Music in East Africa*, 63.
53. George Barz does stress the role and work of known individuals in this work. See Gregory Barz, *Music in East Africa*.
54. Monson, "Riffs, Repetition, and Theories," 25.
55. Weiss, "Permeable Boundaries," 234.
56. Ibid., 234–35.
57. Qureshi, "Sufi Music and the Historicity of Oral Tradition," 103.
58. Weiss, "Permeable Boundaries," 234–35.
59. Blacking, *Music, Culture and Experience*, 151, 161.
60. Barber, "Popular Arts in Africa," 5; quoted in Waterman, "Juju History," 50.
61. Qureshi, "Sufi Music," 103.
62. See Rice, "Towards a Mediation of Field Method and Field Experience in Ethnomusicology," 112–13.
63. Ibid. See also Bruno Nettl, *The Study of Ethnomusicology*, 155.
64. Stokes, "Music and the Global Order," 59.
65. Monson, "Riffs, Repetition, and Theories," 59–60.

Chapter One

1. Such names include Àyángbèmí (Àyàn is good for me); Àyánlérè (Àyán is profitable); Àyántúndé (Àyán has returned).
2. Euba, *Yoruba Drumming*, 90.
3. See Lucas, *The Religion of the Yorubas*; McKenzie, "Yoruba Orisa Cults; Awolalu, *Yoruba Beliefs and Sacrificial Rites*; Alana, "Traditional Religion"; and Falola and Genova, *Yoruba Gods and Spiritual Identity*.

4. For a discussion on the dual role of African masquerades as entertainers and a medium of spiritual communication, see Kasfir, "Elephant Women, Furious and Majestic."

5. Alana, "Traditional Religion," 69.

6. Ibid.

7. Some of these are pan-Yorùbá òrìṣà, that is, deities which are appeased all over Yorùbáland; while some are associated with specific local communities. For example, Òkèbàdàn is associated with Ìbàdàn city, while Ṣàngó and Ògún are pan-Yorùbá deities.

8. Euba, "Gods and Deputy Gods."

9. All these instruments, with the exception of bàtá, are cylindrical in shape, and single-headed membrane drums.

10. Adegbite, "The Drum and its Role in Yoruba Religion," 16.

11. See Johnson, *The History of the Yorubas*. Ṣàngó was an ancient Ọ̀yọ́ king who later became defied as the deity of thunder and lightning. Noted for his expansionist agenda, he was said to have sent one of his rebellious war generals, Tìmì, to Ẹ̀dẹ hoping that he would be attacked and killed there.

12. Waterman, "Our Tradition Is Very Modern," 371.

13. See Adedeji, "Alarinjo"; Euba, "Gods and Deputy Gods"; and Obayemi, "Culture in the Nigerian Economy."

14. See Euba, "Gods and Deputy Gods," 208. I discuss the performance features of eégún apidán later in the chapter.

15. I conducted this interview with Pa Ayandola in July 2006 at the Oshun grove in Òṣogbo.

16. Some of these towns lie outside the Ọ̀yọ́-speaking area. Ẹ̀fọ̀n-Alàyè is, for example in Èkìtì, while Òró, Ìjáráàsin, Ìlá-Ọ̀ràngún and Èsìẹ belong to Ìgbómìnà.

17. For a discussion of Yorùbá opera, see Omojola, "Yorùbá Folk Opera," 633–49.

18. For a study of kìrìbótó music, see Omojola, "Kìrìbótó Music."

19. This, according to my research assistants, was one of a suite of royal gestures marking the movement of Ọ̀yọ́ people from Old Ọ̀yọ́, the erstwhile headquarters of Ọ̀yọ́ kingdom, to their settlement in Àgódọ̀yọ́, the present city of Ọ̀yọ́, in 1836 under Aláàfin Àtìbà, the king at the time.

20. This information was provided during my field research in Ọ̀yọ́ in 1983.

21. Klein, *Yoruba Bata Goes Global*, 115.

22. See Hornbostel, "Ethnology of African Sound Instruments," 129; Nketia, *Ethnomusicology and African Music*, 256; Hornbostel and Sachs, "Classification of Musical Instruments," 83–113.

23. Adegbite, "Drum and Its Role," 19–20.

24. See Adegbite, "Drum and Its Role," 20.

25. See Villepastour, *Ancient Text Messages*, 77.

26. During a processional performance involving bàtá drummers and a masquerade known as Lábúàtá that I witnessed in Òṣogbo in July 2007, the challenge of playing bàtá drums was empirically demonstrated as the procession moved from one part of the city to another. The two master drummers alternated roles three times in the course of the procession to the king's palace, barely one kilometer from where the procession started.

27. This quotation is from an unpublished paper by Segun Oyewo, "Management in Yorùbá Traditional Arts."

28. For the use of these terms, see Adegbite, "Drum and Its Role," 20; and Ortiz, *Los instrumentos de la música afrocubana.*

29. See Beier, "Talking Drums," 30; and Euba, *Essays on Music*, 1:35. Ulli Beier, a German scholar, and Susan Wenger, an Austrian artist, who came to Nigeria in 1950 as a couple, played a major role in promoting indigenous Yorùbá music and musicians. They helped to launch the career of many modern Yorùbá artists and musicians, including the late Duro Ladipo (a performer of Yorùbá folk opera). For further discussion on the activities of Beier and Wenger, see Klein, *Yorùbá Bàtá Goes Global.*

30. Euba, *Yoruba Drumming*, 35.

31. Adegbite, "Drum and Its Role," 21.

32. Duro-Ladipo and Kolawole, "Opera in Nigeria," 126.

33. The musical repertories that form the basis for comparing the speech capabilities of bàtá and dùndún are those usually performed by both categories of drummers, including repertories based on proverbs and those deriving from sacred performances for deities like Ògún, Òṣun and Ṣàngó. They do not include those based on enàan bàtá, a form of coded speech that is exclusive to bàtá drummers.

34. Villepastour, *Ancient Text Messages*, 18.

35. The word *omele* designates not so much a particular drum as the function of accompaniment. The instrument generally used to perform the role of ìyáàlù may also be used to provide accompaniment patterns; at such times, that same instrument would be referred to as *omele.*

36. Not all drummers play ìyáàlù and omele abo bàtá drums this way. For example, bàtá drummers from Iganna in northern Yorùbáland usually play ojú òjò with the left hand, while the right hand, holding a leather beater, is used to play ṣáṣá.

37. See, for example, Villepastour, *Ancient Text Messages*, 5–6.

38. It is important to note that gendered words like ìyáàlù (or *ìyá-ìlù*) mother drum, omele abo (female support drum), *omele akọ* (male support drum) are not exclusive to a particular ensemble. They are used in connection with a variety of sacred and social drum ensembles, denoting musical roles rather than types.

39. Villepastour, *Ancient Text Messages*, 92.

40. Pa Dafidi Ayandola employed this coded language during my interview with him in Òṣogbo in July 2006. He had apparently told one of his bàtá drummer friends that he was hungry and did not have enough energy to pull through the interview that I was conducting with him. He only translated his message to me after I insisted. It was good that I did, for he responded much more enthusiastically to my questions after a lunch break.

41. Drummers' associations are very common in Yorùbá societies. Ethnomusicologists who have reported their work with such associations include Darius L. Thieme, who worked in Ọ̀yọ́ in the mid-1960s, and Akin Euba, who also worked in the Ọ̀yọ́ region. For further details, see Euba, *Yorùbá Drumming*, 101–2; and Thieme, "A Summary Report on the Oral Traditions of Yorùbá Musicians," 359–62.

42. The meeting of Ọ̀yọ́ State Bàtá Drummers Association was held on July 4, 2007, at Ile Oluwole, no. N4/664, Oje, Ìbàdàn, hosted by the Ìbàdàn branch of the association. The meeting was attended by bàtá drummers from all over Ọ̀yọ́ State.

43. This is a rough translation of a very popular Yorùbá proverb "*Ọgbọ́n ọlọ́gbọ́n ni kì í jẹ́ ká pe àgbà ní wèrè.*"

44. See Thieme, "Yoruba Music," 360.

45. Tang, *Masters of the Sabar.*

46. The term "melo-rhythm" was coined by ethnomusicologist Meki Nzewi to capture the melodic character of West African drum patterns. For more information on this, see Nzewi, "Melo-rhythmic Essence," 23–28.

47. Eégún òjè belong to the category of entertaining and friendly masquerades quite distinct and different from those considered ferocious and imbued with the ability to inflict pain, sickness, and even death by means of supernatural power. This second category of masquerades, usually known as *eégún alágbo*, are considered more sacred and are often called upon to spiritually purify the society, ward off enemies, or find solutions to grave situations such as famine, locust attacks, or epidemics, through spiritual appeasement and the enactment of sacred rituals.

48. Universities and colleges at which dùndún rather than bàtá instructors have been hired to teach Yorùbá drumming include the Obafemi Awolowo University, Ile-Ife; the University of Ilorin, Ilorin; The Polytechnic, Ìbàdàn; and Adeniran Ogunsanya College of Education, Lagos. College professors at all these schools told me that the dùndún mode of drumming was more accessible and easier to understand and learn than bàtá.

49. In 2011, when I traveled to Nigeria again to work with Ayanlere's group, two new members played in the ensemble. They were Wasiu Ayangbemi and Isiaka Ayanyemi, who alternated on the part of omele ako.

50. See Blum, Bohlman, and Neuman, *Ethnomusicology and Modern Music History*, 6.

51. See Villepastour, *Ancient Text Messages*; and Klein, *Yoruba Bata Goes Global.*

52. According to Musibau Ayanlere, the triadic drum row, omele mèta, because it may be played by a single person, is also cost-saving. The row consists of three drums, namely omele kúdí èjìn (a deepening secondary drum), omele kúdí ìsáájú (first "secondary" drum) and omele akò (second or male "secondary" drum). Omele kúdí èjìn and omele kúdí ìsáájú are tuned with the aid of ìda, a black paste applied to the drumhead. Omele kúdí èjìn, the deepest of the drums, has the heaviest paste; kudi ìsáájú, which plays a higher sound, has less. The highest of the omele, omele akò, has none.

53. Klein, *Yoruba Bata Goes Global*, xxxv.

54. Ibid.

55. Monson, *Freedom Sounds*, 25.

56. Waterman, "Juju History," 50–51.

57. Askew, *Performing the Nation*, 23.

58. Monson, *Freedom Sounds*, 25.

Chapter Two

1. Locke, "Africa," 101–2.

2. Ibid.

3. Ewe drum ensembles comprise of drums such as *totodzi, kloboto, kidi*, and *kaganu*. See David Locke, "Africa: Ewe, Mande, Shona, Baaka," in *Worlds of Music*, 75–121.

4. Chernoff, *African Rhythm*, 76.

5. King, *Yoruba Sacred Music*; Nketia, *The Music of Africa*; Carrington, "Musical Dimension of Perception"; Euba, *Yoruba Drumming*; Locke, "The Music of Atsiagbeko"; Agawu, *African Rhythm*; Adegbola, "Probabilistically Speaking"; and Tang, *Masters of*

the Sabar. For more discussions on this topic, see Armstrong, "Talking Drums"; Stern, "Drum and Whistle 'Languages'"; Ong, "African Talking Drums"; Locke and Agbeli, "Drum Language in Adzogbo"; Kwami, "Towards a Comprehensive Catalogue"; and Nzewi and Ohiaraumunna, "Beyond Song Texts."

6. See Nketia, *Funeral Dirge*, and Agawu, *African Rhythm*, 105.

7. Agawu, *African Rhythm*, 105.

8. Euba, *Yoruba Drumming*, 197.

9. Agawu, *African Rhythm*, 105–6; see also Euba, *Yoruba Drumming*, 205.

10. Euba, *Yoruba Drumming*, 197.

11. Agawu, *African Rhythm*, 105.

12. I should note that example 2.1 may also be performed during Ifá (divination) rites.

13. Richard Waterman, "African Influence on the Music of the Americas."

14. Hood, *The Ethnomusicologist*, and Kauffman, "African Rhythm."

15. Kubik, *Theory of African Music*, 1:31.

16. See King, "Employment of the 'Standard' Pattern," 51–54.

17. See Kubik, *Theory of African Music*, 1:52.

18. Ibid., 40.

19. This excerpt is only the opening part of an extended performance in honor of Ọ̀ṣun.

20. Ọ̀ṣun is regarded as the most important deity in Oshogbo. The people of the city believe that Ọ̀ṣun is their guardian, the deity who protected the city from attacks of powerful kingdoms in the past and continues to be the source of their blessings. It is generally believed, for example, that the development that the city of Ọ̀ṣogbo has witnessed in recent years is due to blessings from Ọ̀ṣun. Thus, although Ọ̀ṣun is often portrayed in terms of her beauty and her healing powers, this female deity is respected and revered by Oshogbo people for her ability to protect, ward off enemies, and bless in numerous ways.

21. Yorùbá drummers often use and sing these syllables (DA and DIN) to represent melo-rhythmic patterns that do not reference any text.

22. I should note that this groove may also be performed for Ọbàtálá, Egúngún and Ìbejì (twins).

23. *Konkolo* is a mnemonic for Yorùbá standard patterns such as the type played on kánran ìsáájú in example 2.2.

24. Cowry shells (edewó) were used as a form of money in precolonial Yorùbá society.

25. Asked why this particular phrase stands for Ṣàngó, Ayantunde responded, "We have always used it like that." It is however possible that phrases such as this one originally had specific lexical meanings which, in the course of historical time, slipped out of the memory of drummers and other members of the society.

26. Yorùbá bàtá drumming is also now practiced in Cuba because it was brought there by Yorùbá slaves. Afro-Cuban bàtá drumming is however considerably different from Yorùbá bàtá drumming, in spite of the historical and cultural connections between the two. For a discussion on Afro-Cuban bàtá drumming, see Robin Moore and Elizabeth Sayre, "An Afro-Cuban Bata Piece," in *Analytical Studies in World Music*, ed. Michael Tenzer (Oxford: Oxford University Press, 2006), 120–60.

27. Sunday Aladeniyi (a.k.a. Sunny Ade) incorporates this music in in his album Motimo/Destiny. A relatively new release of this album was produced in 2001 on the Masterdisc label (MDCD010).

28. Gbandikan is a vocable.

29. Omele méjì comprises of two omele, namely kúdí and omele ako. Omele kúdí is tuned with the use of *ìda* (black paste affixed to the drum head drum) to generate two tones. Omele ako does not make use of ída, and is made to play the highest of the three tones produced by the two drums.

30. Bàtá drummers generally explain that the role of omele abo is to act as a speech helper (ògbùfọ̀) for ìyáàlù. This process however requires a high degree of coordination between the player of ìyáàlù and that of omele abo, a skill now generally lacked by many modern day bàtá drummers. In the drumming of many such incompetent drummers, the sounds of omele abo, rather than enhancing the "talking" power of many bàtá ensembles, may actually make it much more difficult for the average listener to decipher the speech meanings of ìyáàlù, as I found out through my interaction with many bàtá players.

31. This manner of playing ìyáàlù bàtá is not a universal one. In the more northern part of Oyo state, for example in the town of Ìgànná, ojú ọ̀jò is beaten with the bare left hand while ṣáṣà is played with the right hand holding bílálà. This fact came to light during my work with Musibahu Ayanlere's ensemble when I noticed that the player of omele abo, Amusa Ayanwole, held the drum differently from Ayanlere. That was how I discovered that he originally hailed from Ìgànná.

32. Phillips, *Yoruba Music*, 1953.

33. When all the instruments of a traditional bàtá ensemble, namely, ìyáàlù bàtá, omele abo, omele akọ, kúdí, and èjìn, play together, a variety of pitches, both clear and vague, are activated. The sounds of the various instruments are often not synchronized toward the reflection of the Yorùbá text of ìyáàlù bàtá. It is however possible for a knowledgeable listener who is familiar with the particular text being played to aurally sieve through the density of musical material, connecting and linking pitch areas from different instruments of the ensemble to generate a melo-rhythmic line that reflects the tonal inflection of the Yorùbá text. In such cases, it is the listener who is "composing" the vocal inflections through the use of his or her ears in a process of creative listening even when the parts of ìyáàlù and omele abo are not necessarily synchronized by the musicians to articulate such a pattern. I was able to do this on a few occasions when I knew beforehand the particular Yorùbá text being played.

34. It is true that this problem applies to dùndún performances as well. The relative clarity of dùndún drumming however often facilitates a much easier process of decoding speech-based phrases not previously known to listeners.

35. On many occasions I asked different categories of listeners, including students, artisans, teachers, bankers, and petty traders to attempt to interpret the speech meanings of bàtá and dùndún drummers. Responses clearly indicated that it is far more challenging to decode speech meanings of bàtá drumming that those of dùndún.

36. Oyelami, *Yoruba Bàtá Music*.

37. Villepastour, *Ancient Text Messages*, 48.

38. Regarding the linguistic notion of Intrinsic Intensity, Villepastour explains that "soft vowels [i] and [u], [have] the lowest Intrinsic Intensity." These are vowels that are "spoken with the mouth relatively closed, [and] will take less time to articulate and will also register a lower volume." These contrast with the vowels [a], and, to an extent, [o] and [e], which "are the 'longest' and 'loudest.'" See Amanda Villepastour, *Ancient Text Messages* (Ashgate, London: SOAS Musicology Series, 2010), 52.

39. Villepastour, *Ancient Text Messages*, 57.

40. Sahlins, *Historical Metaphors and Mythical Realities*; and Waterman, "Juju History," 51.

41. Those who do not understand the speech meanings of speech-based drum patterns are often referred to as "ọ̀gbẹ̀rì aláìgbọ́lù."

Chapter Three

1. Shehan, "Balkan Women as Preservers," 45; Cohen, "Ya Salió," 55; and Sakata, "Hazara Women in Afghanistan," 85.

2. Post, "Professional Women in Indian Music," 107.

3. Koskoff, "An Introduction to Women, Music, and Culture," 11; Turner, *Music as Social Life*, 184; and Basso, Musical Expression and Gender Identity in the Myth and Ritual of the Kalapalo of Central Brazil," 163.

4. Auerbach, "From Singing to Lamenting," 25.

5. See Barber, *I Could Speak*. Oríkì, literally "head-praise," refers to the genre of the Yorùbá attributive praise poetry. It is often categorized according to its thematic focus. For example, individuals have their own oríkì, which may be performed at both formal and informal contexts. Such oríkì may be performed informally to pacify an angry child or formally to praise a king in public. In its genealogical focus, oríkì would typically recount the heroic activities of the ancestors of the person being praised in addition to cataloguing his or her notable achievement and attributes. Individuals, towns, families, and communities typically have their own oríkì.

6. The Èkìtì State, which was created in 1996, has a population of close to three million people. It is divided into twenty-six local government areas. Adó-Èkìtì, the main city, is the administrative and commercial capital of the state.

7. Askew, *Performing the Nation*, 23.

8. Turner, *Dramas, Fields, and Metaphors*; see Askew, *Performing the Nation*, 19.

9. Drewal, "The State of Research"; see Askew, *Performing the Nation*, 21.

10. Fabian, *Power and Performance*; Askew, *Performing the Nation*, 21.

11. Bauman, *Verbal Art as Performance*; Bauman, *Story Performance and Event*.

12. Butler, *Excitable Speech*, 40.

13. Most Yorùbá kings are polygamists; but not all olorì have sexual relationships with the reigning king. Tradition prescribes that newly installed kings "inherit" the wives of previous ones, a custom meant to guarantee that the new king fends for such women. Many of the women that I interacted with in Emùré explained to me that they are regarded as the wives of the reigning king, though are not married to him.

14. The Èkìtì people represent one of the many sub-ethnic groups that make up the Yorùbá. Other such groups include Ọ̀yọ́, Ìjẹ́ṣà, Ẹ̀gbá, Ìjẹ̀bú, and Ìgbómìnà, to mention just a few. Each of these groups speaks a dialect of the Yorùbá language, most of which are largely mutually intelligible.

15. Elémùré (literally, the owner of Emùré) is the official title of the king of Emùré-Èkìtì. Rulers are chosen through consultation with the ifá oracle from established royal families in a hereditary succession that is similar to what obtains in other parts of Yorùbáland. Elémùré rules in consultation with a council of chiefs, membership of which is also largely hereditary.

16. The tradition of orin olorì (songs or music of the king's wives) is unique to the Èkìtì part of Yorùbáland. I have yet to come across this tradition in non-Èkìtì parts of

Yorùbá land. Mosunmola Omibiyi-Obidike, a professor of ethnomusicology who has conducted extensive research in many parts of Yorùbáland, told me in an informal discussionthat she had yet to come across any such palace-affiliated all-female musical ensemble in any other part of Yorùbáland. She agreed with this writer that this tradition is unique to the Èkìtì-Yorùbá.

17. Ìkọ́lé-Èkìtì is the administrative headquarters of the Ìkọ́lé local government area of the Èkìtì State.

18. Oyewumi, *The Invention of Women*, 31.

19. Koskoff, "An Introduction to Women, Music, and Culture," 5.

20. Ṣàngó, believed to be an ancient king of the old Ọ̀yọ́ kingdom, is now the Yorùbá deity of thunder and lightning. Yemoja is a Yorùbá female deity often described as a patron deity of women.

21. Matory, *Sex and the Empire That Is No More*, 519.

22. Ibid., 521–22.

23. Koskoff, "An Introduction to Women, Music, and Culture," 9.

24. Oyeronke Olajubu, *Women in the Yoruba Religious Sphere*, 22.

25. Ibid.

26. For further discussions on this issue see Ogundipe, Molara, "The Invention of Women"; Okome, "African Women and Power"; Oyewumi, "Visualizing the Body," 3–22; and Amadiume, *Re-inventing Africa*.

27. Koskoff, "An Introduction to Women," 10.

28. Yorùbá culture boasts of a range of performances and rituals that may be enacted to punish erring members of a community. Kings and highly placed leaders are not exempt from such punishing performances. For example, a townwide processional performance by singing naked women is a rare form of punishment against a ruling king, sending a message that he should abdicate. The efficacy of this form of protest derives from the belief that a king is tabooed from seeing a naked body.

29. Barber, "*Oriki*, Women and Proliferation," 328–29. See also Barber, *I Could Speak*, 96–105.

30. This seems to be a general trend in Africa. For studies devoted to this issue, see Beverly, *Muslim Women Sing*; and Nannyonga-Tamusuza, *Baakisimba*.

31. Musibau Ayanlere told me, for example, that his sisters joined the family ensemble performances on many occasions when they were young, but that the boys were encouraged to master the drum, since it was believed that they were more likely to continue the family tradition than the girls, who would leave the home when they got married.

32. The annual festival in Òṣogbo is an extended event running into weeks. My discussion here refers to the final day, the grand finale that attracts participants from all over the world. Two most important activities leading up to the final day of the festival are a town-wide procession (*ìwọ́-pópó*) and the lighting of the sixteen-burner lamp (*àtùpà olójú mẹ̀rìndínlógún*). The townwide procession is conceived to sensitize the people about the various activities leading up to the final festival, while the lighting of the sixteen-burner lamp is a nighttime ritual involving the king, his family and some devotees, including the chief priestess (the Ìyá Òṣun). In the ritual, the king dances around the burner while offering prayers for the people of the town. For further discussions on the Òṣun deity and festival, see Adepegba, "Òṣun and Brass"; Abiodun, "Hidden Power"; Alcamo, *Iya Nla*; Badejo, *Òṣun Seegesi*; Badejo, "Authority and Discourse in the Orin Ọdún Òṣun"; and Olupona, "Imagining the Goddess."

33. My discussion here focuses on the Òṣun festival as practiced in Nigeria. For studies devoted to the practice of the Òṣun religion in Yorùbá Diaspora communities, see Castellanos, "A River of Many Turns"; Ribeiro dos Santos, "Nesta cidade todo mundo"; Murphy, "Yeye Cachita"; Flores-Pena, "Overflowing with Beauty"; Brandon, "Ochun in Bronx."

34. The Igbó Òṣun or Odò Òṣun is the sacred grove housing the main Òṣun shrine. Located in what used to be the center of Òṣogbó town, the seventy-five-hectare grove was in 2005 inscribed a world heritage center. It is an expansive piece of land and forest on the Òṣun River.

35. The votary maid is a virgin chosen from the royal family. A new one is chosen each year to perform the role of carrying the calabash of sacrifice from the palace to the grove during the festival. Her arrival at the scene of the shrine marks the climax of the festival. She is seen as the embodiment of the spirit of Òṣun. Participants at the festival would, on sighting her, intensify their prayers that Òṣun should bless, protect, and heal them, and provide for their needs. These prayers are believed to be most efficacious when the votary maid moves to a secret location within the grove to empty the items of sacrifice. Tradition prescribes that the votary maid be given in marriage immediately after performing this role. Usually the bridegroom for the votary is known before the festival, and wedding arrangements are already in top gear by the time the festival is held.

36. Drewal and Drewal, *Gelede*, xv.

37. Apter, *Black Critics and Kings*, 112.

38. King, *Yoruba Sacred Music*, 1961.

39. Anthony King's study is based on the music of a group of Òyọ́ settlers in Ìfàkì-Èkìtì, a small Yorùbá town in Èkìtì State, just a few miles from Adó-Èkìtì, the state capital.

40. See Euba, "Multiple Pitch Lines," for a discussion of these features in the vocal musics of Èkìtì and Ìjèṣà sub-ethnic groups.

41. See Euba, *Yoruba Drumming*, 28–29.

42. Examples of this include the exclusive use of a shaken cylindrical idiophone, known as pàṣọ́ọ̀rọ̀ by Ogori women in Kogi State, and the exclusive use of àpíìrì clay drums by women in towns like Ìjerò, Ìlawẹ́ and Òkèmẹ̀sí in Èkìtì State.

43. The use of music to distinguish the identity of a female group here differs from those in which music is used as a tool of oppositional gendering. For examples of the later type, see Rothenbusch, "The Joyful Sound"; Petersen, "An Investigation into Women-Identified Music in the United States"; and Robertson, "Power and Gender in the Musical Experiences of Women."

44. Turino, *Music as Social Life*, 95.

Chapter Four

1. Ampene, *Female Song Tradition*, 11.

2. Ibid., 8.

3. Merriam, "Characteristics of African Music,"165–84; and Ampene, *Female Song Tradition*, 11.

4. Dor, "Communal Creativity," 26.

5. Waterman, "Juju History," 50.

6. I was commuting from Adó-Èkìtì, a distance of about 25 miles, during my field-work in Emùré-Èkìtì.

7. Olorì Qṣìn is the widow of the immediate past king who died early 2007. As an Emùré chief, she holds regular meetings with other female chiefs. And because of her position as the immediate past main olorì, she provides guidance and leadership to other female chiefs as well as to other olorì, even though her position has now been taken over by the first wife of the incumbent king.

8. A short comment on the etymology of these two words is instructive. Ègbè liter-ally means "support," while èṣà means "the chosen." Ègbè, a noun, derives from the verb gbè, which means "to support," while èṣà derives from the verb "to choose."

9. Gbàmọ is an exclusive male group comprising of an elite group of young men trained as soldiers and hunters and on whom the defense of Emùré depends. Gbàmọ may be compared to a modern elite military unit with a rapid response capability.

10. Owálúayé translates as "the owner of the earth." Titles such as this show that Yorùbá kings are held in great awe. A related title is Ekeji Orisa, by which any Yorùbá king may be addressed. It translates as "the companion of the gods."

11. Barber and Waterman, "Traversing the Global," 256. It should also be noted that fújì belongs to the category of Yorùbá Islam-influenced popular music, which I discuss in chapter 8. For other relevant discussions, see Omibiyi-Obidike, "Islamic Influence on Yoruba Music"; and Euba, "Islamic Musical Culture among the Yoruba."

12. Barber and Waterman, "Traversing the Global," 241.

13. Ìwí, another form of Yorùbá chant, is associated with the Yorùbá egúngún [traditional mask]. For an introductory discussion on Ìwí, see Oludare Olajubu, "Ìwí Egúngún Chants," 31–51.

14. Òwọ̀ is a major Yorùbá town in Oǹdó state.

15. Adó-Èkìtì is the capital of Èkìtì state of Nigeria.

16. Ìkọ̀lé, about forty miles from Emùré-Èkìtì, is the headquarters of the Ìkọ̀lé-Èkìtì local government area of Èkìtì state (the Federal Republic of Nigeria is made of up thirty-six states, which are subdivided into smaller administrative formations known as local government areas).

17. The Qlọ́wọ̀ (king of) Òwọ̀ is unique for his ceremonial dress, made completely of beads.

18. Yorùbá crowned kings are traditionally defined as those whose ancestors received a special crown from the first major Yorùbá king, Odùduwà. Although newly crowned kings have emerged in recent years through promotion by modern political leaders, crowned kings, in traditional Yorùbá parlance, are those whose crowns ante-dated the colonial era and were given to them directly by Odùduwà.

19. The "ordinary eye" figuratively refers to the average person who has neither the spiritual powers nor the requisite knowledge of charms to engage supernatural forces or deal with men or women who have extraordinary powers. This statement serves once again to depict the power of the Yorùbá king and the respect that his subjects, men and women, accord him. Although the king is loved by everyone and is indeed accessible to all his subjects, he is also seen as someone with supernatural powers by virtue of his position as king. The process of installing a Yorùbá king often takes many days and involves elaborate rituals through which, it is believed, the king becomes transformed from an ordinary person into a "companion of the gods." For a discussion on the music which helps to define the status of kings, see Euba, "Gods and Deputy Gods."

20. Waterman, "Big Man, Black President," 23. This idea is vividly conveyed in the popular Yorùbá saying: "Ènìyàn laṣọ ọ̀ mi" which translates as: "My people are the "clothes" that I wear; without them, I am naked."

21. Although I could hear clear European-type metric orientation in this song, my transcription of "Ọba Kọ Yẹ Á" conveys only pitch relationships. It is also important to note that there is significant disparity between the fixed nature of the notes in my transcription and the flexible, often microtonal, nature of the performance.

22. Agawu, *Representing African Music*, 99–100.

23. This statement was made in an interview I conducted with them in July 2009.

24. Sowande cautioned against making general statements that suggest that all African songs are short, fragmentary and percussive. See Sowande, "The African Musician in Nigeria," 27.

25. See Blum, Bohlman, and Neuman, *Ethnomusicology and Modern Music History*, 4.

26. Rice, "Disciplining *Ethnomusicology*, 322.

Chapter Five

1. Turino, *Music as Social life*, 121.

2. See appendix A for details.

3. See also Kidula, "Making and Managing Music," 106.

4. I have provided a fairly detailed historical background of modern Nigerian music in two earlier works. See Omojola, *Nigerian Art Music*; and Omojola, *Music of Fela Sowande*. In order to locate my present discussion within its appropriate socio-musical milieu, however, I provide a brief summary here, based on my earlier discussions in the two aforementioned publications.

5. Leonard, *Growth of Entertainment*, 29–33.

6. For a detailed discussion on the growth of Victorian art forms, including music, in Nigeria, see Leonard, *Growth of Entertainment*.

7. Omojola, *Nigerian Art Music*, 14.

8. Roberta King, "Global Church: Lessons from Africa," 136.

9. See Omojola, *Nigerian Art Music* for a discussion of these composers and their works.

10. This point has been variously and extensively discussed by many scholars, including Euba, "Multiple Pitch Lines in Yorùbá Choral Music," 66–71; and Ekwueme, "Linguistic Determinants of Some Igbo Musical Properties."

11. Church Missionary Society, *Iwe Orin Mimo*.

12. This was not possible within the orthodox churches, many of which remained largely controlled by Western missionaries far into the second half of the twentieth century. Yorùbá translations of European hymns continue to feature in these and other Yorùbá churches to this day.

13. See King, "Beginnings," 6; and "Music Culture: Euro-American Christianity," 34. The Yorùbá Aládǔrà movement refers to churches that lay a strong emphasis on the incorporation of Yorùbá cultural practices into Christian worship. The churches include the African Church, the Cherubim and Seraphim Church, the Christ Apostolic Church, and the Celestial Church of Christ, a relatively new arrival to the fold, which I discuss in chapter 6. For more details, see Webster, *The African Church*.

14. Emmanuel Sowande was Fela Sowande's father.

15. The Reverend J. J. Kuti was the grandfather of Nigeria's late Afro-beat king, Fela Anikulapo-Kuti. For further discussions on the Kuti family, see Delano, *The Singing Minister of Nigeria*; and Delano, *Josiah Ransome-Kuti*.

16. The man who trained many of Nigeria's composers of art music, including Fela Sowande, Ayo Bankole, and Sam Akpabot.

17. Akin George was the maternal grandfather of Ayo Bankole.

18. Phillips, *Yoruba Music*.

19. Exceptions to this neglect exist in the following works: Olatunji, "The Biography of T. K. E. Phillips," and Sadoh, *Thomas Ekundayo Phillips*.

20. Phillips, *Yoruba Music*, 5.

21. Scholes, *The Oxford Companion*; and Grove, *Grove's Dictionary of Music*.

22. Phillips, *Yoruba Music*, 9.

23. Ibid., 34.

24. Ibid.

25. Dedeke, *Má Gbàgbé Ilé*. The title translates in English as *Remember Your Roots*.

26. As a pupil at Christ's School, Ado-Ekiti, this writer was part of the school choir that Dedeke came to train on many occasions between 1973 and 1976.

27. The Pratt School of Music, which was affiliated to the Royal Academy of Music, London, was established in 1940 by one Professor Pratt. The school was one of the institutions that initiated professional training in European music in Nigeria.

28. Phillips, *Vesicles and Responses*. For a list of works by other Nigerian composers, see Akin Euba, *Modern African Music*; and Omojola, *Nigerian Art Music*, 135–47.

29. Phillips's *Vesicles and Responses* is still in use in all the Yorùbá speaking Anglican churches across the country.

30. Phillips, *Vesicles and Responses*.

31. This modal practice recalls a similar procedure in the traditional Yorùbá song, "Ọba Kọ Yẹ Á," which I discussed in chapter 4.

32. The word "lyrics" is used by Nigerian local church organists to refer to church anthems by nonprofessional composers. Such works are usually set to Yorùbá lyrics, written in solfège notation, sung in unison, taught by rote, and accompanied by drums, shakers, metal gong, and organ. These works are different from those by Western-educated composers like Phillips and Christopher Ayodele, whose compositions are written in European staff notation and display a more intimate knowledge of European harmonic and formal procedures.

33. Anthems are also rendered to accompany thanksgiving processions by congregational members as they dance from their seats to the altar.

34. Oriere's songs are printed under the title *Orin Ìtùnú* (Songs of Consolation). The songs, which are now rarely used, were widely popular from the mid-1960s till the early 1980s, especially in the old Oǹdó Anglican Diocese, which was comprised of all the churches in the present states of Èkìtì and Oǹdó.

35. I recall singing these songs as a young boy at the Emmanuel Anglican Church Cathedral in Adó-Èkìtì, the church that my parents and my entire family attended when I was growing up.

36. I worked with Chief I. F. Ayelaagbe as an assistant choirmaster and organist at the Saint Stephen's Anglican Church, Ináléndé, in Ìbàdàn in the early 1980s, and I had a firsthand experience of the process of composing and performing anthems. On many occasions, we encouraged talented choristers with virtually no musical training to compose songs for the choir. Chief Aiyelaagbe or I would thereafter

improvise an organ accompaniment. Drummers who were also members of the choir provided improvised accompaniment to the music.

37. The Ìgbàjà style is popular in Kwara and Kogi states where the Evangelical Church of West Africa (ECWA) has a strong presence.

38. In another example, *Kì í ṣe Gbogbo Ẹniti ń Pè Mí* (Not Everyone That Calls Me God), the piano is used to reinforce the ternary division of the piece. The middle section contrasts with the outer sections through its irregular phrases. This contrast is further articulated through the harmonic interpretation of m. 16 as an added-sixth chord, which helps to bring a suspended quality to the section. The suspension is resolved in the re appearance of the opening section.

39. Yemi Olaniyan holds a PhD in ethnomusicology and teaches at the Obafemi Awolowo University, Ile-Ife; while Christopher Ayodele, a music graduate of Ibadan Polytechnic, teaches music in the department of music technology. Ayo Ogunranti, a doctoral student at the University of Pittsburgh, has held the position of organist in several churches in Ibadan.

40. William, "A Theory of Structure," 25.

Chapter Six

1. Friedson, *Dancing Prophets*. See also Kidula, "Music Culture," 47.
2. Muller, *Rituals of Fertility and the Sacrifice of Desire*, 20.
3. Ibid., 18.
4. Ibid., 20.
5. See also Weman, "African Music and the Church in Africa," 20.
6. Muller, *Rituals of Fertility and the Sacrifice of Desire*, 18.
7. Ibid.
8. King, "Bible: Lex Canendi, Lex Credendi,"118.
9. According to Helen Crumbley, "AICs, two-thirds of which are in three countries—South Africa, Congo, and Nigeria—are estimated to have had 42,000 members in early 1900s and grew to 54 million adherents by 2000, making up 14 percent of the African population." See Crumbley, *Spirit, Structure, and Flesh*, 18.
10. Peel, *Aladura*; Adegboyega, *A Short History*; Omoyajowo, *Cherubim and Seraphim*; Olupona, "New Religious Movements"; and Oduro, "Church Music in the Life." See also Opoku, "A Brief History," 22–26.
11. Crumbely, *Spirit, Structure, and Flesh*, 28.
12. See the following: Adegboyin and Ademola, *African Indigenous Churches*; Olayiwola, "The Social Impact of New Aladura Movements on Contemporary Yoruba Life"; Olayiwola, "Church and Healing in Nigeria"; Mbon, "The Quest for Identity"; Peel, *Religious Encounter and the Making of the Yoruba*; Anderson, *African Reformation*; and Ositelu, *African Instituted Churches*.
13. See, for example, Oshun, "The Pentecostal Perspective of the Christ Apostolic Church."
14. See Adogame, *Celestial Church of Christ*.
15. Henning, Klaus, and Ritz-Müller, *Soul of Africa*, 472.
16. Ibid., 470.
17. Ibid.
18. Ibid.

19. Candles, honey, and sugar are symbolic of the light, joy and abundant life that come with worshipping God as a member of the Celestial Church of Christ.

20. Processions such as this typify the celebration of Yorùbá religious festivals, which are also performed as thanksgiving ceremonies. I discuss examples of such processions in chapter 1.

21. In the Celestial Church of Christ, individuals are generally encouraged to build sanctuaries as donations to the church.

22. The University of Nigeria, Nsukka (UNN) is Nigeria's first indigenous university, but not the first university in Nigeria. The first university in Nigeria, the University of Ibadan, remained a campus of the University of London until 1962, two years after UNN was founded. For many years the UNN was the only university in Nigeria offering degree and diploma programs in Music. It was not until 1977, that another university, the University of Ife (now Obafemi Awolowo University) started a degree program in music. Today, however, music can be studied in many federal, state and private universities in the country.

23. This is another example of how dùndún drums have been incorporated into modern performance traditions in Yorùbáland. See chapters 1 and 2 for a detailed discussion of this issue.

24. This song reminds me of a popular Yorùbá folk tune entitled "Ògòngò Baba Ẹyẹ," whose text goes as follows: "Ògòngò Baba ẹyẹ, kìnìún baba ẹranko, àwá jù wọ́n lọ tẹ́lẹ̀tẹ́lẹ̀, ojú ni wọ́n yá, àwa rèé o." The English translation is as follows: "Ògòngò (ostrich), king of birds, kìnìún (lion), king of all animals, we are greater than our enemies; we are here, formidable as ever." This is a song of abuse, and often rendered during competitions between local youth clubs engaged in wrestling competitions or in soccer competitions. I recall singing this song along with my high school mates to intimidate rival schools during inter-school soccer, hockey and volleyball competitions. The CCC song attempts to symbolize the supremacy of God through references to the superiority of the lion over other animals.

25. See chapter 8 for a discussion of fújì music.

26. It must be noted however that such prolongations are uncommon at concert performances outside the church, especially when they are attended by nonmembers of the CCC. In such performances, a more formal concert presentation is typical. Adetiran's conducting approach at such concerts is also very professional and businesslike, as expected of a highly trained musician.

27. Waterman, "Our Tradition Is Very Modern," 371; and Geertz, *The Interpretation of Cultures*, 451.

28. Crumbley, *Spirit, Structure, and Flesh*, 18.

29. Floyd, *The Power of Black Music*, 6.

Chapter Seven

1. Slobin, "Micromusics of the West," 2, 4, 61.
2. Erlmann, "Aesthetics of Global Imagination," 467–87.
3. Monson, "Riffs, Repetition, and Theories," 48–49.
4. Ibid., 49.
5. Ibid., 60.

6. Bakhtin, *The Dialogic Imagination*, 358–59.

7. Ibid.

8. Stokes, "Music and the Global Order," 60–61.

9. Bhabha, *The Location of Culture*, 112.

10. Bakthin, *The Dialogic Imagination*, 358. See also Clifford, *The Predicament of Culture*, 23; Young, *Colonial Desire*, 23; and Bakrania, "Hybridity."

11. Stokes, "Music and the Global Order," 59.

12. Valdivia, "Geographies of Latinidad," 309–10.

13. Alaja-Browne, "A Diachronic Study of Change in Juju Music"; Waterman, *Jùjú*; Veal, "Jazz Music Influences"; Veal, *Life and Times*; Olaniyan, "The Cosmopolitan Nativist"; and Olaniyan, *Arrest the Music!* For similar studies on Nigeria and on other parts of Africa, see Bender, *Sweet Mother: Modern African Music*; Collins, *West African Pop Roots*; Erlmann, *Night Song*; Agawu, *Representing African Music*; Barz, *Music in East Africa*; Schoonnmaker, *Fela*; Muller, *South African Music*; and Tang, *Masters of the Sabar*.

14. Waterman, "Our Tradition Is Very Modern," 372.

15. Ibid., 374.

16. Weiss, "Permeable Boundaries, 205.

17. The concept of the average Yorùbá person is not easily defined. In the colonial era, there was a considerable social gap between members of the Western-educated Yorùbá elite in cities like Lagos and Ìbàdàn and the ordinary people whose lives revolved around traditional institutions, and who constituted the majority of the population.

18. I. K. Dairo was honored with the title of MBE (Member of the British Empire) by the Queen of England in 1963 (see http://en.wikipedia.org/wiki/Music_of_Nigeria).

19. Àpàlà music, which was pioneered by Haruna Ishola, dates back to the 1940s and represents the earliest medium for popularizing indigenous Yorùbá drumming outside religious and social ceremonies. One of the more recent examples of such Islam-affiliated musical genres is *fújì*. Popularized by musicians like Kolawole Ayinla (a.k.a. Kollington) and Alhaji Ayinde Barrister, *fújì* remains one of the most widely patronized examples of Yorùbá popular music today. For a detailed discussion of Yorùbá Islamic music, see chapter 8.

20. Euba, *Essays on Music*, 1:129.

21. Waterman, *Juju*, 45.

22. Ibid., 48.

23. For Olaiya's full biography, see Omojola, "Politics, Identity, and Nostalgia."

24. Victor Olaiya, "Ìlú Le" (Times are hard), LP Polydor [Lagos] POLP 096, 1983. For further details about Olaiya's albums and recordings, see http://en.wikipedia.org/wiki/Victor_Olaiya.

25. The konkolo is the Yorùbá antecedent of the Afro-Cuban clave pattern.

26. Please note that there are different rerecordings of this music, and indeed of the two other songs analyzed in this chapter. The timeline and duration provided in my tables for each of the songs may therefore be slightly different from the recordings in the possession of the reader.

27. Olaiya's Stadium Hotel, which has been functioning since the early 1970s, is the most popular spot for the performance of highlife music in Lagos, Nigeria's commercial capital. The hotel houses Olaiya's business office, a performance arena, a bar, and some shops and suites. The size of the hotel speaks to the success of Olaiya's

musical career. Apart from the late Bobby Benson, who had a thriving, but now abandoned nightclub, the Caban Bamboo, also in Lagos, no other highlife musician owns such an edifice.

28. I discuss this and other forms of Islamic popular music in chapter 8.

29. Olaniyan, "The Cosmopolitan Nativist"; and Veal, *Fela*.

30. Victor Olaiya provided this information when I interviewed him in February 2003 and 2006. He explained that Fela Anikulapo-Kuti worked with him before proceeding to England and that some of the early songs of the Koola Lobitos (the name of Anikulapo-Kuti's first band) were those which Fela had performed while working with him prior to his departure for England.

31. It has been suggested that his visit to the US marked the beginning of his political music career. This is a plausible suggestion, given the considerable scope of political exposure that he gained during his tour. But Fela Anikulapo-Kuti's personal brushes with the Nigerian police also represented a major factor in his transformation from an apolitical musician to an activist.

32. See Rotberg, *Nigeria*; Paden, *Faith and Politics*; Kalu, *State Power, Autarchy*; and Adekunle, *Religion in Politics*.

33. For ease of reading, all music examples are written in one key.

34. See Moore, and Sayre, "An Afro-Cuban Bata Piece for Obatala, King of the White Cloth," 126.

35. Olaniyan, "The Cosmopolitan Nativist."

36. See appendix A for a list of some of Lagbaja's albums.

37. See chapter 1 for a discussion of an example of the Yorùbá egúngún performance.

38. J. J. Hensley, "Behind the Mask," *Pitch*, July 12, 2001, http://www.pitch.com/kansascity/behind-the-mask/Content?oid=2163656.

39. "Africano," *Lágbájá*.com, accessed May 24, 2012, http://www.lagbaja.com/africano/africano.php.

40. These are descriptive labels for the shapes of the headgear. "National theatre," for example, refers to headgear that has a shape similar to that of the Nigeria's national theatre in Lagos.

41. These are the tonal areas that I deciphered aurally when I listened to the music. It is not certain whether Lagbaja is aware of these specific tonal areas in his music. What is clear, however, is the fact that the opening section, because of the use of the guitars and heptatonic melodies, bears a strong influence of European music. The Yorùbá ceremonial section, on the other hand is dominated by pentatonic folksongs rendered without the accompaniment of any melodic instrument.

42. Turino, *Music as Social Life*, 106.

43. Monson, "Riffs, Repetition, and Theories," 36.

44. Ibid., 36, 44.

Chapter Eight

1. Omojola, *Popular Music in Western Nigeria*.

2. Nigeria, with a population of about 150 million people, is today roughly equally divided between Christians and Muslims. The northern part is a predomi-

nantly Muslim region, while the southern part is predominantly Christian. The Yorùbá ethnic group, although predominantly Christian, has the largest Islamic population among the ethnic groups in southern Nigerian. Some Yorùbá families are split down the middle between Christianity and Islam. A man may be a Muslim while his wife is a Christian, with the children having the freedom to choose to belong to either of the two religions. The mixed nature of religious affiliation within Yorùbá families provides the demographic setup for the popularity of Islamic popular music across religious divides in Yorùbá society.

3. Omojola, *Popular Music in Western Nigeria*, 50.

4. See Priscilla Starrati, "Islamic Influences on Oral Traditions," 159–75.

5. See Brenner, *Muslim Identity and Social Change*, 1–20.

6. Omojola, "History, Style and Identity," 189–210.

7. Euba, *Essays on Music*, 2:126–27.

8. Musiliu Haruna's main album, *Soyoso*, released in 2004, was conceived to promote àpàlà music to a younger generation of listeners.

9. The Yorùbá lamelaphone, àgídìgbo, is much bigger than the Shona mbira, and plays a limited range of notes—just about three or four. Unlike the Shona mbira, it plays mainly bass ostinato patterns.

10. In 1981, Haruna Ishola was given the national award of Member of the Order of Nigeria (MON) by the federal government of Nigeria in acknowledgment of his contributions to cultural development and the promotion of Yorùbá music.

11. Ìjèbú-Igbó is a town located in Ògùn State.

12. One of the pioneers of jùjú music discussed briefly in chapter 7.

13. See Banning Eyre's short biography of Haruna Ishola at Afropop.org, accessed December 19, 2009, http://www.afropop.org/explore/artist_info/ID/375/Haruna%20Ishola/.

14. For a fairly comprehensive list of Ishola's discography, see "Discography of Haruna Ishola: The Late Great Apala Singer," updated October 22, 2010, http://biochem.chem.nagoya-u.ac.jp/~endo/EAIshola.html.

15. Herbert Macaulay was a prominent Nigerian nationalist of the colonial era.

16. Bode Thomas was a prominent Yorùbá politician of the early 1960s.

17. Aláàfin is the title of the king of the ancient Yorùbá kingdom of Òyó. Following the demise of the kingdom, the title now refers to the king of Òyó town.

18. Chief Obafemi Awolowo was the first premier of Western Region, a predominantly Yorùbá geopolitical region of Nigeria, in the late 1950s and early 1960s. He was also Nigeria's leader of the Opposition during the same period. Between 1979 and 1983, he led the Unity Party of Nigeria, a political party which controlled five of the former nineteen states in the country. The party also played the role of opposition within the presidential system of government during the period.

19. The cockerel and the palm tree were the symbols of two of Nigeria's political parties in the late 1950s and the early 1960s. The palm tree was the symbol of the Action Group (AG), a political party led by Chief Obafemi Awolowo, while the cockerel was adopted by another political party, the National Council for Nigerian and Cameroon (NCNC), led by Nigeria's foremost nationalist leader, Herbert Macaulay.

20. Euba, *Essays on Music*, 2:11.

21. See Ahmed, *Women and Gender*; Strobel, *Muslim Women in Mombasa*.

22. Salawa Abeni was at some point married to Kolawole Ayinla Kollington. Her music was substantially influenced by that of Kollington, notably in the incorporation of Western musical instruments like the synthesizer keyboard and the drum set.

23. There is a sense in which the use of the keyboard by Islamic music singers represents an attempt to compete with Christian gospel artists who typically feature the keyboard more prominently than Islamic singers. In both cases, the use of the keyboard helps to attract the patronage of younger generation of listeners, thus boosting the evangelical mission of the two religions. The increasing use of other Western musical instruments, like the guitar and the Western drum set, by Muslim singers could also be seen from this perspective. It must, however, be stressed that Muslim musicians do not use these instruments in the same way that they are used in Christian-affiliated music. In Yorùbá Islamic popular music, they are used rhythmically rather than harmonically, a practice guided by an attempt to carve an identity that is different from that of the Christian-affiliated music.

24. See Alidou, *Engaging Modernity*, 1.

25. White, "Congolese Rumba and Other Cosmopolitanism," 663–86.

26. See Brenner and Last, "The Role of Language"; Starrati, "Islamic Influences"; McLaughlin, "Islam and Popular Music"; and Charry, "Music and Islam."

Conclusion

1. Monson, *Freedom Sounds*, 24. See also Foucault, *The Archeology of Knowledge*.

2. See Askew, *Performing the Nation* 19; and Turner, *Dramas, Fields, and Metaphors*, 38.

3. Guilbault, "On Redefining the 'Local,' 138.

4. Gutting, *Foucault*, 6.

5. Ibid.

6. Phillips, *Yorùbá Music*, and *Awon Adura Kukuru.*

Selected Discography and Videography

Highlife

Akinsanya, Adeolu, with the Western Toppers Band. *Original Highlife.* Afrodisa DWAPS 2257, 1986, LP.

Benson, Bobby. "Taxi Driver." Available online at OnlineNigeria.com, accessed February 9, 2008. http://www.onlinenigeria.com/music/Bobby%20Benson/.

Campbell, Ambrose. *Great African Highlife Music.* Melodisc MLP 12-131, n.d., LP.

Chicago, Roy. *Dancing Time No. 1.* Phillips 402016PE, n.d., LP.

Ige, Kayode, with his Mainland Orchestra. *Top Hits from Nigeria: Late Shonibare.* Philips 420022PC, n.d., LP.

King, Kenny Tone, with theWestern Toppers Band. *Dancing Time No. 2.* Philips 420017PE, n.d., LP.

Lawson, Rex. "Love Me Adure." Available online at OnlineNigeria.com, accessed February 9, 2008. http://www.onlinenigeria.com/music/Rex%20lawson/.

Lawson, Rex, and his Mayors Dance Band. *Top Hits from Nigeria.* Sawale Philips 420022PC, n.d., LP.

Ojo, Dele, and his Stars Brothers Band. *Top Hits from Nigeria: Eni A Fe L'amo.* Philips 420022PC, n.d., LP.

Olaiya, Victor. *Leading Gentleman.* 2 vols. Premier Music, n.d., compact disc.

———. *Three Decades of Highlife.* Premier Records Limited, 2002, compact disc.

Olaiya, Victor et al. *Saturday Highlife.* Philips 402021PE, n.d., LP.

Juju

Ade, Sunny. *Sunny Ade and His African Beats.* SALPS 1, 1971, LP.

———. *Juju Music of the 80s.* SALPS 24, 1981, LP.

———. *Ijinle Odu.* SALPS 32, 1982, LP.

———. *Ariya Special.* SALPS 27, 1982, LP.

———. *Togetherness/Kajose.* SALPS 42, 1985, LP.

———. *Otito.* SALPS 46, 1984, LP.

Dairo, Isaac Kehinde, and his Blue Spot Band. *Elele Ture.* NWA 5079, 1962, single.

———. *Chief Awolowo.* EMI NEMI LP 0044, 1979, LP.

Obey, Ebenezer. *Mo Tun Gbede.* WAPS 138, 1979, LP.
———. *Ota Mi Dehin Lehin Mi.* WAPS 248, 1974, LP.
———. *Chief Commander Obey and His Inter-Reformer's Band.* Decca WAPS 418, 1978, LP.
———. *Eyi Yato.* OTI 508, 1980, LP.
———. *Solution Sterns Africa.* STERNS 1005, 1984, LP.
Peters, Sina. *Omo Nbo.* Africa Never Stand Still 3. Ellipsis Arts, 1994, LP.

Waka

Abeni, Salawa. *Queen Salawa Abeni.* Leader Records LRCLS 44, 1983, LP.

Sakara

Olatunji, Yusuf. *Yusuf Olatunji (Baba Legba) and His Sakara Group.* Zaresco OSRL 1729, 1976, LP.
———. *O'Wole Olongo,* vol. 2, Premier Music, OLCD 002, [1977?], compact disc.

Apala

Ishola, Haruna. *Haruna Ishola and His Apala Group.* Star Records SRPS 40, n.d., LP.
———. *Late Oba Adeboye—The Orimolusi of Ijebu Igbo.* Star Records SRPS 49, 1955, LP.
———. *Late Oba Adeboye—The Orimolusi of Ijebu Igbo.* Star Records and Lati Alagbada & Sons Co. Ltd., n.d., compact disc.
Omowura, Ayinla. *Ayinla Omowura and His Apala Group.* EMI HNLX 5085, n.d., LP.

Fuji

Ayinla Kollington. *Ibi Eri E Kigbe Mi Lo.* EMI NEMI (LP) 0145, 1979, LP.
———. *Esin O Faja.* Olumo Records ORPS 12, 1981, LP.
Barrister, Sikiru Ayinde. *Iwa.* Silky Oluyole Records SKOLP 18, 1982, LP.
———. *Ise Loogun Ise.* Silky Oluyole Records SKOL 19, 1982, LP.
———. *Refined Juju Garbage.* Africa Never Stand Still 1. Ellipsis Arts, 1994, compact disc.

Afro-Beat

Anikulapo-Kuti, Fela. *Expensive Shit.* SWS 1001, 1975, LP.
———. *No Bread.* SWS 1003, 1976a, LP.
———. *Zombie.* CRLP 511, 1977, LP.

———. *VIP: Vagabond in Power.* KILP 001, 1979, LP.

———. *Unknown Soldier.* SKLP 0003, 1979, LP.

———. *ITT: International Thief Thief.* K203554, 1979, LP.

———. *Shuffering and Shmiling.* PMLP 1005, 1980, LP.

———. *Coffin for Head of State.* KALP 003, 1981, LP.

———. *Teacher Don't Teach Me Nonsense.* LONDP 28, 1987, LP.

Asha (Bukola Elemide). *Aṣa.* Downtown, 2007, compact disc.

———. *Live in Paris.* Naïve, 2009, compact disc.

———. *Beautiful Imperfection.* Naïve, 2010, compact disc.

Lagbaja. *C'est Un African Thing.* Motherlan' Music MM049603, 1996, compact disc.

———. *Me.* Motherlan' Music MM040004, 2000, compact disc.

———. *We.* Motherlan' Music MM040005, 2000, compact disc.

———. *Abami.* Motherlan' Music MM040006, 2000, compact disc.

———. *We Before Me.* Indigedisc B00005K129, 2001, compact disc.

———. *Africano, the Mother of Groove.* Motherlan' Music MM0507, 2005, compact disc.

———. *African Party.* Motherlan' Music MM0508, 2005, compact disc.

Videography

Adelakun, J. A. *Amona Tete Mabo.* Ibadan: Ayewa Gospel Music Ministry, VCD 01, n.d., video compact disc.

Adeniyi-Babalola, Kemi. *Segan Mi D'ogo.* Remdel Optimum Communication, ROCOM 031, n.d., video compact disc.

Ayefele, Yinka. *Aspiration.* Aloy Productions International, n.d., video compact disc.

Umosen, Folake. *The King's Praise.* King's Glory Music, n.d., video compact disc.

Osupa, Saheed. *Matagbamole Son.* K. K. Entertainment, n.d., video compact disc.

Bibliography

Abiodun, Rowland. "Hidden Power: Oshun the Seventeenth Odu." In Murphy and Sanford, *Oshun across the Waters*, 10–33.

Adebonojo, Mary Bunton. "Text-Setting in Yoruba Secular Music." Master's thesis, University of California, Berkeley, 1967.

Adedeji Joel. "Alarinjo: The Traditional Yoruba Travelling Theatre." In *Drama and Theatre in Nigeria: A Critical Source Book*, edited by Yemi Ogunbiyi, 221–47. Lagos: Nigeria Magazine, 1981.

Adegbite, Ademola Moses. "*Oriki*: A Study in Yoruba Musical and Social Perception." PhD diss., University of Pittsburgh, 1978.

Adegbite, Ademola. "The Drum and Its Role in Yoruba Religion." *Journal of Religion in Africa* 18, no. 1 (1988): 15–26.

Adegbola, Tunde. "Probabilistically Speaking: A Question of Quantitative Exploration of Yoruba Speech Surrogacy." Unpublished paper, 1988.

Adegboyega, S. G. *A Short History of the Apostolic Church in Nigeria*. Ibadan: Rosprint Industrial Press, 1978.

Adegboyin, Deji, and Ademola S. Ishola. *African Indigenous Churches: An Historical Perspective*. Lagos: Greater Heights Publications, 1997.

Adekunle, O. Julius, ed. *Religion in Politics: Secularism and National Integration in Modern Nigeria*. Trenton, NJ: Africa World Press, 2009.

Adepegba, Cornelius O. "Osun and Brass: An Insight into Yoruba Religious Symbology." In Murphy and Sanford, *Oshun across the Waters*, 102–12.

Adogame, Afe. *Celestial Church of Christ: The Politics of Cultural Identity in a West African Prophetic-Charismatic Movement*. Frankfurt: Peter Lang, 1999.

Agawu, Kofi. *African Rhythm: A Northern Ewe Perspective*. Cambridge: Cambridge University Press, 1995.

———. "The Impact of Language on Musical Composition in Ghana: An Introduction to the Musical Style of Ephraim Amu." *Ethnomusicology* 28, no. 1 (1984): 37–73.

———. *Representing African Music: Postcolonial Notes, Queries, Positions*. New York: Routledge, 2003.

———. "Structural Analysis or Cultural Analysis? Competing Perspectives on the "Standard Pattern" of West African Rhythm." *Journal of the American Musicological Society* 59, no. 1 (2006): 1–46.

Ahmed, Leita. *Women and Gender in Islam*. New Haven, CT: Yale University Press, 1992.

Alaja-Browne, Afolabi. "A Diachronic Study of Change in Juju Music." *Popular Music* 8, no. 3 (1989): 231–42.

Alana, Olu. "Traditional Religion." In *Understanding Yoruba Life and Culture*, edited by Nike Lawal, Matthew Sadiku, and Ade Dopamu, 65–80. Trenton, NJ: African World Press, 2004.

Alcamo, Iyalaja Ileana. *Iya Nla: Primordial Yoruba Mother: The Source*. Bloomington: Indiana University Press, 2005.

Alidou, Ousseina D. *Engaging Modernity: Muslim Women and the Politics of Agency in Postcolonial. Niger*. Madison, Madison: University of Wisconsin Press, 2005.

Amadiume, Ifi. *Re-inventing Africa: Matriarchy, Religion and Culture*. London: Zed Books, 1998.

Ampene, Kwasi. *Female Song Tradition and the Akan of Ghana*. Hampshire: Ashgate Publishing Company (SOAS Musicology Series), 2005.

Anderson, Allan. *African Reformation: African Initiated Christianity in the Twentieth Century*. Trenton, NJ: African World Press, 2001.

Anku, Willie. "Principles of Rhythmic Integration in African Drumming." *Black Music Research Journal* 17 (1997): 211–38.

Apter, Andrew. *Black Critics and Kings: The Hermeneutics of Power in Yoruba Society*. Chicago: University of Chicago Press, 1992.

Armstrong, Robert G. "Talking Drums in the Benue-Cross River Region of Nigeria." *Phylon* 15, no. 4 (1954): 355–63.

Askew, M. Kelly. *Performing the Nation: Swahili Music and Cultural Politics in Tanzania*. Chicago: University of Chicago Press, 2002.

Atanda, J. Adebowale. *An Introduction to Yoruba History*. Ibadan: Ibadan University Press, 1980.

Auerbach, Susan. "From Singing to Lamenting: Women's Musical Role in a Greek Village." In Koskoff, *Women and Music in Cross-Cultural Perspective*, 25–43.

Awolalu, W. *Yoruba Beliefs and Sacrificial Rites*. London: Longman, 1979.

Ayandele, E. A. *The Missionary Impact on Modern Nigeria*. London: University of London Press, 1960.

Ayelaagbe, I. F. *O Dun Yungbayungba*. Unpublished compilation of Yoruba anthems. 1985.

Babalola, S. Adeboye. *The Content and Form of Yoruba Ijala*. London: Oxford University Press, 1966.

Badejo, L. Diedre. "Authority and Discourse in the Orin Odun Osun." In Murphy and Sanford, *Oshun across the Waters*, 128–40.

———. *Osun Seegesi: The Elegant Deity of Wealth, Power, and Feminity*. Trenton, NJ: African World Press, 1995.

Bakhtin, Mikhail M. *The Dialogic Imagination*. Translated by Caryl Emerson and Michael Holquist. Austin: University of Texas Press, 1981.

Bakrania, Falu. "Hybridity." In *International Encyclopedia of the Social Sciences*. 2008. http://www.encyclopedia.com/doc/1G2-3045301063.html.

Bankole, Ayo, Judith Bush, and Sadek H. Samaan. "The Yoruba Master Drummer." *African Arts* 8, no. 2 (1975): 48–56, 77–78.

Barber, Karin. "Popular Arts in Africa." *African Studies Review* 30, no. 3 (1987): 1–78.

———. "*Oriki*, Women and the Proliferation and Merging of *Orisha*." *Africa: Journal of the International African Institute* 60, no. 3 (1990): 313–37.

———. *I Could Speak Until Tomorrow: Oriki, Women and the Past in a Yoruba Town.* London: Edinburg University Press (for the International African Institute), 1991.

Barber, Karin, and Christopher Waterman. "Traversing the Global and the Local: Fuji Music and Praise Poetry in the Production of Contemporary Yoruba Popular Culture." In *Worlds Apart: Modernity through the Prism of the Local,* edited by Daniel Miller, 240–62. London: Routledge, 1995.

Barz, Gregory. *Music in East Africa: Expressing Music, Expressing Culture.* New York: Oxford University Press, 2004.

Basso, B. Ellen. "Musical Expression and Gender Identity in the Myth and Ritual of the Kalapalo of Central Brazil." In Koskoff, *Women and Music in Cross-Cultural Perspective,* 163–76.

Bauman, Richard. *Story, Performance and Event.* Cambridge: Cambridge University Press, 1986.

———. *Verbal Art as Performance.* Prospect Heights, IL: Waveland Press, 1977.

Bhabha, Homi K. *The Location of Culture.* London: Routledge, 1994.

Beier, Ulli. "Oshun Festival." *Nigeria Magazine* 53 (1957): 170–87.

———. "The Talking Drums of the Yoruba." *African Music* 1, no. 1 (1954): 29–31.

———. "Yoruba Folk Operas." *African Music* 1, no. 1 (1954): 32–34.

———. "Yoruba Vocal Music." *Journal of the African Music Society* 1, no. 3 (1956): 23–28.

Bender, Wolfgang. *Sweet Mother: Modern African Music.* Chicago: University of Chicago Press, 1991.

Blacking, John. *Music, Culture and Experience: Selected Papers of John Blacking.* Edited and with an introduction by Reginald Bryon. Chicago: University of Chicago Press, 1995.

Blum, Stephen. "Prologue: Ethnomusicology and Modern Music History." In Blum, Bohlman, and Neuman, *Ethnomusicology and Modern Music History,* 1–23.

Blum, Stephen, Philip V. Bohlman, and Daniel M. Neuman, eds. *Ethnomusicology and Modern Music History.* Urbana: University of Illinois Press, 1993.

Bourdieu, Pierre. *Outline of a Theory of Practice.* Cambridge: Cambridge University Press, 1977.

Brandel, Rose. "Africa." In *Harvard Dictionary of Music,* edited by Willi Apel, 17–24. 2nd ed. Cambridge, MA: Harvard University Press, 1969.

Brandon, George. "Ochun in Bronx." In Murphy and Sanford, *Oshun across the Waters,* 155–64.

Brenner, Louis, ed. *Muslim Identity and Social Change in Sub-Saharan Africa.* London: Hurst, 1993.

Brenner, Louis and Murray Last. "The Role of Language in West African Islam." *Africa* 55, no. 4 (1985): 443–46.

Bruce, Lee. "Introducing the Highlife." *Jazz Monthly* 3, 1969: 3–8.

Burns, James. *Female Voices from an Ewe Dance-Drumming Community in Ghana: Our Music Has Become a Divine Spirit.* SOAS Musicology Series. Surrey: Ashgate Publishing Limited, 2009.

Butler, Judith. *Excitable Speech: A Politics of the Performative.* New York: Routledge, 1997.

Caroll, K. "Yoruba Religious Music." *Journal of the African Music Society* 1, no. 3 (1956): 45–47.

Carrington, F. John. "The Musical Dimension of Perception in the Upper Congo, Zaire." *African Music* 5, no. 1 (1971): 46–51.

Certeau, Michel de. *The Practice of Everyday Life*. Berkeley: University of California Press, 1984.

Castellanos, Isabel. "A River of Many Turns: The Polysemy of Ochun in Afro-Cuban Tradition." In Murphy and Sanford, *Oshun across the Waters*, 34–45.

Charry, Eric. "Music and Islam in Sub-Saharan Africa." In *The History of Islam in Africa*, edited by Nehemia Levtzion and Randall L. Pouwels, 545–73. Athens: Ohio University Press, 2000.

Chernoff, John Miller. *African Rhythm and African Sensibility: Aesthetics and Social Action in African Musical Idiom*. Chicago: University of Chicago Press, 1979.

Church Missionary Society. *Iwe Orin Mimo Fun Ijo Enia Olorun Ni Ile Yoruba* [Yoruba hymn book with an appendix of sacred native songs]. Lagos: Church Missionary Society (CMS), 1923.

Clifford, James. *The Predicament of Culture: Twentieth-Century Ethnography, Literature, and Art*. Cambridge, MA: Harvard University Press, 1988.

Cohen, R. Judith. "Ya Salió: Judeo-Spanish Wedding Songs among Moroccan Jews in Canada." In Koskoff, *Women and Music in Cross-Cultural Perspective*, 55–67.

Collins, John. *West African Pop Roots*. Philadelphia: Temple University Press, 1992.

Crumbley, Deidre Helen. *Spirit, Structure, and Flesh: Gendered Experiences in African Instituted Churches among the Yoruba of Nigeria*. Madison: University of Wisconsin Press, 2008.

Dedeke, Dayo. *Ma Gbagbe Ile*. London: Oxford University Press, 1963.

Delano, Isaac O. *The Singing Minister of Nigeria: The Life of the Rev. Canon J. J. Ransome-Kuti*. London: United Society for Christian Literature, 1942.

Delano, Isaac O. *Josaiah Ransome-Kuti: The Drummer Boy Who Became a Canon*. Ibadan: Oxford University Press, 1968.

DjeDje, C. Jacqueline. *Fiddling in West Africa: Touching the Spirit in Fulbe, Hausa, and Dagbamba Cultures*. Bloomington: Indiana University Press, 2008.

Dor, George. "Communal Creativity and Song Ownership in Anlo Ewe Musical Practice: The Case of Havolu." *Ethnomusicology* 48, no. 1 (2004): 26–51.

Drewal, Henry and Margaret Drewal. *Gelede: Art and Female Power Among the Yoruba*. Bloomington: Indiana University Press, 1983.

Drewal, Margaret Thompson. "The State of Research on Performance in Africa." *African Studies Review* 34, no. 3 (1991): 1–64.

———. *Yoruba Ritual: Performers, Play, Agency*. Bloomington: Indiana University Press, 1992.

Duro-Ladipo, Abiodun and Gboyega Kolawole. "Opera in Nigeria: The Case of Duro Ladipo's *Oba Koso*." *Black Music Research Journal* 17, no. 1 (1992): 101–29.

Ekwueme, Lazarus. "Linguistic Determinants of Some Igbo Musical Properties." *Journal of African Studies* 1, no. 3 (1974): 335–53.

Erlmann, Veit. "The Aesthetics of the Global Imagination: Reflections on World Music in the 1990s." *Public Culture* 8, no. 3 (1996): 467–87.

————. *Night Song: Performance, Power, and Practice in South Africa*. Chicago: University of Chicago Press, 1996.

Euba, Akin. "Concept of Neo-African Music as Manifested in Yoruba Folk Opera." In *The African Diaspora: A Musical Perspective*, edited by Ingrid Monson, 202–41. London: Routledge, 2003.

————. *Essays on Music in Africa*. 2 vols. Bayreuth: Bayreuth African Studies and Elekoto Music Center, 1988.

————. "Gods and Deputy Gods: Music in Yoruba Religious and Kingship Traditions." In *The Interrelatedness of Music, Religion, and Ritual in African Performance*, edited by Daniel K. Avorgbedor, pp: 39–64. London: Edwin Mellen Press, 2003.

————. "Ilu Esu/Drumming for Esu: Analysis of a Dundun Performance." In *Essays for a Humanist: An Offering to Klaus Wachsmann*, 137–45. New York: Town House Press, 1977.

————. "Islamic Musical Culture among the Yoruba: A Preliminary Survey." In *Music and History in Africa*, edited by Klaus Wachsmann, 178–88. Evanston: Northwestern University, 1971.

————. "Multiple Pitch Lines in Yoruba Choral Music." *Journal of the International Folk Music Council* 19 (1967): 66–71.

————. "Music Adapts to a Changed World: A Leading Composer Looks at How Africa's Musical Traditions Have Expanded to Suit Contemporary Society." *Africa Report* (1970): 24–27.

————. *Yoruba Drumming: The Yoruba Dundun Tradition*. Bayreuth: Bayreuth African Studies, 1991.

Fabian, Johannes. *Power and Performance: Ethnographic Exploration through Proverbial Wisdom and Theater in Shaba, Zaire*. Madison: University of Wisconsin Press, 1990.

Falola, Toyin and Ann Genova, eds. *Orisa: Yoruba Gods and Spiritual Identity in Africa and the Diaspora*. Trenton, NJ: Africa World Press, 2006.

Falola, Toyin and Dare Oguntomisin. *Yoruba Warlords in the 19th Century*. Trenton, NJ: Africa World Press, 2000.

Fiagbedzi, Nissio. "The Music of the Anlo." PhD diss., UCLA, 1977.

Furniss, Susan. "Aka Polyphony: Music, Theory, Back and Forth." In *Analytical Studies in World Music*, edited by Michael Tenzer, 163–204. Oxford: Oxford University Press, 2006.

Flores-Pena, Ysamur. "Overflowing with Beauty: The Ochun Alter in Lucumi Aesthetic Tradition." In Murphy and Sanford, *Oshun across the Waters*, 155–64.

Floyd, Samuel A. Jr. *The Power of Black Music: Interpreting Its History from Africa to the United States*. New York: Oxford University Press, 1995.

Friedson, Stephen. *Dancing Prophets: Musical Experience in Tumbuka Healing*. Chicago: University of Chicago Press, 1996.

Foucault, Michel. *The Archeology of Knowledge and the Discourse on Language*. New York: Pantheon, 1972.

Geertz, Clifford. *The Interpretation of Cultures*. New York: Basic Books, 1973.

Grove, George. *Grove's Dictionary of Music and Musicians*. London: Macmillan, 1920.

Guilbault, Jocelyne. "On Redefining the 'Local' through World Music." In *Ethnomusicology: A Contemporary Reader*, edited by Jennifer Post, 137–46. New York and London: Routledge, 2006.

Gutting, Gary. *Foucault: A Very Short Introduction.* Oxford: Oxford University Press, 2005.

Hale, Thomas. *Griots and Griottes: Masters of Words and Music.* Bloomington: Indiana University Press, 1998.

Hannerz, Ulf. "The World in Creolization." *Africa* 57, no. 4 (1987): 546–59.

Henning, Christoph, Müller E. Klaus, and Ute Ritz-Müller. *Soul of Africa: Magical Rites and Traditions.* Cologne: Köneman Verlagsgesellschaft mbH, 1999.

Hood, Mantle. *The Ethnomusicologist.* New York: McGraw Hill, 1971.

Hornbostel, Erich M. von. "African Negro Music." *Africa* 1, no. 1 (1928): 30–62.

———. "The Ethnology of African Sound Instruments." *Africa* 6, no. 2 (1933): 129–57.

Hornbostel, Eric M. von, and Curt Sachs. "Classification of Musical Instruments." Translated from the original German by Anthony Baines and Klaus P. Wachsmann. *Galpin Society Journal* 46: (1961): 83–113.

Idowu, Bolaji. *Olodumare in Yoruba Belief.* London: Oxford University Press, 1962.

Johnson, Samuel. *The History of the Yorubas.* Lagos: CSS (new edition), 1977.

Jones, A. M. "African Rhythm." *Africa* 1, no. 24 (1954): 26–47.

———. *Studies in African Music.* 2 vols. London: Oxford University Press, 1959.

Kalu, N. Kalu. *State Power, Autarchy, and Political Conquest in Nigerian Federalism.* Lanham, MD: Lexington Books, 2008.

Kasfir, Sidney Littlefield. "Elephant Women, Furious and Majestic: Women's Masquerades in Africa and the Diaspora." *African Arts* (Spring 1998): 18–27, 92.

Kauffman, Robert. "African Rhythm: A Reassessment." *Ethnomusicology* 24, no. 3 (1980): 393–415.

Kidula, Jean N. "Making and Managing Music in African Christian Life." In King et al., *Music in the Life of the African Church,* 101–16.

———. "Music Culture: African Life." In King et al., *Music in the Life of the African Church,* 37–56.

King, Anthony. "Employment of the 'Standard' Pattern in Yoruba Music." *African Music* 2, no. 3 (1960.): 51–54.

———. "Nigerian Music." In *New Grove Dictionary of Music,* edited by Stanley Sadie, 13:239. London: MacMillan, 1980.

———. *Yoruba Sacred Music from Ekiti.* Ibadan: Ibadan University Press, 1961.

King, Roberta. "Beginnings: Music in the African Church." In King et al., *Music in the Life of the African Church,* 1–16.

———. "Bible: Lex Canendi, Lex Credendi." In King et al., *Music in the Life of the African Church,* 117–32.

———. "Global Church: Lessons from Africa." In King et al., *Music in the Life of the African Church,* 133–50.

———. "Music Culture: Euro-American Christianity." In King et al., *Music in the Life of the African Church,* 17–35.

King, Roberta, J. N. Kidula, James R. Krabill, and Thomas Oduro, eds. *Music in the Life of the African Church.* Waco, TX: Baylor University Press, 2008.

Klein, L. Debra. *Yoruba Bata Goes Global: Artists, Culture Brokers, And Fans.* Chicago: University of Chicago Press, 2007.

Koetting, James. "Analysis and Notation of West African Drum Ensemble Music." *Selected Studies in Ethnomusicology* 1, no. 3 (1970): 115–46.

Koskoff, Ellen. "An Introduction to Women, Music, and Culture." In Koskoff, *Women and Music in Cross-Cultural Perspective*, 1–23.

———, ed. *Women and Music in Cross-Cultural Perspective*. Urbana: University of Illinois Press, 1989.

Krabill, James R. "Encounters: What Happens to Music When People Meet." In King et al., *Music in the Life of the African Church*, 57–79.

Kubik, Gerhard. *Theory of African Music*. 2 vols. Chicago: University of Chicago Press, 2010.

Kwami, Robert. "Towards a Comprehensive Catalogue of Eve Drum Mnemonics." *Journal of African Cultural Studies* 11, no. 1 (1998): 27–38.

Law, R. C. C. "The Heritage of Oduduwa: Traditional History and Political Propaganda among the Yoruba." *Journal of African History* 14, no. 2 (1973): 207–22.

Laoye 1, Timi of Ede. "Yoruba Drums." *Odu* 7 (1959.): 10–11.

Leonard, Lynn. "The Growth of Entertainment of Non-African Origin in Lagos." Master's thesis, University of Ibadan, 1967.

Levine, E. "Constructing a Market, Constructing an Ethnicity: U.S. Spanish-Language Media and the Formation of a Syncretic Latinola Identity." *Studies in Latin American Popular Culture* 20 (2001): 33–50.

Linton, Ralph. *The Study of Man*. New York: Appleton-Century-Crofts, 1936.

Lloyd, P. C. *The Political Development of Yoruba Kingdoms in the Eighteenth and Nineteenth Centuries*. London: Royal Anthropological Institute (Occasional Publication Series), 1971.

Lucas, J. Olumide. *The Religion of the Yorubas*. Lagos: Church Missionary Society, 1941.

Locke, David. "Africa: Ewe, Mande, Shona Baaka." In *Worlds of Music: An Introduction to the Music of the World's Peoples*, edited by Jeff Todd Titon, 75–121. Belmont, CA: Schirmer, 2005.

———. "The Music of Atsiagbeko." PhD diss., Wesleyan University, 1978.

Locke, David, and Agbeli, Godwin. "Drum Language in Adzogbo." *The Black Perspective in Music* 9, no. 1 (1981): 25–50.

Mack, Beverly B. *Muslim Women Sing: Hausa Popular Song*. Bloomington: Indiana University Press, 2004.

Matory, J. Lorand. "Is There Gender in Yoruba Culture?" In *Orisa Devotion as World Religion: The Globalization of Yoruba Religious Culture*, edited by Jacob K. Olupona, and Terry Rey, 513–58. Madison: University of Wisconsin Press, 2008.

———. *Sex and the Empire That Is No More: Gender and the Politics of Metaphor in Oyo Yoruba Religion*. Minneapolis: University of Minnesota Press, 1994.

Mbon, Friday M. "The Quest for Identity in African New Religious Movements." In *New Religious Movements and Society in Nigeria*, edited by Gudrun Ludware-Ene, 7–29. Bayreuth: Bayreuth University Press, 1991.

McKenzie, P. R. "Yoruba Orisa Cults: Some Marginal Notes Concerning Cosmology and Concepts of Deitey." *Journal of Religion in Africa* 8, no. 3 (1976): 189–207.

McLaughlin, Fiona. "Islam and Popular Music in Senegal: The Emergence of a 'New Tradition.'" *Africa* 67, no. 4 (1997): 560–81.

Merriam, Alan P. *The Anthropology of Music.* Evanston, IL: Northwestern University Press, 1964.

———. "Characteristics of African Music." *International Folk Music Journal* (XI) (1959): 13–19.

Monson, Ingrid. *Freedom Sounds: Civil Rights Call Out to Jazz and Africa.* New York: Oxford University Press, 2007.

———. "Riffs, Repetition, and Theories of Globalization." *Ethnomusicology* 43, no. 1 (1999): 31–65.

Moore, Robin and Elizabeth Sayre. "An Afro-Cuban Bata Piece for Obatala, King of the White Cloth." In *Analytical Studies in World Music*, edited by Michael Tenzer, 120–60. Oxford: Oxford University Press, 2006.

Muller, Carol Ann. *Rituals of Fertility and the Sacrifice of Desire: Nazarite Women's Performance in South Africa.* Chicago: University of Chicago Press, 1999.

———. *South African Music: A Century of Traditions in Transformation.* Santa Barbara, CA: ABC-CLIO, 2004.

Munoz, Louis J. *A Living Tradition: Studies in Yoruba Civilization.* Ibadan: Bookcraft LTD, 2003.

Murphy, Joseph M. "Yeye Cachita: Oxun in a Cuban Mirror." In Murphy and Sanford, *Oshun across the Waters*, 87–101.

Murphy, Joseph M., and Mei-Mei Sanford, eds. *Oshun across the Waters: A Yoruba Goddess in Africa and the Americas.* Bloomington: Indiana University Press, 2001.

Nacify, H. *The Making of Exile Cultures: Iranian Television in Los Angeles.* Minneapolis: University of Minnesota Press, 1993.

Nannyonga-Tamusuza, Sylvia A. *Baakisimba: Gender in the Music and Dance of the Baganda People of Uganda.* New York: Routledge, 2005.

Nettl, Bruno. *The Study of Ethnomusicology: Thirty-One Issues and Concepts.* Champaign: University of Illinois Press, 2005.

Nketia, Kwabena J. H. *Ethnomusicology and African Music: Collected Papers.* Vol. 1, *Modes of Inquiry and Interpretation.* Accra: Afram Publications, 2005.

———. *Funeral Dirges of the Akan People* New York: Negro Universities Press, 1962.

———. *The Music of Africa.* New York: W. W. Norton, 1974.

———. "Yoruba Musicians in Accra." *Odu* 6 (1958): 43.

Nzewi, Meki. "Melo-Rhythmic Essence and Hot Rhythm in Nigerian Folk Music." *The Black Perspective in Music* 2, no. 1 (1974): 23–28.

Nzewi, Meki, Israel Anyahuru, and Tom Ohiaraumunna. "Beyond Song Texts: The Lingual Fundamentals of African Drum Music." *Research in African Literatures* (Special edition: The Landscape of African Music) 32, no. 2 (2001): 90–104.

Obayemi, Ade. "Culture in the Nigerian Economy: Some 1989 Perspectives." In *Culture, Economy, and National Development*, edited by Sule Bello and Yabuku Abdullahi Nasadi, 21–30. Lagos: National Council for Arts and Culture, 1991.

Oduro, Thomas, A. "Church Music in the Life of African Church Communities." In King et al., *Music in the Life of the African Church*, 81–100.

Ogundipe, Molara. "The Invention of Women: Theorizing African Women and Gender: Now and into the Future," Lecture presented at Round Table: The Invention of African Women and Gender at the African Studies Association Meeting, 2002.

Okome, Mojubaola Olufunke. "African Women and Power: Reflections on the Perils of Unwarranted Cosmopolitanism," *JENDA*: A Journal of Cultural and African Women Studies 1, no. 1.

Olajubu, Oludare. "Iwi Egungun Chants: An Introduction." *Research in African Literatures* 5, no. 1(1974): 31–51.

Olajubu, Oyeronke. *Women in the Yoruba Religious Sphere*. New York: State University of New York, 2003.

Olaniyan, Oluyemi. "Compositional and Performance Technique in Yoruba Dundun-Sekere Music." PhD diss., Queen's University of Belfast, 1984.

Olaniyan, Tejumola. *Arrest the Music! Fela and His Rebel Art and Politics*. Bloomington: Indiana University Press, 2004.

———. "The Cosmopolitan Nativist: Fela Anikulapo-Kuti and the Antinomies of Postcolonial Modernity." *Research in African Literatures* 32, no. 2 (2001): 76–89.

Olatunji, Michael Olutayo. "The Biography of T. K. E. Phillips: Nigeria's Foremost Contemporary Art Musician." *Institute of African Studies: Research Review* 21, no. 2 (2005): 11–16.

Olayemi, Val. *Orin Ibeji*. Ibadan: Institute of African Studies, University of Ibadan, 1971.

Olayiwola, D. O. "Church and Healing in Nigeria." *Asia Journal of Theology* 4, no. 2 (1990): 417–23.

———. "The Social Impact of New Aladura Movements on Contemporary Yoruba Life." *Africana Marbuguensia* 22, no. 2 (1989): 33–44.

Olupona, Jacob Kayode. "Imagining the Goddess: Gender in Yoruba Religious Traditions and Modernity." *Dialogue and Alliance* 18, no. 1 (2005): 71–86.

———. "New Religious Movements and the Nigerian Social Order." In *New Religious Movements and Society in Nigeria*, edited by Gudrun Ludware-Ene, 231–52. Bayreuth: Bayreuth University Press, 1989.

Omibiyi-Obidike Mosunmola. "Islamic Influence on Yoruba Music." *African Notes* 8, no. 2 (1979): 37–54.

Omojola, Bode. "History, Style and Identity in Yoruba Popular Music." *Jazz Forschung* 33 (2001): 189–210.

———. "Kiriboto Music in Yoruba Culture." *Bulletin on Urgent Anthropology and Ethnographic Research* 32–33 (1990): 121–42.

———. *The Music of Fela Sowande: Encounters, African Identity and Creative Ethnomusicology*. Point Richmond, CA: Music Research Institute, 2009.

———. *Nigerian Art Music*. Ibadan: Institut Français de Recherche en Afrique (IFRA), University of Ibadan, 1995.

———. "Politics, Identity, and Nostalgia in Nigerian Music: A Study of Victor Olaiya's Music." *Ethnomusicology* 53, no. 2 (2009): 249–76.

———. *Popular Music in Western Nigeria: Theme, Style and Patronage System*. Ibadan: Institut Français de Recherche en Afrique (IFRA), University of Ibadan, 2006.

———. "Yoruba Folk Opera." In *Understanding Yoruba Life and Culture*, edited by Nike Lawal, Mathew Sadiku, and Ade Dopamu, 633–49. Trenton, NJ: African World Press, 2004.

Omoyajowo, J Akinyele. *Cherubim and Seraphim: The History of an African Church*. New York: Nok Publishers, 1982.

Ong, Walter J. "African Talking Drums and Oral Noetics." *New Literary History* 8, no 3 (1977): 411–29.

Opoku, Kofi Asare. "A Brief History of Independent Church Movements in Ghana since 1862." In *The Rise of Independent Churches in Ghana*, 22–26. Accra, Ghana: Asempa Publishers, 1990.

Oriere, G. B. *Orin Itunu*. 2 vols. Unpublished compilation, 1959.

Ortiz, Fernando. *Los instrumentos de la música afrocubana*. 5 vols. Havana: Ministerio de Educación, 1954–55.

Oshun, Christopher Olubunmi. "The Pentecostal Perspective of the Christ Apostolic Church." *Orita* 15, no. 1 (1983): 105–14.

Ositelu, Rufus Okikiolaolu Olabiyi. *African Instituted Churches*. New Brunswick, NJ: Transactions Publishers, 2002.

Oyelami, Muraina. *Yoruba Bata Music: A New Notation with Basic Exercises and Ensemble Pieces*. Bayreuth, Germany: Iwalewa Haus, 1991.

———. *Yoruba Dundun Music: A New Notation with Basic Exercises and Five Yoruba Drum Repertoires*. Bayreuth, Germany: Iwalewa Haus, 1989.

Oyewo, Segun. "Management in Yorùbá Traditional Arts." Unpublished paper.

Oyewumi, Oyeronke. *The Invention of Women: Making an African Sense of Western Gender Discourses*. Minneapolis: University of Minnesota Press, 1997.

———. "Visualizing the Body: Western Theories and African Subjects." In *African Gender Studies: A Reader*, edited by Oyerionke Oyewumi, 3–32. New York: Palgrave Macmilian, 2005.

Paden, John N. *Faith and Politics in Nigeria: Nigeria as a Pivotal State in the Muslim World*. Washington, DC: United State Institute of Peace Press, 2008.

Pantaleoni, Hewitt. The Rhythm of Atsia Dance Drumming Among the Anlo (Eve) of Anyako. PhD diss., SUNY Oneonta, 1972.

Peel, John. *Aladura: A Religious Movement Among the Yoruba*. London: Oxford University Press, 1968.

———. "Religious Change in Yorubaland." *Africa* 37, no. 4 (1967): 292–310.

———. *Religious Encounter and the Making of the Yoruba*. Bloomington: Indian University Press, 2000.

Petersen, Karen E. "An Investigation into Women-Identified Music in the United States." In Koskoff, *Women and Music in Cross-Cultural Perspective*, 203–12.

Phillips, Ekundayo. *Awon Adura Kukuru: Vesicles and Responses* London: Novello and Co. Ltd., 1926.

———. *Yoruba Music*. Johannesburg: African Music Society, 1953.

Pobee, John. "Foreword." In *African Reformation: African Initiated Christianity in the 20th Century*, edited by Allan Anderson, ix–xvi. Trenton, NJ: Africa World Press, 2001.

Post, Jennifer. "Professional Women in Indian Music: The Death of the Courtesan Tradition." In Koskoff, *Women and Music in Cross-Cultural Perspective*, 97–109.

Qureshi, Regula Burckhardt. "Sufi Music and the Historicity of Oral Tradition." In Blum, Bohlman, and Neuman, *Ethnomusicology and Modern Music History*, 102–20.

Rattray, R. Sutherland. "The Drum Language of West Africa." *African Affairs* 22 (1923): 226–36.

Reed, Daniel. *Dan Ge Performance Masks and Music in Contemporary Côte d'Ivoire.* Bloomington: Indiana University Press, 2003.

Reily, Suzei Ana. "Discipline or Dialogue: A Response to Tim Rice." *Ethnomusicology* 54, no. 2 (2010): 331–33.

Ribeiro dos Santos, Ieda Machado. "Nesta Cidade Todo Mundo e d'Oxun: In This City Every One is Oxun's." In Murphy and Sanford, *Oshun across the Waters,* 68–83.

Rice, Timothy. "Disciplining *Ethnomusicology:* A Call for a New Approach." *Ethnomusicology* 54, no. 2 (2010): 318–25.

———. "Toward a Mediation of Field Method and Field Experience in Ethnomusicology." In *Shadows in the Field: New Perspectives for Fieldwork in Ethnomusicology,* edited by Gregory F. Barz and Timothy J. Cooley, 101–20. New York: Oxford University Press, 1997.

Robertson, Carol E. "Power and Gender in the Musical Experiences of Women." In Koskoff, *Women and Music in Cross-Cultural Perspective,* 225–44.

Rotberg, I. Robert. *Nigeria: Elections and Continuing Challenges.* New York: Council of Foreign Relations. 2007.

Rothenbusch, Esther. "The Joyful Sound: Women in the Nineteenth-Century United States." In Koskoff, *Women and Music in Cross-Cultural Perspective,* 177–94.

Sachs, Curt. *The History of Musical Instruments.* New York: W. W. Norton, 1940.

Sadoh, Godwin. *Thomas Ekundayo Phillips: The Doyen of Nigerian Church Music.* iUniverse.com, 2009.

Sahlins, Marshall. *Historical Metaphors and Mythical Realities: Structure in the Early History of the Sandwich Island Kingdoms.* Ann Arbor: University of Michigan Press, 1981.

Sakata, Hiromi Lorrain. "Hazara Women in Afghanistan: Innovators and Preservers of a Musical Tradition." In Koskoff, *Women and Music in Cross-Cultural Perspective,* 85–95.

Schäfer, Henning. "A Celebration of Impurity, Locating Syncretism and Hybridity in Native Canadian Theatre." *Textual Studies in Canada,* Summer Issue 17 (2004): 79–96.

Schoonnmaker, Trevor, ed. *Fela: From West Africa to West Broadway* New York: Palgrave Macmillan, 2003.

Schneider, Marius. "Tone and Tune in West African Music." *Ethnomusicology* 5, no. 3 (1961): 204–15.

Scholes, Percy. *The Oxford Companion to Music.* London: Oxford University Press, 1938.

Sewell, Jr., William H. "A Theory of Structure: Duality, Agency and Transformation," *American Journal of Sociology* 98, no. 1 (1992): 25.

Shehan, K. Patricia. "Balkan Women as Preservers of Traditional Music and Culture." In Koskoff, *Women and Music in Cross-Cultural Perspective,* 45–53.

Shelemay, Kay Kaufman. "The Ethnomusicologist, Ethnographic Method, and the Transmission of Tradition." In *Shadows in the Field: New Perspectives for Fieldwork in Ethnomusicology,* edited by Gregory F. Barz and Timothy J. Cooley, 189–204. New York: Oxford University Press, 1997.

Slawek, M. Stephen. "Ravi Shankar as Mediator between a Traditional Music and Modernity." In Blum, Bohlman, and Neuman, *Ethnomusicology and Modern Music History,* 161–80.

Slobin, Mark. "Micromusics of the West: A Comparative Approach." *Ethnomusicology* 36, no. 1 (1992): 1–87.

Smith, S. Robert. *Kingdoms of the Yoruba.* Madison: University of Wisconsin Press, 1988.

Sowande, Fela. "The African Musician in Nigeria." *Worlds of Music* (1967): 27–36.

———. "The Catholic Church and the Tone Languages of Nigeria." Unpublished paper.

Starrati, Priscilla. "Islamic Influences on Oral Traditions in Hausa Literature." In *The Marabout and the Muse: New Approaches to Islam in African Literature,* edited by Kenneth W. Harrow, 159–75. Portsmouth, NH: Heinemann, 1996.

Stern, Theodore. "Drum and Whistle 'Languages': An Analysis of Speech Surrogates." *American Anthropologist* (New Series) 59, no. 3 (1957): 487–506.

Stokes, Martin, ed. *Ethnicity, Identity and Music: The Musical Construction of Place.* Oxford: Berg, 1997.

———. "Music and the Global Order." *Annual Review of Anthropology* 33 (2004): 47–72.

Strobel, Margaret. *Muslim Women in Mombasa: 1890–1975.* New Haven, CT: Yale University Press, 1979.

Tang, Patricia. *Masters of the Sabar: Wolof Griot Percussionists of Senegal.* Philadelphia: Temple University Press, 2007.

Thieme, Darius. "A Descriptive Catalog of Yoruba Musical Instruments." PhD diss., Catholic University of America, 1969.

———. "A Summary-Report on the Oral Traditions of Yoruba Musicians." *Africa: Journal of the International African Institute* 40, no. 4 (1970): 359–62.

———. "Three Yoruba Members of the Mbira-Sanza Family." *Journal of the International Folk Music Council* XIX (1967): 42–48.

———. "Yoruba Music." *African Notes* 3, no. 3 (1966): 9–12.

Turino, Thomas. *Music as Social Life: The Politics of Participation.* Chicago: University of Chicago Press, 2008.

Turner, W. Victor. *Dramas, Fields, and Metaphors: Symbolic Action in Human Society.* Ithaca, NY: Cornell University Press, 1974.

———. *The Ritual Process: Structure and Anti-Structure.* Chicago: Aldine, 1969.

Valdivia, Angharad N. 2005. "Geographies of Latinidad: Deployment of Radical Hybridity in the Mainstream." In *Race, Identity, and Representation in Education.* Critical Social Thought, edited by Cameron McCarthy, Warren Crichlow, Greg Dimitriadis, and Nadine Dolby, 307–17. New York, NY: Routledge 2005.

Veal, Michael. *Fela: Life and Times of an African Musical Icon.* Philadelphia: Temple University Press, 2000.

———. "Jazz Music Influences on the Music of Fela." *Glendora Review* 1, no. 1 (1995): 8–13.

Vidal, A. O. "Oriki, Praise Chants of the Yoruba." Master's thesis, UCLA, 1971.

Vidal, Tunji. "Oriki in Traditional Yoruba Music." *African Arts* 3, no. 1 (1969): 56–59.

Villepastour, Amanda. *Ancient Text Messages of the Yoruba Bàtá Drum.* SOAS Musicology Series. London: Ashgate, 2010.

Ward, W. E. "Music in the Gold Coast." *Gold Coast Review* 3 (1927): 199–223.

Waterman, Christopher. "Big Man, Black President, Masked One: Models of the Celebrity Self in Yoruba Popular Music in Nigeria." In *Playing with Identities in Contemporary Music in Africa,* edited by Mai Palmberg and Annemette Kirkegaard, 19–34. Uppsala: Nordiska Afrikainstitutet, 2002.

———. "'I'm a Leader, Not a Boss': Social Identity and Popular Music in Ibadan, Nigeria." *Ethnomusicology* 26, no. 1 (1982): 59–71.

———. *Juju: A Social History and Ethnography of an African Popular Music.* Chicago: University of Chicago Press, 1990.

———. "Juju History: Towards a Theory of Sociomusical Practice." In Blum, Bohlman, and Neuman, *Ethnomusicology and Modern Music History,* 49–67.

———. "'Our Tradition Is a Very Modern Tradition': Popular Music and the Construction of a Pan-Yoruba Identity." *Ethnomusicology* 34, no. 3 (1990): 367–79.

Waterman, Richard Alan. "African Influence on the Music of the Americas." In *Acculturation in the Americas,* edited by Sol Tax, 207–18. New York: Cooper Square Publishers, 1967.

Webster, James Bertin. *The African Church among the Yorubas.* London: Clarendon Press, 1964.

Weiss, Sarah. "Permeable Boundaries: Hybridity, Music, and the Reception of Robert Wilson's *I La Galigo.*" *Ethnomusicology* 52, no. 2 (2008): 203–38.

Welch, David. "Ritual Intonation of Yoruba Praise-Poetry (Oriki)." *Yearbook of International Folk Council* 5 (1973): 156–64.

Weman, Henry. *African Music and the Church in Africa.* Also published as *Studia Missionalia Upsaliensia.* Uppsala: Svenska Institutet for Missionsforkning, 1960.

White, Bob W. "Congolese Rumba and Other Cosmopolitanisms." *Cahiers études africaines.* 42, no. 168 (2002): 663–86.

Young, Robert. *Colonial Desire: Hybridity in Theory, Culture, and Race.* London: Routledge, 1995.

Index

Page numbers in italics indicate illustrations or tables.

www.ingramcontent.com/pod-product-compliance
Lightning Source LLC
Chambersburg PA
CBHW070603290326
41929CB00061B/2655